WALDECK (GERMANY) SOLDIERS
OF THE
AMERICAN REVOLUTIONARY WAR

I0129842

BRUCE E. BURGOYNE

HERITAGE BOOKS
2008

HERITAGE BOOKS

AN IMPRINT OF HERITAGE BOOKS, INC.

Books, CDs, and more—Worldwide

For our listing of thousands of titles see our website
at
www.HeritageBooks.com

Published 2008 by
HERITAGE BOOKS, INC.
Publishing Division
100 Railroad Ave. #104
Westminster, Maryland 21157

International Standard Book Numbers
Paperbound: 978-1-55613-480-1
Clothbound: 978-0-7884-7603-7

TABLE OF CONTENTS

iii

Waldeck

Rhoden •

• Kohlgrund

• Vasbeck

• Arolsen

Mengeringhausen •

Rhenegge • • Adorf

Landau •

Twiste •

Sudeck •

• Nieder-
Waroldern

• Willingen

Usseln •

Lengefeld • • KORBACH

• Meineringhausen

• Sachsenhausen

• Waldeck

• Goddelsheim

• Kleinern

Hof Dampf
Dalwigkstha

Bad Wildungen •

chsenberg •

Gershausen •

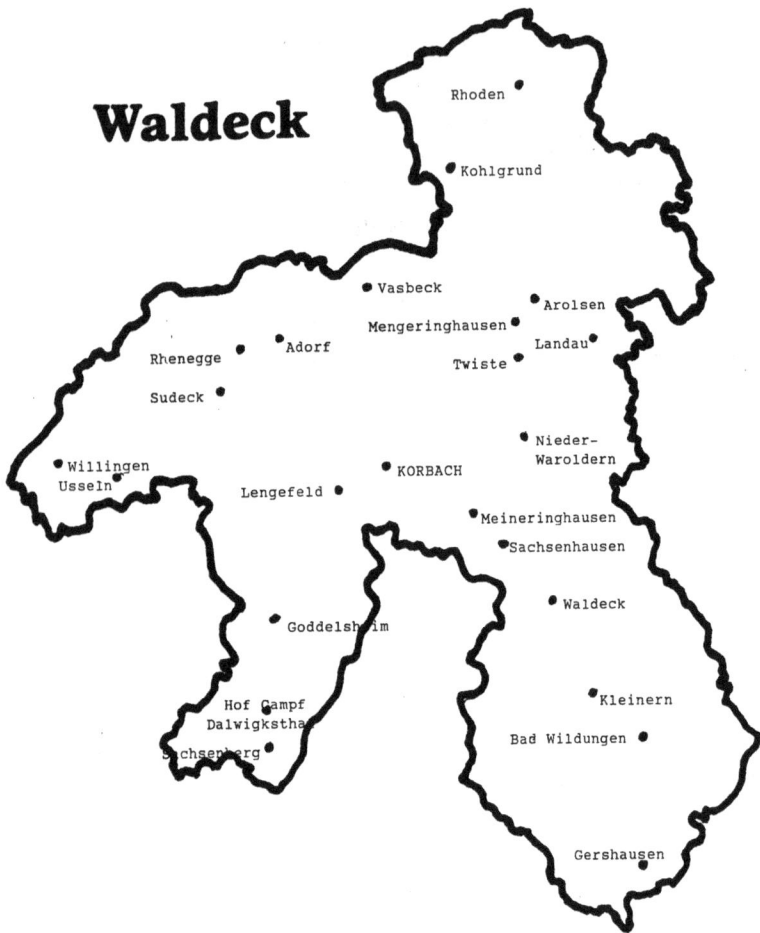

3RD WALDECK REGIMENT

in New York and New Jersey

1776-1783

1. 1st encampment, New Rochelle, October 1776.
2. Encampment, Ft. Independence, November 1776.
3. Attack on Ft. Washington, November 16, 1776.
4. Winter quarters, area of Springfield, N.J., winter of 1776-1777; loss of two patrols totaling eighty men, January 1777.
5. Encampment, Staten Island, most of 1777-1778.
6. Engaged General Sullivan on Staten Island, August 1777.
7. Sailed up Hudson River as part of abortive relief force for General Burgoyne, October 1777.
8. Sailed for West Florida, October 1778.
9. Returned to Newtown, Long Island, from Florida, summer 1781.
10. Departed for Europe, summer 1783.

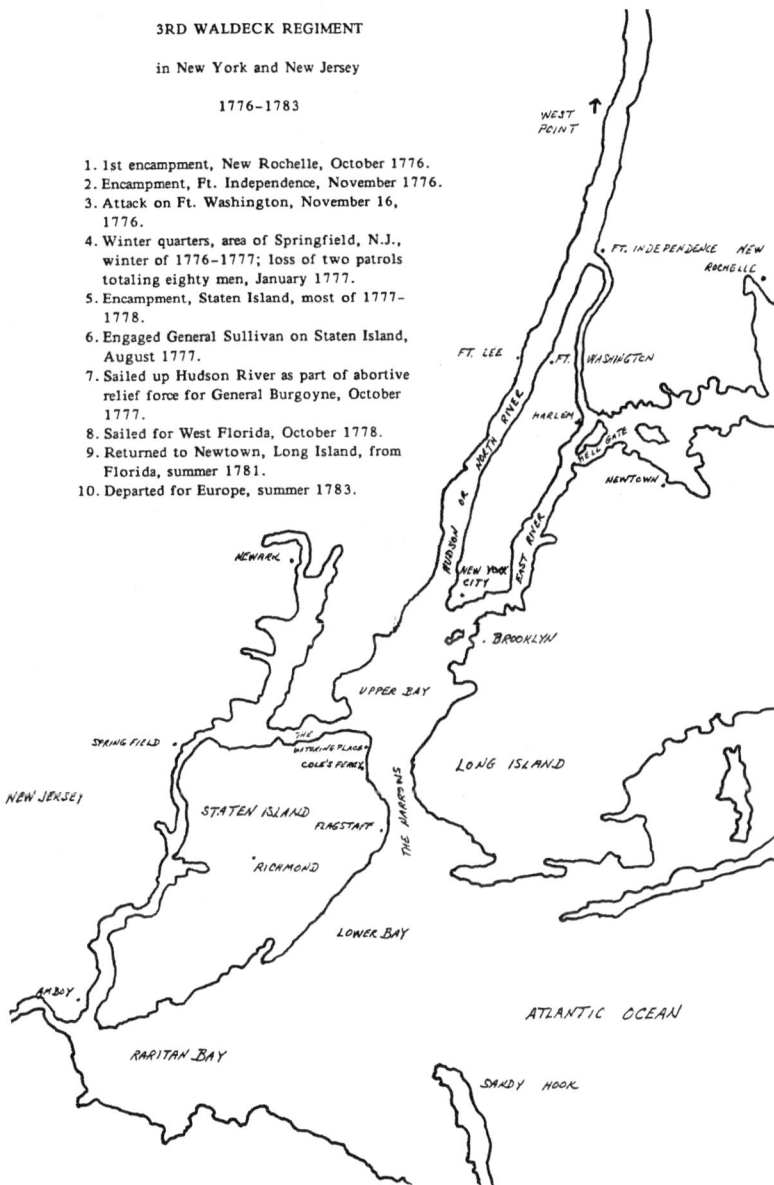

WEST POINT

FT. INDEPENDENCE   NEW ROCHELLE

FT. LEE   FT. WASHINGTON

HARLEM

HELL GATE

NEWTOWN

HUDSON OR NORTH RIVER

EAST RIVER

NEWARK

NEW YORK CITY

BROOKLYN

UPPER BAY

SPRINGFIELD

THE WATERING PLACE

COLE'S FERRY

LONG ISLAND

NEW JERSEY

STATEN ISLAND

FLAGSTAFF

THE NARROWS

RICHMOND

LOWER BAY

AMBOY

ATLANTIC OCEAN

RARITAN BAY

SANDY HOOK

--courtesy of the author

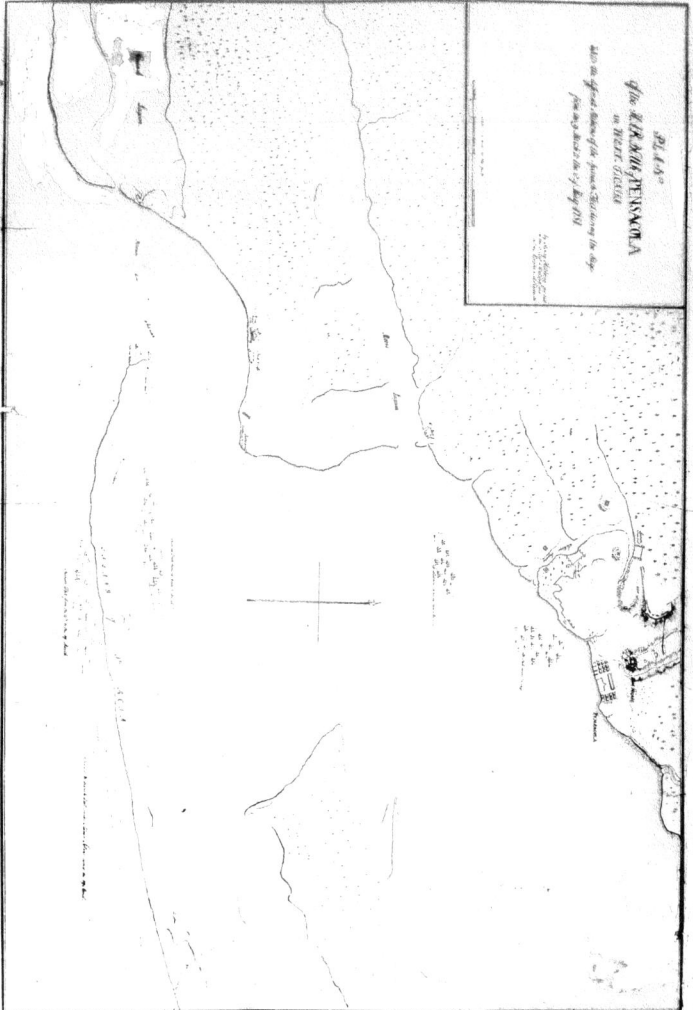

Plan of the Harbour of Pensacola in West Florida, by Henry Heldring

--*courtesy of the Clements Library, University of Michigan*

INTRODUCTION

Having served over a quarter of a century with the American military on land, on sea, and in the air, during World War II, the Korean War, and the Vietnam War, as an enlisted man and as a common soldier, I have always felt a bond with soldiers of all nations, both friends and foes. I do not wish to glamorize the military nor make heroes of the men who fight the world's wars. They are only ordinary persons, like all others, and I want to give recognition to them as such. They are men who leave home and loved ones, to suffer and die; they are men who revert to the ordinary activities of life, work, and family when the fighting is over or they become too old or broken to serve.

In an effort to show the humanity of soldiers, I have written brief biographies of every man who served in one country's war--not many men and not a big country, but a war as difficult and deadly as any in history. The country was the eighteenth-century German principality of Waldeck and the men were the members of the 3rd English-Waldeck Regiment who traveled to the Western Hemisphere to fight against the American colonists during the American Revolutionary War.

Of all the so-called Hessian units employed by England during the American Revolutionary War, none traveled more widely nor had more interesting experiences than the 3rd English-Waldeck Regiment. This contingent of men from the smallest of the six lands which provided soldiers for England--Anhalt-Zerbst, Ansbach-Bayreuth, Brunswick, Hesse-Cassel, Hesse-Hanau, and Waldeck--served against more nations, in more widely scattered areas, traveled to more places, and suffered a greater percentage of losses than any other contingent.

Originally scheduled to be sent to Canada in 1776, the regiment was sent instead to New York to join the army of General William Howe. After service in the New York-New Jersey area, during which time men from the regiment who were captured were sent to prison facilities in Pennsylvania and Maryland and some entered the American army, the regiment was ordered to West Florida. En route to West Florida the transports carrying the Waldeck Regiment stopped at Jamaica to regroup and to take on provisions and water. They then

vii

sailed to Pensacola. From Pensacola part of the regiment was sent to the area of the Mississippi River where the men were captured by the Spanish forces commanded by Don Bernardo Galvez. After being held captive at New Orleans for about a year, the men were transferred to Cuba, sailing first to Vera Cruz, Mexico. Following their exchange, the men returned to New York. Some of the men held prisoner in New Orleans deserted, went up the Mississippi River, and joined George Rogers Clark to fight against the English in the Illinois Country.

A part of the regiment which remained in Pensacola participated in an unsuccessful attack against The Village, a Spanish strongpoint near present-day Mobile, Alabama. Then the Pensacola garrison was besieged by a vastly superior Spanish-French combined command. The siege ended when the garrison surrendered on 9 May 1781. According to the terms of the capitulation the members of the garrison were allowed to return to New York on condition that they would not take up arms against Spain or France (the Americans were not mentioned) until exchanged. Again, as in earlier situations, some of the Waldeckers taken prisoner by Spain, both on the Mississippi and at Pensacola, chose to serve in the Spanish army rather than remain as prisoners for an indefinite period of time.

Finally, the men of the 1782 recruit shipment--recruits were sent from Germany each year to replace losses--stopped at Halifax, Nova Scotia, and the following year returned to Germany. However, during their assignment at Nova Scotia, some of the men may have participated in an expedition to the Penobscot, Maine, area.

When hostilities ended in 1783 the regiment returned to Germany, arriving back in Waldeck in September and October of that year.

It is interesting to note that the 3rd Waldeck Regiment, later designated the 5th Battalion, saw many years of employment in the service of Holland. This service included duty from 1802 to 1806 at the Cape of Good Hope, where some of the men who had fought beside the English in America fought against their former comrades-in-arms.

In the pages which follow, an attempt has been made to focus on the men of the regiment rather than on the unit. About 1,225 men served in the regiment during the course of the American Revolutionary War, of which 470 so far have been identified as native Waldeckers. Of the total number, about 500 men returned to Waldeck after the war and another 250 stayed in the New World as deserters or after being released from the regiment. The others died in America, primarily of disease. In fact, the smallest contingent of Hessians suffered the highest loss ratio of all the units which fought in America.

As fighting men, the Waldeckers have generally had a poor reputation, but seem to have fought well at Fort Washington in November 1776. They conducted themselves well and received English approval for helping to repulse General John Sullivan's attack on Staten Island in August 1777. Also, they were a significant portion of the Pensacola garrison which for a time withstood a combined Spanish and French siege force, although outnumbered more than eight to one. However, many of the men were captured during the war, some two or three times, and most of the men spent some time as prisoners of war.

While the desertion rate was high, it was not out of proportion to that of other nationals, Germans, English, or even Americans. Surprisingly, desertion was not always undertaken to avoid military service. Many of the Waldeck deserters joined the American or Spanish armies, sometimes as a means of getting out of prisoner-of-war conditions. While this was often a ploy used to facilitate escape back to their own unit, they sometimes served their new employers faithfully and well. Other nationals, including American soldiers, participated in similar activities.

But the Waldeckers were not just fighting men, they were human beings with all the characteristics that the term implies. Most military historians describe battles and leaders, both military and civilian, but the "Mini-Bios" which follow describe the Waldeck soldiers who were called upon to serve and if need be, to die. All the men of the Waldeck Regiment served, and the reader will quickly notice that a great many died.

It has taken years to assemble the information on the Waldeckers and more information will come to light in the future, but enough data is now available to indicate the heartbreak and suffering endured by the men and their families. There is also information which indicates courage, determination, intelligence, and professional skill, as well as the less desirable human traits of greed, cowardice, weak will, drunkenness, and infidelity.

As with all studies of men, on some there is a wealth of information and on others very little. *The Hessische Truppen im Amerikanischen Unabhaengigkeitskrieg (HETRINA)*, vol. V, was and remains the basis for this collection of Mini-Bios, but it was the Steuernagel and Waldeck manuscripts from the Bancroft Collection of the New York Public Library and my friendship with Guenter Jedicke of Arolsen, Germany, which stimulated my interest in the men of the 3rd English-Waldeck Regiment.

To facilitate understanding the Mini-Bios, a brief organizational summary of the regiment, a chronological table of events, explanation of certain aspects of the Mini-Bios, and a list of alternate spellings have been added. Because material has been gathered over many years, and because footnotes would be repetitious and superfluous, none have been used. Instead the reader can probably determine the source of most information by checking the bibliography.

Maybe readers will provide me with additional information about the men of the Waldeck Regiment. It would be welcome. Perhaps those same readers can help me correct errors so that the Mini-Bios will be more accurate. Perhaps some of the readers will select other military units and follow my example of granting recognition to other men called soldiers or ship's crew members.

Many people have contributed to this collection of Mini-Bios, which I hope is a different and more humane approach to writing history. While I cannot list everyone, the following have been especially helpful: Guenter Jedicke and Frau Ingeborg Moldenhauer of the Waldeck Historical Society; their fellow Waldeckers and historical society members, Karl and Hilda Bracht, Linde Freifrau von Dalwigk, Wilhelm Hellwig, Klaus Peter Scholz, and the Vesper Family; Dr. Gerhard Menk and the personnel of the Hessen State Archives, Marburg, Germany; Susan Davis and the personnel of the New York Public Library; Galen R. Wilson of the Clements Library of the University of Michigan, Ann Arbor; James Servies of the Pace Library of the University of West Florida, Pensacola; and personnel of the Alderman Library of the University of Virginia, Charlottesville, and the Library of Congress. Roald Tichelaar and his family of DeLier, Holland, helped with Dutch translations and took me to the National Archives at the Hague and the Army Museum at Delft. Finally, none of the Mini-Bios could have been written without the loving and constant support, encouragement, and assistance in all phases by my wife, Marie.

Bruce E. Burgoyne
Dover, Delaware
1991

ORGANIZATION
of the
3rd English-Waldeck Regiment

According to a treaty dated 20 April 1776, the German principality of Waldeck sold a 670-man infantry regiment into English service for use against the American colonists who were in revolt. The staff and five companies of the regiment were accompanied by a 14-man artillery detachment with two small field pieces. The key positions and personnel of the 12-man staff were:

Commander, Lieutenant Colonel/Colonel Johann Ludwig
 Wilhelm von Hanxleden
Major/Lieutenant Colonel Ludwig von Dalwigk
Adjutant, Ensign/Lieutenant Johann Henrich Stierlein
Regimental Quartermaster, Lieutenant Karl Theodor
 Wiegand
Regimental Drummer Christian Glaentzer
Provost Konrad Glaentzer
Regimental Surgeon Christian Mattern
Commissary (Auditor/Paymaster) Philipp Marc
Chaplain Philipp Waldeck

Other positions on the staff were an assistant provost and two wagon servants.

The 1st, or Grenadier Company, was organized with:

3 Officers	1 Solicitor
3 Batmen	6 Corporals
3 Sergeants	2 Fifers
1 Quartermaster Sergeant	3 Drummers
1 Captain at Arms	110 Privates
1 Medic	131 Total

The 2nd, 3rd, 4th, and 5th Companies were musket companies organized with:

3 Officers	1 Solicitor
3 Batmen	1 Free Corporal
3 Sergeants	6 Corporals

1 Quartermaster Sergeant	1 Fifer
1 Captain at Arms	3 Drummers
1 Medic	107 Privates
	131 Total

Company commanders, all of whom arrived in America with the regiment in 1776, were:

1st Company - Captain/Major (later Lieutenant Colonel) Konrad Albrecht von Horn until 1778, and then Captain Georg von Haacke.

2nd Company - Major/Lieutenant Colonel von Dalwigk until March 1777, Captain Christoph Alberti, Sr., until March 1781, and later, Captain Augustin Alberti.

3rd Company - Lieutenant Colonel/Colonel von Hanxleden until January 1781, and later, Captain Alexander von Baumbach

4th Company - Captain/Major Christian Friedrich Pentzel

5th Company - Captain Georg von Haacke until August 1778, and then Major/Lieutenant Colonel Konrad von Horn.

Other officers when the regiment arrived in America in October 1776 and their company of assignment:

Lieutenant Wilhelm Leonhardi - 5th Company
Lieutenant/Captain Lieutenant Gerhard Henrich Heldring
    4th Company
Lieutenant Wilhelm Keppel - 2nd Company
Lieutenant Friedrich von Wilmowsky - 3rd Company
Lieutenant Karl Henrich Strubberg - 1st Company
Ensign/Lieutenant Andreas Brumhard - 5th Company
Ensign/Lieutenant and after January 1781, Adjutant,
    Henrich Jakob Knipschild - 3rd Company
Ensign Friedrich Noelting - 2nd Company
Ensign/Lieutenant Karl Hohmann, Sr. - 4th Company

Other officers subsequently assigned to the regiment and who served in America as ensigns were:

Friedrich von Axleben	Theodor Ursall
Karl von Horn	August Mueller. Jr.
Christian Schmidt	Franz Philipp Wirths
Karl Mueller	Bernhard Schreiber
August Hohmann, Jr.	

CHRONOLOGY OF EVENTS

1776

20 April – Treaty signed in Arolsen (W) between Waldeck and England. Waldeck to provide a 670-man regiment for use in America. The customary two regimental guns and a 14-man artillery section were also sent by Waldeck.

20 May – The regiment marched out of Korbach (W) and spent the first night at Kuelte (W).

21 May – The regiment stopped at night at Borgentreich.

22 May – During the afternoon the regiment embarked on boats on the Weser at Beverungen.

23 May – The boats passed Hoexter at 8 AM, Corvey at 9 AM and Holzmuenden at 10 AM.

24 May – The regiment arrived at Hameln.

25 May – Early in the morning the boats passed the pontoon bridge at Rinteln.

26 May – Pentecost services were held underway with the singing of hymns.

27 May – The regiment stopped at Hoya and bivouacked in the Verden area.

28 May – The regiment passed through Bremen in the afternoon.

29 May – The regiment arrived at Vegesack at noon and transferred to larger boats.

30 May – The regiment arrived at Bremerlehe early in the morning. The men were landed, mustered by the English commissary, Colonel William Faucitt, and sworn into English service. The regiment then went back aboard the boats.

31 May – The regiment went aboard three Dutch transport ships, which were to carry them to America, as follows:
Jacob Cornelius, Master John Waterson – Staff ship, Lieutenant Colonel von Hanxleden, part of the staff, 144 men of the 3rd Company, and 115 men of the 2nd Company. 271 men.
John Abraham, Master Martin Digby – 1st Company and part of the 4th Company. 196 men.
Benjamin, Master George Knight – Captain Pentzel and 78 men of the 4th Company. 35 men of the 2nd Company, and 131 men of the 5th Company. 249 men.

3 June - The Waldeckers sailed from Bremerlehe very early in the morning.

20 June - The transports carrying the Waldeckers arrived at Spithead, England, during the morning.

21 June - The Waldeckers, who originally were to have gone to Canada, were ordered to proceed to America with the 2nd division of Hessians and to join General William Howe's army. Escort of the fleet was to be the *Diamond*, Captain Charles Fielding, the *Ambuscade*, the *Unicorn*, and the *Lark*. The *Lark* later was sent to Cork, Ireland.

24 June - Eighty men of the 2nd Company and 35 men of the 4th Company were transferred to an additional transport, *Adamant*, Master Josias Walker, at Spithead. As 35 men of the company were transferred from *Benjamin*, another 45 men of the 2nd Company must have been transferred from *Jacob Cornelius*. Probably men of the 4th Company were taken from *Benjamin* and *John Abraham*. The officers of the 2nd Company and Chaplain Waldeck, as well as Private Volcke of the 4th Company who served as the chaplain's batman, were aboard the *Adamant*.

28 June - A flotilla of 64 ships, including the Waldeck transports, set sail but made little headway.

7 July - The fleet entered Plymouth Harbor, in England.

20 July - The fleet again set sail for America.

12 Aug - The 1st Division of Hessians arrived at New York.

27 Aug - The Battle of Long Island.

9 Sept - Fire broke out at sea aboard the *Benjamin*, but was brought under control.

17 Sept - A severe storm struck the fleet.

21 Sept - The Great Fire in New York City.

25 Sept - Another severe storm struck, causing the *John Abraham* to lose its middle mast.

18 Oct - *Diamond* and *Ambuscade* arrived off Sandy Hook with a convoy of 65 sail carrying 8,000 men.

19 Oct - The fleet entered New York Harbor.

20 Oct - The ships carrying the Waldeckers proceeded to New York.

21 Oct - The Waldeckers transferred to small, single-masted ships and sailed up the East River almost to New Rochelle. One account of the movement of the Hessians and Waldeckers was that they were rowed up the East River in flatboats to a drumbeat, with trumpets and fifes sounding, and colors flying. Those men of the Waldeck Regiment who were sick upon arrival were sent to the hospital on Long Island.

24 Oct - The Waldeck Regiment was mustered and inspected by the Hessian General Leopold Philipp von Heister.

25 Oct - The Waldeck Regiment marched to West Chester, New York, where it was assigned to Lord Cornwallis' brigade on the right wing of the English army.

27 Oct –	While marauding near Maroneck, Corporal Nelle and eighteen privates of the Waldeck Regiment were attacked by an American patrol. The corporal and twelve privates were made prisoners and two of the men were left on the field seriously wounded.
28 Oct –	The brigade moved back to Delaney's Hill. The Battle of White Plains.
29 Oct –	A part of the Waldeck Regiment, forty or fifty men, moved from West Chester to New Rochelle and remained in camp there until 5 November 1776. Those men may have been assigned later to guard duty at William's Bridge over the Bronx River. The main part of the Waldeck Regiment marched to Fort Independence by way of Mile Square and Valentine's Hill.
4 Nov –	The regiment arrived at Fort Independence.
5 Nov –	The Waldeckers left at New Rochelle and marched nine miles to a new camp, the Sun Redoubt, where they arrived about 2 PM. They were then ordered to Fort Independence, where they arrived after dark.
6 Nov –	Two companies of Waldeckers were posted in Fort Independence. The other companies were quartered in tents. During this period the regiment sent strong patrols toward Fort Washington.
10 Nov –	Twenty-four men returned to the regiment from the hospital.
16 Nov –	The Waldeck Regiment participated in the attack on Fort Washington as part of Colonel Johann Rall's command of the northern attack force led by the Hessian Lieutenant General Wilhelm von Knyphausen. The Waldeckers suffered six men killed and another seventeen wounded in capturing the fort. The regimental quartermaster sergeant, Carl Philipp Steuernagel, gives a vivid description of a soldier's view of the battle in a diary which is in the New York Public Library. The regiment returned to Fort Independence.
19 Nov –	The regiment moved a half mile from Fort Independence.
22 Nov –	The regiment was ordered to take post at Jones's and to extend toward Delaney's.
25 Nov –	The regiment crossed over Kingsbridge, passed Fort Knyphausen, formerly Fort Washington, and at 4 PM arrived at Delaney's Mill, near Harlem.
28 Nov –	As the tents were useless in such bad weather, the troops were quartered at nearby farms.
1 Dec –	General Henry Clinton sailed with a command from New York to Rhode Island.
5 Dec –	The Waldeck Regiment marched through New York en route to winter quarters at Amboy, New Jersey. They embarked on the North River near the site of their original landing in October.

6 Dec -	The regiment arrived at Amboy in the evening and the men remained aboard ship overnight.
7 Dec -	The troops were landed and marched through Amboy to barracks designed for only 300 men. Clinton's command arrived at Rhode Island.
8 Dec -	Very early in the morning the regiment began a march to Elizabethtown. They spent the night in the open in deep snow and cold weather.
9 Dec -	The regiment entered Elizabethtown at 1 PM.
25 Dec -	Christmas was celebrated in peace and quiet.
26 Dec -	Battle of Trenton.

1777

3 Jan -	Battle of Princeton, New Jersey.
5 Jan -	Captain von Haacke, Lieutenant Heldring, and a command of fifty men were taken prisoner after a skirmish near Springfield, New Jersey.
8 Jan -	Corporal Nelle and a thirty-man command were taken prisoner near Elizabethtown, New Jersey. The regiment was pulled back to the barracks on the outer edge of Amboy and attached to General John Vaughan's Brigade.
13 Jan -	A party of thirteen Waldeckers captured in the East Jersies arrived in Philadelphia.
19 Jan -	A group of Waldeck prisoners of war arrived in Lancaster, Pennsylvania, under escort of the American Lieutenants Jordan and Miller and were put in the barracks.
20 Feb -	Four Waldeckers and two British privates were brought into Windsor, New York, as prisoners of war.
27 Feb -	The four Waldeck prisoners were among 25 prisoners sent to Pennsylvania from Morristown under escort of the American Robert Mullin.
15 May -	A muster of the Waldeck Regiment showed 55 men sick and 101 as prisoners of war.
21 May -	The regiment moved out of winter quarters and into the field about a half mile from Amboy.
22 May -	The regiment moved to Elizabethtown.
3 June -	The *Somerset* and seventeen transports with the 1777 recruits arrived at New York. The *Gale*, Master Henry Jackson, had provisioned 90 Waldeckers from 25 March to 15 June 1777.
11 June -	The Waldeck Regiment, the Anbach-Bayreuth regiments, and the English 55th Regiment were at Amboy under the command of the Ansbach Colonel Friedrich Ludwig Albrecht von Eyb.
18 June -	The 87 recruits of the 1777 recruit shipment joined the regiment. The escort officer, Lieutenant Becker, returned to Germany.

xvi

29 June –	The regiment transferred to Staten Island, crossing at Billop's Ferry, and were placed under the command of the English Brigadier General John Campbell, upon his arrival on the island.
1 July –	The Waldeck Regiment encamped at the Watering Place near the redoubts, present-day Fort Hill, and called Fort Knyphausen.
6 July –	The British forces under Lieutenant General John Burgoyne entered Fort Ticonderoga in New York.
12 July –	Lieutenant Colonel von Dalwigk, Sergeant Henrich Schumacher, and Quartermaster Sergeant Franz Arnold Riemenschneider departed for Waldeck.
19 July –	Eighteen men of the regiment were sent to the hospital in New York due to illness.
23 July –	General William Howe sailed from New York for the Philadelphia campaign.
16 Aug –	Battle of Bennington, Vermont.
23 Aug –	A scheduled review ended with the Waldeck Regiment and the English 52nd Regiment being sent to repulse an American attack on Staten Island led by General John Sullivan. There were no Waldeck battle casualties but three men died of fatigue and heat exhaustion on the return march to camp.
26-30 Aug –	Waldeck and Hessian prisoners of war were moved from Lancaster to Lebanon, Pennsylvania, and quartered in the Moravian parsonage.
11 Sept –	The Waldeck Grenadiers were part of a command sent to Elizabeth Point and which crossed into New Jersey to procure fodder. Battle of Brandywine in Pennsylvania.
16 Sept –	The above-mentioned command returned.
19 Sept –	Battle of Freeman's Farm near Saratoga in New York.
26 Sept –	Howe's army entered Philadelphia.
1 Oct –	Commissary Marc visited the camp on Staten Island from New York and brought mail from Waldeck.
4 Oct –	Battle of Germantown, Pennsylvania.
5 Oct –	Only eighteen men of the regiment were in the hospital and all but two of them were up and dressed.
7 Oct –	Second Battle of Freeman's Farm.
14 Oct –	At 10 PM the Waldeck Regiment went aboard ships which sailed at midnight as part of General Clinton's force to assist General Burgoyne.
15 Oct –	The ships sailed up the North River as far as West Point, where they dropped anchor.
16 Oct –	The ships returned down river and anchored off Fort Knyphausen.
17 Oct –	General John Burgoyne surrendered to the American General Horatio Gates at Saratoga.
19 Oct –	The Waldeck Regiment left the ships and camped near Kingsbridge.

20 Oct –	The regiment returned aboard ship at noon and sailed down the North River in a snow storm.
21 Oct –	The ships arrived at Staten Island but the troops remained aboard ship.
22 Oct –	The Waldeckers landed and pitched camp at the former site on Staten Island.
23 Oct –	In General Campbell's absence, Colonel von Hanxleden took command on Staten Island until 2 November 1777. There were heavy rains and strong winds during this period.
29 Oct –	The prisoners at Lebanon were moved into the Lutheran Church.
1 Nov –	Colonel von Hanxleden quartered the men in houses as the tents were in tatters.
4 Nov –	General Campbell ordered the Waldeckers back into camp to insure a rapid command response should the Americans attack again. Johann Conrad Doehla, an Ansbach-Bayreuth soldier diarist, reported that the Waldeck Regiment revolted at this time because of the bad living conditions, but I have found no other such reference.
12 Nov –	Men of the regiment were engaged in building huts and blockhouses against the cold.
17 Nov –	General Campbell mustered the Waldeck Regiment.
27 Nov –	The regiment was divided into sections and sent out to repel an American attack which failed to materialize.
1 Dec –	Rain and wind had so damaged the huts, which partially collapsed, that repairs were undertaken. The huts were called Waldeck Town.
25 Dec –	Christmas divine services were held under open skies in pleasant weather.

1778

6 Feb –	French alliance with the American colonies.
5 Apr –	The 1778 recruits for the Waldeck Regiment were mustered at Bremerlehe by Colonel William Faucitt.
23 Apr –	Regimental strength in America was 636 men, 34 short of treaty strength.
May –	Regimental strength in America was 646 men, with two officers and 94 men prisoners of war and thirty men sick.
8 May –	General Clinton assumed command of British forces in America.
2 June –	Captain Alberti, Sr., and the 2nd Company were ordered to a fortification named *N* at the mouth of New York Harbor.

17 June –	Twenty-nine Waldeckers were on a list of prisoners of war to be sent to Philadelphia from Lancaster under escort of the American Captain Michale Opp, to be exchanged. One of the men, Wilhelm Henrich Neumeyer, was not included in the 1778 exchange, however.
18 June –	The British evacuated Philadelphia.
21 June –	The Waldeck Grenadiers were in camp at the Flagstaff on Staten Island, about two miles from the regimental camp near Cole's Ferry. Mosquitoes were thick, rations scarce.
28 June –	The Battle of Monmouth Courthouse in New Jersey.
29 June –	Three Waldeckers were on a list of prisoners of war to be sent to Philadelphia for exchange under escort of Lieutenants William Vanlear and Stephen Stephenson of the 5th Pennsylvania Regiment.
18 July –	39 more exchanged prisoners of war returned to regiment.
23 July –	There were no sick in the regimental hospital.
25 July –	The regiment was mustered and the muster master was surprised at the regimental strength.
27 July –	Captain Pentzel and the 4th Company relieved the grenadiers at the Flagstaff.
3 Aug –	A great fire in New York caused everyone in the regiment concern because all had sent their personal belongings to the regimental baggage house in New York, where their property could be protected.
4 Aug –	A powder ship blew up in New York Harbor after being struck by lightning.
8 Oct –	Major von Horn and eleven Waldeck invalids sailed for Europe on the *Echo*, Master J. Menenir, which arrived in Portsmouth, England, on 1 January 1779.
13 Oct –	A detail of men was sent to New York to get the regimental baggage which was to be put aboard ship.
16 Oct –	The regimental baggage was put aboard ship. An embarkation list of the Waldeck Regiment when it went aboard ship at Staten Island contained the following figures: **Staff:** 5 officers; 2 NCOs; 2 corporals and privates; 2 servants = Total 11. **1st Company:** 3 officers; 6 NCOs; 5 musicians; 126 corporals and privates; 3 batmen; 11 wives; 5 children = Total 159. **2nd Company:** 3 officers; 8 NCOs; 4 musicians; 123 corporals and privates; 2 batmen; 7 wives; 1 child = Total 148. **3rd Company:** 4 officers; 8 NCOs; 4 musicians; 124 corporals and privates; 4 batmen; 8 wives; 5 children = Total 157. **4th Company:** 3 officers; 7 NCOs; 4 musicians; 121 corporals and privates; 2 batmen; 4 wives; 4 children = Total 145. **5th Company:** 3 officers; 6 NCOs; 3 musicians; 123 corporals and privates; 2 batmen; 5 wives = Total 142. **Artillery:** 2 NCOs and 10 corporals and privates = Total 12.

18 Oct –	During church service transports approached Staten Island from New York.
19 Oct –	The remaining regimental baggage was put aboard ship.
20 Oct –	By 11 AM the entire regiment was aboard ship: *Springfield* – The colonel and key staff and 3rd Company. *Britannia* – The 2nd and 5th Companies. *Crawford* – The 4th Company, chaplain and possibly other staff members. *Christian* – The 1st Company and possibly the artillery.
28 Oct –	Colonel von Hanxleden sent a detail from the *Springfield* to load General Campbell's baggage.
31 Oct –	The fleet set sail, but anchored again near Sandy Hook.
3 Nov –	At 7 AM the fleet raised anchor and sailed for West Florida and the West Indies.
9 Nov –	The *Soleby*, 28 guns, Captain Thomas Symonds, and the nine transports carrying the Waldeck Regiment and the provincial troops to West Florida separated from the other ships in the convoy.
10 Nov –	The *Crawford* became separated from the other ships. The *Soleby* found the *Crawford* but then could not find the other ships.
2 Dec –	The *Soleby* and *Crawford* arrived at Jamaica, entered Port Royal, and anchored at Kingston. The other ships had already arrived.
5 Dec –	The *Crawford* sailed toward Rockford in order to take on water. Chaplain Waldeck baptized two children on the *Christian*.
27 Dec –	All the transports carrying Waldeckers were anchored at Port Royal.
29 Dec –	The English captured Savannah.
31 Dec –	The fleet set sail from Port Royal for West Florida.

1779

5 Jan –	Men of the Waldeck Regiment caught sight of the coast of West Florida.
18 Jan –	The ships carrying the Waldeck Regiment entered Pensacola Harbor, but the men remained aboard ship as the barracks for their quarters were not ready.
30 Jan –	The Waldeck soldiers were landed from the transports *Springfield*, *Crawford*, and *Christian*, and officers and men of those three companies went into the barracks.
2 Feb –	Men of the two companies on the transport *Britannia* landed. During the Waldeckers' stay at Pensacola they met a former comrade-in-arms, Brandenstein, a native of Koenigshagen who had deserted in Waldeck and become a chief among the American Indians.

6 Mar – A Corporal Nain, native of Berlin and a member of the Pensacola garrison, went aboard the sloop *West Florida* with a detail of twelve men for the purpose of reconnoitering the region of the Mississippi River.

19 Mar – The Waldeck Regiment had a strength of 707 men; 1 sergeant, 2 corporals, 1 medic, and 33 privates over strength.

1 Apr – Lieutenant Heldring was doing duty as assistant engineer of the Pensacola garrison. Maps he made of Pensacola are in the Clements Library at the University of Michigan.

1 May – The 1779 recruits for the Waldeck Regiment were embarked on the transport *Joseph*, 253 tons, Captain Mapp, after nearly a month of waiting for a ship at Bremerlehe. The Waldeckers were 1 NCO, 19 recruits, 2 batmen, 1 provost, and 1 wife, who had sailed down the Weser River from Beverungen. Captain von Horn and his son Karl, an ensign, were also with the recruits, as well as Sergeant Stuckenbrock, acting as the escort officer. There were also 160 Hessian recruits on board.

19 June – The Waldeck Grenadiers were ordered aboard ship.

20 June – The grenadiers sailed from Pensacola en route to the Mississippi area.

21 June – Spain declared war on England.

3 July – The Spanish governor of Louisiana, Don Bernardo de Galvez, reported to Havana that there were 400 men in the English defenses at Manchac, near Baton Rouge, and 300 Waldeckers were expected as reinforcements.

2 Aug – The 5th Company of the Waldeck Regiment plus a corporal and fourteen privates of the 3rd Company were sent to Baton Rouge from Pensacola.

29/30 Aug – Captain Alberti's 2nd Company was ordered to the Mississippi area.

4 Sept – A small Spanish force ambushed the ships carrying Captain Alberti's company on the Amite River. In the very brief engagement, Lieutenant Noelting was wounded, dying that evening, and the entire 2nd Company was captured.

4 – 7 Sept – Eight Waldeck soldiers were made prisoners of war at Thompson's Creek (?), and the English Fort Butte at Manchac was captured by the Spaniards. Twenty-three English soldiers were made prisoners at Manchac but the Waldeckers had previously been ordered to Baton Rouge.

8/9 Sept – The packet boat *Carteret* delivered the news to Pensacola that Spain had declared war on England on 21 June 1779.

12 Sept – Don Galvez invested the position at Baton Rouge.

21 Sept – After a three-hour bombardment, Lieutenant Colonel Alexander Dickson of the 60th Regiment, commanding at Baton Rouge, surrendered, and the entire command was made prisoners of war.

16 Nov – The Pensacola garrison received the report that the wives and children of the Waldeck soldiers at Baton Rouge had been sent into the nearby forest so as not to be in danger in the pending battle. However, they were attacked by Indians and all were massacred. (I have found no confirmation of this report.)

25 Nov – The British evacuated Rhode Island.

22 Dec – Strength of the Waldeck Regiment was estimated at 600 men, including prisoners of war and the recruits en route from Europe.

1780

3 Feb – Captain Pentzel was sent as escort officer under a flag of truce with Spanish officers returning to New Orleans on parole, on the ship *Christiana*. Commissary Marc went along to arrange financial accounts of the prisoners.

6 Feb – An earthquake shook Pensacola and was accompanied by a possible hurricane.

14/15 Feb – A hurricane struck Pensacola. Because of weather-caused damage, and the awareness of a pending Spanish attack, the garrison at Pensacola was constantly employed on work details and guard duty.

5 Mar – General Campbell sent the remnants of the 60th Regiment on a 72-mile march to relieve the besieged forces under the Lieutenant Governor, Captain Elias Durnford, at Mobile.

6 Mar – The remaining Waldeckers marched out at 6 AM to strengthen the relief force. After crossing the Perdido River they advanced to the Tensa River, where they halted. Officers of the Waldeck Regiment left at Pensacola were Colonel von Hanxleden, Lieutenants Heldring and Wiegand, Ensign Knipschild, and Chaplain Waldeck.

14 Mar – Fort Charlotte at Mobile surrendered to the Spaniards.

17 Mar – The relief force was reported on the way back to Pensacola.

19 Mar – The Waldeckers of the relief force arrived back in camp at 4 PM. The others had returned the same day or possibly one day earlier.

28 Mar – A Spanish fleet consisting of 29 ships, including 2 ships-of-the-line, appeared off Pensacola. The Waldeck Regiment marched to camp at Fort George at 10 AM with flags flying. At the camp the men slept in tents. The other troops at Pensacola moved to Fort George.

1 Apr – Colonel von Hanxleden was given overall command on Gage Hill, including Fort George and the other redoubts. He also served as official greeter of the Indian allies who came to Pensacola.

5 Apr – The Spanish fleet which had been off Pensacola was blown away by a strong wind, or possibly mistook an approaching English supply fleet for reinforcements for the Pensacola garrison.

6 Apr – It became known that the new fleet had Lieutenant Colonel von Horn, his sons, Sergeant Stuckenbrock, and the nineteen men of the 1779 recruit shipment on board.

8 Apr – All but two of the recently arrived ships entered the harbor at Pensacola. Lieutenant Colonel and Ensign von Horn landed.

9 Apr – On this Sunday the recruits landed in good health after having been aboard ship for a full year.

17 Apr – A defensive position behind the camp at Fort George was named Waldeck as it had been constructed entirely by the regiment.

25 Apr – Captain Pentzel and Commissary Marc returned from their mission to New Orleans.

12 May – General Benjamin Lincoln surrendered Charleston, South Carolina, to the English.

1 June – The 1780 recruit shipment for the Waldeck Regiment consisted of only Cadet Friedrich Boehme, who embarked on the transport *Castor* at Bremerlehe on this date, and who was in charge of clothing being sent to the regiment.

7 July – George Germain, secretary of state for the colonies, wrote to the Prince of Waldeck, who had inquired as to the whereabouts of his regiment in March 1779! Germain explained that part of the regiment had been captured and made prisoners of war in West Florida. However, an exchange was being sought and later the regiment would be given better posting, if possible.

18 July – Figures in use in Waldeck indicated the regiment was 106 men under strength.

19 July – Ensign von Horn, recently arrived at Pensacola, died and was buried the next day.

July – At least 35 Waldeck soldiers deserted from prisoner of war status at New Orleans and joined the Spanish army. One of these, Wilhelm Pique, then apparently deserted from the Spanish army, as a William Pique was a member of George Rogers Clark's command in the Illinois Country at a later date. Others, including George Rupert and John Coldwater (Kaltwasser), who deserted at New Orleans but did not join the Spanish army, journeyed up the Mississippi and joined Clark's American troops. During the closing days of the month the Spaniards sent the Waldeck prisoners of war who had been held at New Orleans to Vera Cruz, Mexico, on the *Nuestra Senora del Carmen*. This may have caused the increased July desertion rate among the Waldeck soldiers.

Aug – The Waldeck prisoners of war were sent from Vera Cruz to Havana, Cuba, on the El Cayman.

16 Aug –	Battle of Camden, South Carolina.
Sept –	There was a serious outbreak of illness among the Waldeck soldiers at Pensacola at this time caused by the continuous duty requirements and the shortage of food and medicine.
7 Oct –	Battle of King's Mountain, South Carolina.
16 Oct –	Don Galvez sailed for Pensacola from Havana with a fleet of 64 warships and transports carrying 4,000 men.
30 Oct –	Figures in use in Waldeck indicated the regiment was 156 men under strength.
Oct –	During October five 32-pound cannon were moved from Fort George to The Cliffs which overlook the present-day Pensacola Naval Air Station.
8 Nov –	Captain Pentzel was given command of the artillery position at The Cliffs. He had fifty Waldeck rank and file, plus officers and NCOs.
17 Nov –	Don Galvez arrived back in Havana after having encountered a hurricane during the period 20 to 26 October, which scattered his fleet.
31 Dec –	Colonel von Hanxleden was sent to attack The Village, also known as Frenchtown, a Spanish strongpoint near Mobile. He had 100 infantry, 11 mounted provincials, and 300 Indians. The Waldeckers of his command were Captain von Baumbach, Lieutenants von Wilmowsky and Stierlein, Ensign Ursall, 3 NCOs, 3 corporals, 1 fifer, 1 drummer, and 7 privates.

1781

7 Jan –	The attack on The Village was unsuccessful and the attack force suffered heavy losses. Waldeck losses included Colonel von Hanxleden, Ensign Stierlein, and three soldiers killed, and Captain von Baumbach and seven men wounded.
9 Jan –	The remnants of the command sent against The Village returned to Pensacola. A Spanish fleet of twenty ships arrived off Pensacola from Havana with 1,600 soldiers. Others were on the way.
15 Mar –	Battle of Guilford Courthouse in North Carolina.
18 Mar –	Galvez led a reconnoitering force of ships into Pensacola Harbor.
19 Mar –	The Spanish fleet, 88 ships, entered the harbor.
22/23 Mar –	Spanish reinforcements arrived at Pensacola from New Orleans and Mobile.
25 Mar –	Ten ships sailed from Pensacola, returning Sergeant Stuckenbrock and four invalids, plus one invalid's wife, to Germany. Colonel von Hanxleden's son probably sailed with this fleet, also.

12 Apr – The Waldeck Regiment suffered one man killed and one man wounded from friendly fire from Fort George.

21 Apr – A combined Spanish-French fleet landed 3,000 men at Pensacola. During the siege of Pensacola, according to sketches drawn by Captain Heldring, the defenses included batteries at The Cliffs and a line from the city northward and supporting one another, including Fort George, the Prince of Wales Battery, and the Queen's or Advanced Redoubt.

24 Apr – A sortie by 300 Spaniards was repulsed by the Provincials with artillery support after the Indians had failed to hold the Spaniards. The Spanish sortie was a preliminary move to planning an attack and lasted until about 9 AM. The original Spanish force was supported by five companies of light infantry. At noon an armed Spanish brigantine approached to determine the effectiveness of their naval gunfire and the British counter-fire. The British artillery drove the ship off. At 2 PM a Spanish brig approached and fired on Fort George. The garrison returned the fire and at 3 PM the English artillery officer and Captain von Baumbach with a party of Waldeckers took a howitzer to the water's edge and drove the Spaniards away. At 4 or 5 PM the Spanish infantry tried unsuccessfully to take an elevated position near the English defenses. The Pensacola garrison fired a feu de joie in the evening to celebrate news of the British victory at Guilford Courthouse.

26 Apr – The 1781 Waldeck recruit shipment of 144 men embarked at Bremerlehe with their escort officer, Major Sebisch. They were to sail north of the British Isles to avoid the French fleets.

4 May – The Provincials, supported by Lieutenant Colonel von Horn and the Waldeck troops, made a sortie against some new Spanish positions and spiked six cannon.

7 May – Two Waldeck soldiers were captured by Indians making a reconnaissance against The Cliffs.

8 May – At 9 AM a Spanish shell exploded in a British powder magazine in the Queen's Redoubt killing 81 and injuring 24, but no Waldeckers. The survivors fell back to the Prince of Wales Battery and the Spaniards advanced, capturing heights above Fort George. General Campbell raised a white flag at 3 PM and called a truce to discuss a capitulation.

9 May – At 2 PM negotiations were completed and at 3:30 PM Galvez and two companies of Spanish grenadiers took possession of the city of Pensacola.

10 May – The garrison marched out and laid down its arms. The garrison numbered about 1,200 men plus 1,500 Negroes and Indians. Casualties amounted to about 90 killed and 50

wounded, with Waldeck losses being 5 killed and 6 wounded. About 50 men had deserted from the garrison. Spanish losses were 119 killed and 133 wounded, including Don Galvez.

11 May - The surrender at The Cliffs took place. The combined Spanish-French force consisted of many warships of all sizes, 7,000 Spanish and 3,000 French soldiers, some Americans and Indians, plus an immense artillery train. One estimate of the opposing forces gave the figures as 7,800 effectives for the Spanish-French force and 800 regulars, 200 seamen, and 1,000 Indians for the Pensacola garrison.

29 May - Members of the Waldeck Regiment in the Pensacola garrison boarded the Spanish transports *San Pedro and San Pablo* and *Santa Rosalie*. There were 113 persons, including dependents, on the first and 6 officers, 85 men, 5 women, and 7 children on the latter, whose captain was Pedro Gatell.

1 June - The entire Pensacola garrison, except for the sick, were on board Spanish transports.

4 June - The eleven ships carrying the Pensacola garrison sailed for Havana.

15 - 20 June - The fleet carrying the Pensacola garrison arrived at Havana.

30 June - The ships carrying the Pensacola garrison departed Havana for Fort Reinfort in New York.

12 July - The transports with the Pensacola garrison arrived at New York. The men were landed near Brooklyn and the Waldeckers marched to cantonments at Newtown on Long Island.

15 July - A company of 40 German deserters from the Pensacola garrison had been formed in the Spanish army. As the English 60th Regiment also contained many Germans, all the deserters were not necessarily Waldeckers.

11 Aug - The 1781 Waldeck recruit shipment arrived at New York. The recruits included 1 staff officer, 6 NCOs, 8 drummers, 128 rank and file, 8 women, and 2 children. Seven Waldeckers had died on the crossing and one man died aboard ship in New York Harbor.

26 Aug - The 1781 Waldeck recruits were in the New York area near Hornshook.

1 Sept - Strength figures for the Waldeck Regiment in the New York area showed 124 fit for duty, 127 sick, and 504 effectives. Apparently the 124 fit for duty were the 1781 recruits, the 127 sick from the Pensacola garrison and possibly the 1781 recruits, and both the recruits and former Pensacola garrison totaled 504 men. The recruits were quartered at Hallet's Cove.

5 Sept - Battle of the Chesapeake Capes.

22 Sept - Prior to this date the Prince of Waldeck had offered more than the 140 recruits sent in the 1781 shipment, if the Waldeck officers who were prisoners of war could be exchanged.

7 Oct - Eighty 1781 Waldeck recruits were transferred to Paulus Hook in New Jersey to relieve 120 Brunswickers who were then moved to Denyse's Ferry.

13 Oct - Paulus Hook was attacked by a party of Americans which captured 1 Waldeck soldier, Christian Mueller, who was released in August 1782, and 1 soldier from Anhalt-Zerbst.

15 Oct - Duty at Paulus Hook was being performed by 113 men of the 1781 Waldeck recruit shipment and 373 men of the Anhalt-Zerbst contingent.

19 Oct - The British at Yorktown, Virginia, surrendered.

16 Nov - The Waldeck and Anhalt-Zerbst troops at Paulus Hook were relieved by English troops. The men relieved of duty were moved to Brooklyn in sloops and the Waldeckers then marched to Newtown on Long Island.

1782

20 Mar - Spain still held 145 Waldeck soldiers as prisoners of war and the Americans held 15. Those reported as held by the Americans had probably deserted from prisoner status as early as 1777.

31 May - The 1782 recruit shipment for the Waldeck Regiment, escorted by Sergeant Stuckenbrock, included 1 officer, 5 NCOs, 1 medic, 4 drummers, and 124 recruits, plus either 13 or 16 wives. They boarded the transport *Enterprise* at Bremerlehe with recruits from Anhalt-Zerbst and Brunswick. The *Neptune* carried equipment for the Waldeck Regiment and the convoy was escorted by the frigates *Emerald*, *Cyclops*, and *Pettipoint*.

24 June - The 1781 recruits, who had been kept separated from the former members of the Pensacola garrison, were integrated into the regiment.

24 July - The Waldeck Regiment, although not prohibited from fighting against the Americans by terms of the Pensacola capitulation, had been treated as prisoners on parole by General Clinton, but on this date they were ordered to resume duty.

29 July - The regiment broke winter quarters and camped at Brooklyn together with other units under the command of the Hesse-Hanau Colonel Lentz. The other units included escaped Brunswick Convention prisoners, exchanged officers, Brunswick recruits, Hesse-Hanau Jaeger recruits, the 2nd Battalion of Anhalt-Zerbst, and the "last" Ansbach recruits plus some "picked men of the old corps."

13 Aug –	Eighty-two Waldeck recruits arrived at Halifax, Nova Scotia.
12 Sept –	The Waldeck Regiment was at Brooklyn.
14 Sept –	The regiment was transferred to New York to do garrison duty in the city.
23 Oct –	A Waldeck detail of two officers and fifty men buried the Hessian Lieutenant Hartmann.
1 Nov –	Prior to this date a Major Neumann of the Hessian Seitz Regiment was detached to Penobscot, Maine, from Halifax, with Anhalt-Zerbst, Ansbach-Bayreuth, Hesse-Hanau, and Waldeck recruits to prevent a possible French expedition against that place.
Nov –	Preliminary peace treaty signed by England and the American colonies.
31 Dec –	Estimated strength of the Waldeck Regiment was 500 men with 15 men still held prisoner by the Americans.

1783

15 July –	The Waldeck Regiment, 418 men and women and 13 children, was embarked at New York for the return to Europe. Some men had been released to remain in the New World.
9 Sept –	The transport *Ocean*, with Major Pentzel and 170 Waldeckers, anchored at Cuxhaven in Germany, but the troops were not allowed to land and the ship sailed to Bremerlehe.
23 Sept –	En route home on the Weser, Major Pentzel apparently shot and killed himself.
Sept and Oct –	The men of the Waldeck Regiment arrived in Korbach (W) and many were released. Others, who remained with the regiment under a new designation, the 5th Battalion, were to serve later in the Dutch army and even saw service in South Africa where they fought against the English.
25 Nov –	The British evacuated New York.

SHIP LIST

In addition to the *Adamant*, the *John Abraham*, the *Benjamin*, and the *Jacob Cornelius*, which were used to transport the Waldeck Regiment to America in 1776, the following ships were used to carry recruits to America.

1777 – *Gale*, Master Jefferson, embarked recruits at Bremerlehe on 25 March and debarked the men at Amboy on 15 June, having victualed ninety persons.

1778 – *Two Brothers*, Master Joseph Patten, embarked recruits at Spithead on 6 April and debarked the men at New York on 13 September, having victualed 142 persons, escorted by Captain Sebisch.

1779 – *Seven Brothers*, Master William Dawson, embarked recruits at Spithead on 20 May 1779 and victualed twenty persons. Probably these men were initially landed at New York and then transferred to another ship for the voyage to Pensacola. The recruits landed at Pensacola on 9 April 1780.

1781 – *Castor*, carried the lone recruit for the year for the Waldeck Regiment, Cadet Friedrich Boehme.

1781 – I have not found the name of the ship which carried the recruits in 1781.

1782 – *Enterprise*, transported 1 officer, 134 men, and 13 women of the Waldeck recruits, plus Brunswick and Anhalt–Zerbst recruits to America.

1783 – Fifteen officers, 7 staff, 20 sergeants, 21 drummers, and 335 soldiers, plus 20 women and 13 children were expected "hourly" at Bremerlehe as of 10 September 1783. This number apparently did not include the 170 men who returned to Europe on the *Ocean* with Major Pentzel.

EXPLANATION
of Certain Aspects of the Mini-Bios

The most difficult problem of writing the short biographies, as can easily be imagined, was the identification of individuals. Men with the same or similar names are often encountered, names are misspelled in the records, and men often used given names not even in the birth records, or changed their given names at various times. They even changed the spelling or anglicized their names. As a result, the most common error in the Mini-Bios is probably in assigning the correct name to an individual. In several cases letters in parentheses have also been used with given names to indicate names used but not included on birth records, or a name frequently used. A list of variable spellings has been added at the end of the Mini-Bios, but all possible variations would make the list excessively long. Letters which might be used single or double, such as in 'Man' or 'Mann', have not been indicated. When names begin with C or K, each should be checked. The same is true with T and D, F and V, and other phonetically variable letters. Names such as Heinrich and Henrich, Friedrich and Frederick, have been standardized as Henrich and Friedrich. In general, the name is listed as most often used, or when known, as the individual himself used it. The umlauted letters a, o, and u have been spelled in the following pages as ae, oe, and ue. Designations "senior" and "junior" were sometimes used to indicate earliest or latest assignment to the unit of persons with the same name, as well as age variations and father-son relationships.

Because of the difficulty in identifying individuals with the same last name, when only the name was used in the records, a serial numbering system was developed which could be applied to all the Hessian soldiers. A letter prefix designated the country of origin, in this case "W" for Waldeck. Next, a six-digit number allows for any country to have provided up to 99,999 men, with the number assigned at random, but with the first number of the six digits having a special meaning--1 for commissioned personnel, 2 for foot soldiers, 3 for artillery personnel, and 4 for staff positions. These were the only categories supplied by Waldeck. To allow for a change of status, a letter suffix is used, with "A" indicating transfer to the artillery, "C" receiving a commission, and "S" assignment to the staff.

The next portion of the information in the Mini-Bios contains birth data as accurate as possible, but of necessity often being years in error. The older men were made to seem younger and the little boys were made to seem like men by using false information concernages. This was sometimes done to try to fool the British muster masters who inspected the troops taken into English service. The birthplace is listed as shown in the records, although current spelling corrections have been made, when known.

Religion, height, and trade information is given as presented in the records. Family information is a compilation of information from military church records, as well as genealogical and historical publications.

Information on travel to America, rank, and unit of assignment was compiled from military records, HETRINA, and an analysis of information available.

The next block of information in each individual Mini-Bio is a summary of his service in America, including assignments, promotions, transfers, battles, illness, desertion, captivity, etc.

While the dates are probably accurate in most cases, some information was recorded after the events and the writers' memories may not have been as good as desired. Also, the men captured by the Spaniards in present-day Louisiana are generally listed as returned to duty in January 1782, as shown in the HETRINA. That seems to have been a date when an exchange was agreed upon and the actual date of return may have been sometime later, even as late as March 1782.

Men released as invalids in America probably returned to Europe, as a rule. There are also indications that the boys, who accompanied their soldier fathers to America, were taken into the regiment as batmen or even as privates as they grew up. This would not only have justified their rations, but would have filled vacancies in the organization as well.

It is necessary to make a few remarks concerning geographical places mentioned. In 1776 Waldeck was a principality of some 4,000 square miles and a population of 37,000 persons in 7,000 families, living in 6,000 homes. In the Mini-Bios a (W) indicates Waldeck cities, towns, etc. Other European place names are as found in source documents if a modern spelling was not known.

American places which figured prominently in the life of the Waldeckers included New York City, then a rather small city on the southern end of present-day Manhattan Island. Fort Washington (or later, Fort Knyphausen) and Harlem are also on 'Manhattan Island; Brooklyn, Flatbush, and Newtown were locations where Waldeckers camped on Long Island; Springfield, Amboy, Elizabethtown, and Paulus Hook were locations in New Jersey and places where the Waldeck Regiment suffered casualties as well. Philadelphia, Lancaster, Bethlehem, and Reading were Pennsylvania localities which the Waldeckers visited as prisoners of war. In what was then West Florida, The Village, or Frenchtown, on Mobile Bay, and Manchac, Baton Rouge, and New Orleans were locations where the Waldeckers suffered and died, as was Pensacola. York Point had not been fully identified but was apparently a crossing point on the Delaware River in Pennsylvania.

The final section of the Mini-Bios contains information on military experience prior to assignment to the 3rd regiment and, in some cases, a summary of post-war activities.

Summary

In the following pages 1,194 men who sailed to America with the 3rd English-Waldeck Regiment and the yearly replacements, not counting escort personnel, have been identified, as well as another 64 who either sailed to America or joined the regiment in America; 18 died en route. I have been unable to identify family members who went to America. Regimental losses were 37 combat deaths; 358 deaths due to illness or accidents; 225 men deserted in America, Cuba, and Europe; and 224 men were released from the regiment, about 50 in America.

Private of the Third English-Waldeck Regiment

--reproduced from an original oil painting by Klaus P. Scholz

MEN OF THE THIRD ENGLISH-WALDECK REGIMENT

ALBERTI, Augustin Christian   W100008
Sailed to America with the regiment in 1776 as 1st lieutenant of the 1st
or Grenadier Company. He was promoted to captain lieutenant with
date of rank of 5 March 1777. On 14 October 1777 sailed up the
Hudson River on the *Klenehorn* as part of a planned reinforcement for
General Burgoyne, which, however, returned down river on the 16th
and to Staten Island on the 21st. He was transferred to the 5th
Company in August 1778. He was captured at Baton Rouge on 21
September 1779 and is listed in the HETRINA as returning to duty in
June or July 1780. This seems likely as he boarded the *Santa Rosalia*
with his batman on 29 May 1781 to sail to New York after the capitulation at Pensacola. In April 1782 he was promoted to captain and transferred to the 2nd Company in August. He returned to Germany with the
regiment in 1783.

ALBERTI, Franz Christian Johann   W200389
Born 1752/3 in Helsen (W). Sailed to America with the regiment in
1776 as private in the 4th Company. He had transferred from the 1st to
the 4th Company on 16 April 1776 and been over leave on 29 April but
returned to duty on 31 April 1776. Although previously a drummer, he
served throughout the war as a private. He boarded the *Santa Rosalia*
to return to New York on 29 May 1781, after the capitulation of the
Pensacola garrison. He returned to Germany with the regiment in
1783.

ALBERTI, Johann Christoph   W100004
Born 5 April 1736 in Wildungen (W); he was baptized on 10 April, and
confirmed in 1751. Evangelical. Father - Otto Reinhard A.; Mother -
Henrietta. He sailed to America with the regiment in 1776, having
transferred to the *Adamant* at Spithead, England, on 24 June, as captain lieutenant of the 2nd Company. Promoted to captain (grenadier)
with date of rank of 20 September 1777. He was captured on the Amite
River on 4 September 1779, and after being exchanged, he was released from the regiment on 28 February 1781. He went to Nova Scotia
in 1783. He had 21 years' previous military experience in the armies
of Waldeck and Creyes.

ALBRACHT, Johann Friedrich   W200266
Born 20 June 1751 at Wethen (W). Evangelical. Father - Johann
Christoph A.; Mother - Katharina Margareta, nee Flamme. Third of 7
children. Sailed to America with regiment in 1776 as private in 3rd
Company. Died at Pensacola on 5 November 1779, apparently of ill-
ness, although the *Ortssippenbuch for Wethen* states that he was shot.

1

ALBRACHT, Johannes   W200267
Born 1752/53 in Wega (W). Evangelical. Sailed to America with
the regiment in 1776 as private in 3rd Company. Deserted at Flatbush on 5 May 1783. Previous military service was 2.5 months in the
Waldeck army.

ALBRECHT, Christian Peter   W200018
Born 1759 in Barssen, Pyrmont. Evangelical. Sailed to America
with the regiment in 1776 as a private in the 1st Company. Captured on
5 January 1777 in New Jersey. His name was scratched from a list of
prisoners to be exchanged on 17/18 June 1778 and he was carried as a
prisoner of war until 15 July 1783. He was then declared a deserter
from Elizabethtown. A Christian Albrecht is listed in the 1790 census
as living in Bern Township, Berks County, Pennsylvania, in a household with one adult male, four males under sixteen years of age, and
four females.

ALT, Johann Nikolaus   W201105
Born in Dickesbach. Sailed to America with the 1778 recruit shipment,
and was sick upon arrival. He was assigned (as private?) to the 4th
Company. On 15 July 1783 he was released from the regiment at
Flatbush.

ALTNER, Christoph   W200980
Sailed to America with the 1782 recruit shipment and served with
the 5th Company. He returned to Germany with the regiment in 1783
and was released from the regiment at Korbach (W) on 22 October
1783.

ALTVATER, Karl Friedrich   W200510
Born 1760 in Friedburg. Evangelical. 5'2" tall. Sailed to America
with the regiment in 1776 as a member of the 5th Company. He was
reported as a prisoner in New Jersey on 5 January 1777, and as killed
in action on the same day.

AMELUNG, Johann Christian   W200268
Born 13 August 1758 in Wetterburg (W). Evangelical. Father –
Johann Bernhard A., musketeer of the Garde Regiment; Mother – Anna
Catharina·Schluckebier. Third of 3 children. He sailed to America with
the regiment in 1776 as private in the 3rd Company. On 18 March 1777
he died of illness.

AMMENHAEUSER, Karl   W200632
Born at Rittersheim. He sailed to America with the 1777 recruit
shipment and was assigned to the 4th Company. He was released from
the regiment on 15 July 1783 at Flatbush.

2

ANDRE, Christoph (or Christian) Ludwig W200019
Born 26 June 1736 in Wildungen (W); confirmed in 1750. Evangelical. Married with 2 children. Sailed to America with the regiment in 1776 as private in the 1st Company. He was wounded in the attack on Fort Washington on 16 November 1776, but apparently recovered. On 8 September 1779 he died of illness at Baton Rouge.

ANDREAS, Ernst W200981
He sailed to America with the 1782 recruit shipment and was assigned to the 5th Company. He returned to Germany with the regiment in 1783 and was released from the regiment at Korback (W) on 22 October 1783.

ANDREAS, Georg W201106
Born 1757/58 at Harthausen. On September 1778 he transferred from the English army to the 1st Company and served as a private. He did not sail to West Florida with the regiment in 1778. He died in the hospital at New York on 27 May 1779.

AREND, Johann Christoph W200269
Born 26 August 1757 in Bringhausen (W). Evangelical. 5' 1/4" tall. Father - Karl Friedrich A., shepherd; Mother - Anna Marg., nee Wetzel. Third of 5 children. He married Anna Marg. Sachs on 12 April 1793 and fathered one child, Johann Christoph, born 12 September 1794. Arend died 28 July 1795. He sailed to America with the regiment in 1776 as private in the 3rd Company. On 21 September 1779 he was made a prisoner at Baton Rouge. In December 1779 he was transferred to the 5th Company. He returned to duty in January 1782, and in July was transferred back to the 3rd Company. He returned to Germany with the regiment in 1783.

AREND, Henrich W200020
Born 1750 in Voehl, Darmstaft. Evangelical. 5'5" tall. On a four-year enlistment. He sailed to America with the regiment in 1776 as private in the 1st Company. In April 1779 he was transferred to the 3rd Company, and returned to Germany with the regiment in 1783. On 17 October 1783 he was released from the regiment at Korbach (W).

ASCHENHAUSER, Josef W200838
Born in Hildesheim. Sailed to America with the 1781 recruit shipment and was assigned to the 3rd Company as private. He died at Newtown, Long Island, of illness on 23 November 1781.

ASSMANN, Johannes W200511
Born 1760 in Hildesheim. Evangelical. 5' 2 1/2" tall. He sailed to America with the regiment in 1776 as private in the 5th Company. He was made a prisoner at Baton Rouge on 21 September 1779 and deserted on 5 October 1780 at Havana.

3

AXLEBEN, Friedrich von   W200001C
Born 1741 in Fegebuedel, Schlesingen. Evangelical. He sailed to
America with the regiment in 1776 as sergeant in the 1st Company. In
March 1777 he was commissioned an ensign and transferred to the 5th
Company. He was placed under arrest on 1 April 1779 and on 18
November I779 was released from the regiment at Pensacola for
conduct unbecoming an officer.

BACHMANN, Georg   W201084
Born in Goettingen. Entered the regiment as batman in the 2nd
Company in 1781. He was released from the regiment in August 1782,
according to the HETRINA. However, this notation may only mean
that by that date he had been released. Entries for later dates indicate
that he was a private in the 5th Company by June 1782, and
returned to Germany with the regiment. He was released from the
regiment on 19 September 1783 at Bremen. It is possible that he was
released as a batman, and taken back into the regiment as a private in
order to provide him with subsistence and transportation back to
Europe.

BACHSTAEDTER, Ignatius   W200021
Born 1738 in Wuerzburg. Reformed. 5'5" tall. Married with 1 child.
Sailed to America with the regiment in 1776 as private in the 1st
Company. In December 1779 he transferred to the 3rd Company. He
and his wife boarded the *Santa Rosalia* at Pensacola on 29 May 1781,
after the Pensacola capitulation, and returned to New York. In July
1782 he transferred back to the 1st Company. On 15 July 1783 he was
released from the regiment at Flatbush, New York. He had four and
one-half years' previous military experience in the Prussian army.

BACKES, Johannes   W200982
Sailed to America with the 1782 recruit shipment as private and was
assigned to the 5th Company. His initial assignment may have been
to the 3rd Company. He died of illness on 9 November 1782.

BACKHAUS, Henrich Georg   W200022
Born 1754 in Lengefeld (W). Evangelical. 5' 6" tall. Smith by
trade. He sailed to America with the regiment in 1776 as private in the
1st Company. He was killed in action on 16 November 1776 at Fort
Washington.

BANGERT, Jakob Johannes   W200023
Born 8 December 1755 in Meineringhausen (W). Evangelical.
Father - Jost B.; Mother - Juliana. Eighth of 8 children. He sailed to
America with the regiment in 1776 as a private in the 1st Company. He
died 26 July 1779 in the hospital at Manchac, Louisiana, of an
illness.

4

BANGERT, Johannes   W200839
Sailed to America with the 1781 recruit shipment and was assigned
as drummer to the 3rd Company. In July 1782 he was transferred to the
5th Company. He apparently returned to Germany with the regiment in
1783.

BANSE, Dietmar   W200390
Born 1753 in Besse, Hesse. Reformed. 5' 4 1/2" tall. Sailed to
America with the regiment in 1776 as private in the 4th Company.
Made a prisoner, probably in New Jersey, in January 1777; he deserted
from prisoner status at Lancaster, Pennsylvania, on 4 May 1778. He
had one year of previous military experience in Holland, probably in a
Waldeck unit.

BARTH, Adam   W200840
Sailed to America with the 1781 recruit shipment as private in the 3rd
Company. He transferred to the 5th Company in July 1782, and returned to Germany with the regiment in 1783. On 16 October 1783 he
was released from the regiment at Korbach (W).

BATISTER, Johann Henrich   W200391
Born 1755 in Emmern, Hannover. Evangelical. 5' 4 3/4" tall.
Sailed to America with the regiment in 1776 as private in the 4th
Company. He appears to have been made prisoner in January 1777, in
New Jersey, as he deserted from prisoner status at Lancaster, Penn-
sylvania, on 4 May 1778. He had two years of previous military serv-
ice in Holland, probably in a Waldeck unit.

BAUER, Andreas Adam   W200983
Sailed to America with the 1782 recruit shipment and was assigned
as private to the 5th Company. He returned to Germany in 1783 and
was released at Korbach (W) on 14 October 1783.

BAUER, Christian   W200634
Born in Gotha. Sailed to America with the 1778 recruit shipment as
drummer and was assigned to the 1st Company. On 10 July 1779 he
deserted at Manchac, Louisiana.

BAUER, Friedrich   W200270
Born 1752 in Wehrtheim, Loewenstein. Evangelical. He sailed to
America with the regiment in 1776 as private in the 3rd Company. He
died of illness at Pensacola on 8 December 1779.

BAUER, Georg   W200512
Born 1748 in Bergzabern, Zweibruecken. Evangelical. 5'3" tall.
Shoemaker by trade. Married with 2 children. He sailed to America
with the regiment in 1776 as private in the 5th Company. He was made
a prisoner at Baton Rouge on 21 September 1779. On 2 July 1780 he
deserted from prisoner status and joined the Spanish army. He had four
years' previous military experience in Holland, probably in a Waldeck
unit.

5

BAUER, Karl W200841
Born in Asslar. He sailed to America with the 1781 recruit shipment and was assigned as private to the 3rd Company. In July 1782 he was transferred to the 1st Company. He returned to Germany with the regiment in 1783 and was released at Bremen on 19 September 1783.

BAUER, Karl W200984
Sailed to America with the 1782 recruit shipment and was assigned to the 5th Company. He returned to Germany in 1783 and was released from the regiment on 22 October 1783 at Korbach (W).

BAUER, Philipp W201107
Sailed to America with the 1778 recruit shipment and was sick upon arrival. He was probably assigned as a private in the 4th Company. He died of illness on 27 November 1778 on the transport ship *Crawford* en route to West Florida.

BAUERSCHMIDT, Ludwig W200024
Born 1748 in Amt Gifhorn an der Alter. Evangelical. 5' 8 1/2" tall. Sailed to America with the regiment in 1776 as private in the 1st Company. He was made a prisoner in New Jersey on 5 January 1777, and returned from captivity in August 1778. He was captured again on 21 September 1779 at Baton Rouge, and returned to duty in January 1782. In June 1782 he was promoted to corporal and apparently returned to Germany with the regiment in 1783. He had eight months' previous military experience in the Waldeck 2nd Regiment, probably in Holland.

BAUMBACH, Alexander von W100007
Born in Amenau, Upper Hesse. Evangelical. Sailed to America with the regiment in 1776 as captain lieutenant (date of rank of 16 March 1776) in the 1st Company. He was wounded in action at The Village (also known as Frenchtown), near present-day Mobile, Alabama, on 7 January 1781. In April 1782 he was promoted to captain and in July transferred to the 3rd Company. In August he was named company commander, and apparently returned to Germany with the regiment in 1783.

BAUMGARTEN, Georg W200842
He sailed to America with the 1781 recruit shipment and was assigned to the 3rd Company. He returned to Germany with the regiment in 1783 and released at Korbach (W) on 17 October of that year.

BAUMUELLER, Johann Andreas W200513
Born 1757 in Kleinern (W). Evangelical. 5'2" tall. He sailed to America with the regiment in 1776 as private in the 5th Company. He was made a prisoner at Baton Rouge on 21 September 1779 and died of illness at New Orleans on 18 October 1779.

6

BAUS, Andreas (or Adam)   W200635
Born in Enzweihingen. The date and method of his joining the regiment is uncertain. He may have been in the 1777 recruit shipment. His initial assignment was as private in the 3rd Company. He returned to Germany with the regiment in 1783 and was released at Bremen on 19 September 1783.

BECK, Franz Karl   W200636
Born in Pressbach, Bamberg. Date and manner of joining the regiment is uncertain. May have been with the 1777 recruit shipment. Assigned as private to 5th Company. Deserted at Manchac on 2 or 3 September 1779.

BECK, Johann Henrich Daniel   W200255
Born 6 April 1754 in Helsen (W). Evangelical. Surgeon by profession. Father - Bernhard Ludwig B., confectioner in Arolsen (W); Mother - Catherine Marie, nee Thon. Seventh child, and brother of Johann Wilhelm Christoph Beck (W201108). Sailed to America with the regiment in 1776 as medic in the 3rd Company. After the battle at Fort Washington on 16 November 1776, Beck and Corporal Steuernagel took the wounded of the regiment to the hospital at Harlem, arriving early the same evening. He was wounded in action and taken prisoner at Baton Rouge on 21 September 1779. In December 1779 he was transferred to the 5th Company, and probably exchanged in January 1782. In July 1782 he was transferred back to the 3rd Company. He was released from the regiment at Flatbush on 15 July 1783. Previous military experience included 6 months in the Hesse Cassel army, from which he deserted; 9 years in Prussian Service; and 1 year in the Waldeck 2nd Regiment, probably serving in Holland. A Daniel Beck is listed in the 1790 census as living in Flatbush, Kings County, New York, in a household with one adult male, five males under sixteen years of age, and two females.

BECK, Johann Wilhelm Christoph   W201108
Born 25 February 1757 in Helsen (W). Brother of Johann Henrich Daniel Beck (W200255). Eighth child in the family. Date and manner of joining the regiment is uncertain. May have been with the 1777 recruit shipment. Assigned as private in the 3rd Company. Released from the regiment in America on 30 September 1778, he sailed to Europe on the *Echo* on 8 October 1778, arriving at Portsmouth, England, on 1 January 1779.

BECKER, Christian   W200637
Born in Kronweissenburg. Sailed to America with the 1777 recruit shipment and assigned as private in the 3rd Company. Separated at Flatbush on 15 July 1783.

BECKER, Jakob   W200271
Born 1756 in Adorf (W). Evangelical. Sailed to America with the regiment in 1776 as private in the 3rd Company. Returned to Germany with the regiment in 1783 and was released at Korbach (W) on 19 October 1783.

BECKER, Jakob   W201169
Born in Hemmighausen (W). Date and manner of joining regiment is uncertain. By 4 September 1779 he was a batman in the 2nd Company, possibly serving Lieutenant Noelting. He was made a prisoner on the Amite River on 4 September 1779, and died of illness at New Orleans on 20 October 1779 while in prisoner status.

BECKER, Johannes   W200145
Born 1755 in Luezen (W). Evangelical. Shoemaker by trade. Sailed to America with the regiment in 1776 as private in the 2nd Company. He was captured at Springfield, New Jersey, on 5 January 1777, and sent to Philadelphia for exchange on 18 June 1778. In December 1779 he was transferred to the 4th Company, and in June 1782 was transferred back to the 2nd Company. He appears to have returned to Germany with the regiment in 1783.

BECKER, Johannes   W200514
Born Bergheim (W), and baptized 26 October 1752. Evangelical. 5'5" tall. Father - Christoph B. Sailed to America with the regiment in 1776 as private in the 5th Company. He was made prisoner at Baton Rouge on 21 September 1779 and returned to duty in January 1782. He apparently returned to Germany with the regiment in 1783.

BECKER, Lorenz   W200843
He sailed to America with the 1781 recruit shipment and was assigned as private in the 3rd Company. In July 1782 he was transferred to the 1st Company. He returned to Germany with the regiment and was released at Korbach (W) on 17 October 1783.

BECKER, Matthias   W200146
Born 1756 in Rhenegge (W). Evangelical. 5'3" tall. He sailed to America with the regiment in 1776 as private in the 2nd Company. In December 1779 he was transferred to the 4th Company and in June 1782 transferred back to the 2nd Company. He apparently returned to Germany with the regiment in 1783.

BECKMANN, Dietrich Henrich   W200392
Born 1752 in Stadt Roehne, Paderborn. Catholic. 5'2 1/2" tall. Sailed to America with the regiment in 1776 as private in the 4th Company. He served throughout the war in the 4th Company. Following the capitulation at Pensacola, he boarded the *Santa Rosalia* for return to New York on 29 May 1781. He returned to Germany with the regiment and was released at Korbach (W) on 16 October 1783.

BEHR, Johannes   W200638
Born 1745/46 in Landau (W). Sailed to America with the 1778 recruit shipment and was assigned as private in the 1st Company. He died of illness in the hospital at Pensacola on 29 June 1779.

BEISENHERTZ, Daniel   W200147
Born 1755 in Sachsenberg (W). Evangelical. 5'3" tall. Sailed to
America with the regiment in 1776 as private in the 2nd Company. He
was made prisoner on the Amite River on 4 September 1779, and returned to duty in January 1782. He apparently returned to Germany with
the regiment in 1783.

BENDER, Georg   W201109
Born in Malchen. Sailed to America with the 1777 recruit shipment
(as private?) and was assigned to the 4th Company. He died of illness
on 15 October 1777.

BERGER, Justinus   W200639
Date and manner of joining the regiment is uncertain. May have
been with the 1777 recruit shipment. Assigned as drummer in the 4th
Company. He returned to Germany with the regiment and was released
at Korbach (W) on 20 October 1783.

BERGER, Ludwig   W200393
Born 1739 in Spangenberg, Hesse. Evangelical. Married with 2 children. Sailed to America with the regiment in 1776 as private in the 4th
Company. He was wounded on 16 November 1776 at Fort Washington.
On 5 January 1777 he was made prisoner at Springfield, New Jersey,
and sent to Philadelphia for exchange on 18 June 1778. On 24 October
1778 he was released in America as an invalid. He returned to Europe
on the *Echo* on 8 October 1778, arriving at Portsmouth, England, on 1
January 1779.

BERGES, Bernhard   W200501
Born 1754 in Mengeringhausen (W). Evangelical. Sailed to America
with the regiment in 1776 as corporal in the 5th Company. He was
made a prisoner on the Amite River on 4 September 1779 and returned
to duty in January 1782. He apparently returned to Germany with the
regiment in 1783.

BERGES, Henrich   W200148
Born 1734 in Mengeringhausen (W). Evangelical. Miller by trade.
Married with 1 child. Sailed to America with the regiment in 1776 as
private in the 2nd Company. Taken prisoner on the Amite River on 4
September 1779, he died of illness aboard ship near Havana, while
still in PW status, on 27 August 1781. Previous military experience
amounted to 4 years in the Waldeck 2nd Regiment.

BERGES, Johannes   W200515
Born 1756 in Mengeringhausen (W). Evangelical. Miller by trade.
Sailed to America with the regiment in 1776 as private in the 5th
Company. He was taken prisoner at Baton Rouge on 21 September 1779
and returned to duty in January 1782. He apparently returned to
Germany with the regiment in 1783.

BERGES, Ludwig   W200025
Born 30 September 1753 in Berndorf (W). Evangelical. Father -
Arnold Henrich B., miller. Sailed to America with the regiment in 1776
as private in the 1st Company, having joined on the march to Bremerlehe. He was taken prisoner at Baton Rouge on 21 September 1779, and
returned to duty in January 1782. He apparently returned to Germany
with the regiment in 1783.

BERGHOEFER, Wilhelm   W200026
Born 1738 in Twiste (W). Evangelical. Married in 1760, he had 4
children: Johannes, born 20 April 1761, died 23 September 1763;
Johann Henrich, born 6 March 1764, died 20 December 1769; Johannes,
born 15 April 1768, died 17 June 1769; and Anna Margarette Elisa-
beth, born 15 July 1770. Sailed to America with the regiment in 1776
as private in the 1st Company. Taken prisoner at Baton Rouge on 21
September 1779, he returned to duty in January 1782. He returned to
Germany with the regiment and was released at Korbach (W) on 19
October 1783.

BERGMANN, Christian   W200272
Born 1760 in Furstenberg (W). Evangelical. 4'8" tall. Sailed to
America with the regiment in 1776 as private in the 3rd Company,
after having originally enlisted as a drummer. Served in the 3rd
Company throughout the war and apparently returned to Germany with
the regiment in 1783.

BERGMANN, Henrich   W200640
Born in Baccum. Sailed to America with the 1778 recruit shipment
and was assigned as private in the 5th Company. Taken prisoner at
Baton Rouge on 21 September 1779, he died of illness at New Orleans on 9 October 1779.

BERINGER, Michael   W200844
Sailed to America with the 1781 recruit shipment and was assigned
as private in the 3rd Company. In July 1782 he was transferred to the
5th Company. He returned to Germany with the regiment and was
released at Korbach (W) on 16 October 1783.

BERLIN, Christian   W200641
Born in Londorf. Sailed to America with the 1778 recruit shipment and
was assigned as corporal in the 1st Company. He deserted at Manchac
on 19 July 1779.

BERTHOLD, Henrich   W200384
Born in Korbach (W), and baptized 6 November 1746. Evangelical.
Father - Johann B.; Mother - Anna Maria, nee Soebel. Sailed to
America with the regiment in 1776 as corporal in the 4th Company.
After the capitulation at Pensacola, he boarded the *Santa Rosalia* to
return to New York on 29 May 1781. He served throughout the war in
the 4th Company and apparently returned to Germany with the regiment
in 1783. Previous military experience amounted to 10 years' service in
Holland, probably in a Waldeck unit.

10

BERTRAM, Matthias   W200985
Sailed to America with the 1782 recruit shipment and was assigned
to the 5th Company. Died of illness at Halifax on 25 March 1783.

BESSELBACH, Johannes   W200642
Born 1750/51 in Mannheim. Sailed to America with the 1777 recruit
shipment and was assigned as private in the 4th Company. Died of
illness at Pensacola in December 1780.

BESTE, Henrich   W200137
Born 1747/48 in Korbach (W). Evangelical. Sailed to America with
the regiment in 1776 as corporal in the 2nd Company. Deserted on 5
April 1777. Previous military experience either 6 years or 8 years 5
months (records vary) in the Waldeck army.

BESTELMEIER, Wilhelm   W200845
Born in Nuernberg. Sailed to America with the 1781 recruit shipment
and was assigned as private in the 3rd Company. In June 1782 he was
transferred to the 2nd Company. He returned to Germany with the
regiment and was released at Bremen on 19 September 1783.

BETHE, Henrich   W200986
Sailed to America with the 1782 recruit shipment and was assigned
to the 5th Company. Apparently returned to Germany with his unit in
1783.

BETTE, Johann Wilhelm   W200394
Born 1754 in Usseln (W). Evangelical. 5'6" tall. Sailed to America with the regiment in 1776 as private in the 4th Company. Served
throughout the war in the 4th Company and apparently returned to
Germany with the regiment in 1783.

BETZ, Michael   W200643
Born in Rieneck. Sailed to America with the 1778 recruit shipment
and was assigned to the 5th Company. He did not sail to West Florida
with the regiment in 1778, but died of illness in the hospital at New
York on 5 April 1779.

BEUSCH, Philipp   W201193
Born in Neidelheim, Pfalz. Sailed to America with the 1777 recruit
shipment and was assigned as private in the 5th Company. Died of
illness on 20 August 1777.

BEVER, Friedrich   W300001
Born in Goettingen or Hameln. Sailed to America with the regiment
in 1776 as cannoneer in the artillery section. Died of illness on 28
March 1778.

BEYER, Bernhard Leonhard   W200149
Born 1756 in Armsfeld (W). Evangelical. Sailed to America with
the regiment in 1776 as private in the 2nd Company. Taken prisoner on
5 January 1777 at Springfield, New Jersey, he was sent to Philadelphia
to be exchanged on 18 June 1778. In December 1779 he was transferred to the 4th Company. After the capitulation of Pensacola he
boarded the *Santa Rosalia* to return to New York on 29 May 1781. In
June 1782 he transferred back to tbe 2nd Company. He apparently
returned to Germany with the regiment in 1783.

BICKMANN, Johann Christian   W200516
Born 18 June 1749 in Gembeck (W). Evangelical. Father - Konrad
B.; Mother - Maria Katherina, nee Fingerhut. First of 2 children.
Cousin of Johann Friedrich Fingerhut (W200174). Sailed to America
with the regiment in 1776 as private in the 5th Company. Taken prisoner at Baton Rouge on 21 September 1779, he deserted from prisoner
status at New Orleans on 15 July 1780.

BIEBER, Ignatius   W201110
Born 1754/55 in Vienna. Sailed to America with the 1777 recruit
shipment as private in the 2nd Company. He was transferred to the 4th
Company in December 1779. On 17 May 1781, after the fall of Pensacola, he deserted from prisoner status. He may have joined the Spanish army.

BIEG, Jakob   W200644
Sailed to America with the 1777 recruit shipment and was assigned
to the 3rd Company. He served in the 3rd Company during the war and
returned to Germany with the regiment in 1783. He was released at
Korbach (W) on 17 October 1783.

BIGGE, Franz   W200150
Born 1751/52 in Beringhausen, Koeln. Catholic. 5'4 1/4" tall.
Sailed to America with the regiment in 1776 as private in the 2nd
Company. Taken prisoner on 5 January 1777 at Springfield, New
Jersey, he was sent to Philadelphia to be exchanged on 18 June 1778.
He deserted, possibly while still in prisoner status, on 1 August 1778.
Previous military experience amounted to 7 years in the Waldeck 2nd
Regiment.

BIGGE, Franz Christoph Adam   W200846
Born in 1767 in Sudeck (W). Lutheran. 4'9" tall. Sailed to America
with the 1781 recruit shipment and was assigned as fifer in the 3rd
Company. He died of illness at Newtown on 23 December 1781.

BIGGE, Otto   W200517
Born 1754 in Sudeck (W). Evangelical. 5'1" tall. Sailed to America
with the regiment in 1776 as private in the 5th Company. Taken prisoner at Baton Rouge on 21 September 1779, he died of illness at New
Orleans on 7 October 1779 while still a prisoner.

BILLERBECK, Christian   W200987
Sailed to America with the 1782 recruit shipment and was assigned
as private in the 5th Company. He apparently returned to Germany with
his unit in 1783.

BIRCK, Adam   W201111
Born in Mergenthal. Sailed to America with the 1778 recruit shipment
and was sick upon arrival. He was assigned (as a private?) in the 4th
Company. He died of illness in the hospital on 17 December 1778.

BIRCHENHAUER, Christoph Friedrich   W200141
Born in Korbach (W) and baptized 11 February 1753. Evangelical.
Father - Adam B.; Mother - Maria Gerdruth Zimmermann Soebel.
Sailed to America with the regiment in 1776 as fifer in the 2nd
Company. He served throughout the war as a fifer, and was wounded at
The Village on 7 January 1781. He was apparently transferred to the
4th Company later that year, and then returned to Germany with the
regiment in 1783. He had originally joined the Waldeck army on 11
May 1769.

BIRCKMANN, Johannes   W200273
Born 1758 in Reiningen, Wuertemberg. Catholic. 5'3" tall. On a 6-year
enlistment. Sailed to America with the regiment in 1776 as private in
the 3rd Company. He deserted on 3 April 1777.

BLAUFUS, Jakob   W200151
Born 1752 in Ernsthausen, Sachs Eisenach. Evangelical. 5'2 1/2" tall.
Sailed to America with the regiment in 1776 as private in the 2nd
Company. Taken prisoner on the Amite River on 4 September 1779, he
deserted from prisoner status on 2 July 1780 and joined the Spanish
army.

BLESS, Johann Georg   W200646
Sailed to America with the 1778 recruit shipment and was assigned
as private to the 4th Company. After the capitulation of Pensacola he
boarded the *Santa Rosalia* to return to New York on 29 May 1781. He
served in the 4th Company during the war. He returned to Germany
with the regiment and was released at Korbach (W) on 17 October
1783.

BLESS, Johannes   W200647
Born in Erbach. Sailed to America with the 1778 recruit shipment
and was sick upon arrival. He was assigned as private in the 2nd
Company. In December 1779 he transferred to the 4th Company. On
17 May 1781, after the fall of Pensacola, he deserted from prisoner
status and may have joined the Spanish army.

BLESS, Paul   W200648
Born in Erbach. Sailed to America with the 1778 recruit shipment
and was assigned as private in the 1st Company. He died of illness at
Baton Rouge on 19 September 1779.

13

BLOCK, Philipp   W200649
Born in Aalen. Sailed to America with the 1778 recruit shipment and
was assigned as private in the 2nd Company. In December 1779 he
was transferred to the 4th Company. He is listed in the HETRINA as
having deserted in June 1781, after the fall of Pensacola, but in a list
of personnel who died, deserted, or were released from the regiment,
he is listed as having deserted on 24 July 1781 in Havana. By
December 1782 he had apparently rejoined the regiment. He returned
to Germany with the regiment and was released at Bremen on 19
September 1783.

BOB, John   W201170
Date and manner of joining the regiment are uncertain, but by
December 1781 he was a batman in the 4th Company. It appears
likely that he may have been a Negro slave. In June 1782 he was
transferred to the 2nd Company. He may have returned to Germany
with the regiment in 1783. However, a BOB is listed in the 1790
census as living at Maroneck, West Chester County, New York, and
all five persons in the household were "free" people.

BOCK, Georg Andreas   W200027
Born 1754 in Alt Lothheim, Darmstadt. Evangelical. Sailed to
America with the regiment in 1776 as private in the 1st Company.
Taken prisoner at Baton Rouge on 21 September 1779, he deserted
from prisoner status at New Orleans on 13 July 1780 and joined the
Spanish army.

BOCK, Henrich   W200395
Born 1730 in Netze (W). Evangelical. Married. Sailed to America
with the regiment in 1776 as private in the 4th Company. He died of
illness in the hospital on 22 December 1776.

BOCK, Johann Georg   W200518
Born 1756 in Wenzingerode. Evangelical. 5'5 3/4" tall. Sailed to
America with the regiment in 1776 as private in the 5th Company. He
was taken prisoner on 8 January 1777 at Elizabethtown, New Jersey,
and enlisted in the American army. He apparently deserted back to
his own regiment as he was again made prisoner at Baton Rouge on 21
September 1779. He returned to duty in January 1782, but deserted
once again at Flatbush on 8 May 1783. He had 2 years' previous military experience in Holland, probably in a Waldeck unit. A John Bock
is listed in the 1790 census as living at Halfmoon, Albany County,
New York, in a household with two adult males and four females.

BOCK, Konrad   W200847
Sailed to America with the 1781 recruit shipment and was assigned
as private in the 3rd Company. In June 1782 he was transferred to the
1st Company, and apparently returned to Germany with the regiment in
1783.

BOEHLE, Friedrich   W200817
Born 1762/63 in Ober Waroldern (W). Sailed to America with the
1779 recruit shipment and was assigned as private in the 4th Company.
After the capitulation of Pensacola he boarded the *Santa Rosalia* for
return to New York on 29 May 1781. He returned to Germany with the
regiment and was released at Korbach (W) on 20 October 1783.

BOEHLE, Wilhelm Friedrich   W200818
Born 1761/62 in Usseln (W). Sailed to America with the 1779 recruit shipment and was assigned as private in the 3rd Company. He
was transferred to the 5th Company in July 1782 and apparently returned to Germany with the regiment in 1783.

BOEHME, Friedrich   W201112
Born in Cleve. The only man in the 1780 recruit shipment for the
Waldeck Regiment, he sailed to America on the *Castor*. Although a
Cadet, his assignment in America seems to have been as private in
the 3rd Company. He was promoted to corporal on 25 December 1781
and may never have left New York. He was released from the regiment at Flatbush on 15 July 1783, and went to Nova Scotia where he
settled in Clementsport. He died in 1816 and was buried at Edward's
Church in Clementsport.

BOEHMER, Philipp   W200650
Born in Odenbach. Sailed to America with the 1777 recruit shipment
and was assigned as private in the 3rd Company. He deserted at
Pensacola on 17 May 1781, after the fall of Pensacola, and may have
joined the Spanish army.

BOEHNE, Wilhelm   W200651
Born in Twiste (W). Date and manner of joining the regiment are
uncertain, but he may have been with the 1777 recruit shipment. By
April 1779 he was drummer in the 2nd Company. In December 1779 he
was transferred to the 4th Company and in June 1782 transferred back
to the 2nd Company. He apparently returned to Germany with the
regiment in 1783.

BOESAM, Georg   W200988
Sailed to America with the 1782 recruit shipment and was assigned
as private in the 5th Company. He apparently returned to Germany with
his unit in 1783.

BOETTGER, Philipp Friedrich   W200152
Born 1757 in Bremen. Evangelical. 5'2" tall. On 6-year enlistment.
Sailed to America with the regiment in 1776 as private in the 4th
Company. Taken prisoner on the Amite River on 4 September 1779, he
died of illness while in prisoner status at New Orleans on 17 October
1779.

BOLTZE, Henrich   W200819
Born 1759/60 in Hameln. Sailed to America with the 1779 recruit
shipment and assigned as private in the 3rd Company. He deserted at
Flatbush on 4 June 1783.

BORN, Johannes   W200620
Sailed to America with the 1778 recruit shipment. There is no further
information available.

BORNEMANN, Ludwig   W200652
Born in Bovenden. Date and manner of joining the regiment are
uncertain. He may have been with the 1777 recruit shipment. By
April 1779 he was a private in the 5th Company. Taken prisoner at
Baton Rouge on 21 September 1779, he died of illness while in prison-
er status at New Orleans on 26 February 1780.

BRABENDER, Johann Henrich   W201113
Baptized 13 April 1749 in Twiste (W). Father - Johannes B.;
Mother - Marie Katherine, nee Schlingmann. Second of 3 children.
Transferred to the 3rd Regiment from the British army on 8 September
1778 and assigned as private in the 2nd Company. Transferred to the
4th Company in December 1779 and back to the 2nd Company in June
1782. Returned to Germany with the regiment and was released at
Korbach (W) on 24 October 1783.

BRAND, Christian   W200519
Born 1753/54 in Hamburg. Evangelical. 5'3" tall. Blacksmith by
trade. On 6-year enlistment. Sailed to America with the regiment in
1776 as private in the 5th Company. He was made a prisoner of war in
New Jersey on 20 January 1777 and sent into captivity in Pennsylvania. Apparently exchanged in 1778, he was wounded in action and
taken prisoner at Baton Rouge on 21 September 1779. He returned to
duty in January 1782. He returned to Germany with the regiment and
was released at Bremen on 19 September 1783.

BRAND, Friedrich Wilhelm   W200274
Born in Rhoden (W) and confirmed in 1768. Evangelical. 5'2" tall.
Sailed to America with the regiment in 1776 as private in the 3rd
Company. He was killed in action at Fort Washington on 16 November
1776.

BRANDES, Ludwig   W200989
Sailed to America with the 1782 recruit shipment and was assigned
as private in the 5th Company. Apparently returned to Germany with
his unit in 1783.

BRANDSTEIN, Johann Daniel Christian   W200520
Born 1745 in Koenigshagen (W). Evangelical. Sailed to America
with the regiment in 1776 as private in the 5th Company. Taken prisoner at Baton Rouge on 21 September 1779, he returned to duty in Jan.
1782. He apparently returned to Germany with the regiment in 1783.
He had 8 years' previous military experience in the Waldeck army.

BRASSER, Ludwig   W200990
Sailed to America with the 1782 recruit shipment and was assigned
as private in the 5th Company. He returned to Germany with his unit
and then deserted at Bremen on 30 September 1783.

BRAUN, Johannes   W200028
Born 1740 in Giessen, Darmstadt. Evangelical. Sailed to America
with the regiment in 1776 as private in the 1st Company. Released in
Germany as an invalid on 24 June 1778. He had 4 years' previous
military experience in the Darmstadt army.

BRAUN, Johannes   W201114
Born in Brey. Sailed to America with the 1778 recruit shipment and
assigned as private in the 1st Company. He deserted at Manchac on 2
August 1779.

BRAUN, Peter   W201115
Born in Stade. Sailed to America with the 1778 recruit shipment and
was assigned as private in the 3rd Company. He died of illness on 10
November 1778 aboard the transport *Springfield* en route to West Florida.

BRAUNS, Adam   W200820
Born 1739/40 in Battenhausen (W). He Sailed to America with the
1779 recruit shipment and was assigned as private in the 3rd Company. He died of illness on 3 November 1780.

BRAUNS, Carl Philipp   W300002
Born prior to 1740 in Pyrmont. Evangelical. 5'7" tall. Married
Clara Louyse Stoeltingen on 2 March 1756 at Bad Pyrmont. A son,
Johann Ernst Wilhelm Brauns, was born 21 March 1760. He sailed to
America with the regiment in 1776 as cannoneer in the artillery sec-
tion. In June 1781 he was transferred to the 3rd Company, and in 1782
to the 5th Company. He returned to Germany with the regiment and
was released at Korbach (W) on 16 October 1783.

BREMER, Ludwig Lewis   W200848
Sailed to America with the 1781 recruit shipment and was assigned
as private in the 3rd Company. He apparently returned to Germany with
the regiment in 1783.

BRESSLER, Georg   W200991
Sailed to America with the 1782 recruit shipment and was assigned
as private in the 5th Company. He returned to Germany with his unit
and was released at Korbach (W) on 23 October 1783.

BREUNINGER, Anton   W200992
Sailed to America with the 1782 recruit shipment and was assigned
as private in the 5th Company. He returned to Germany with his unit
but deserted at Bremen on 30 September 1783.

BREUNINGER, Friedrich   W200029
Born 1753/54 in Neustadt, Hohen. Evangelical. Brickmaker by trade.
Sailed to America with the regiment in 1776 as private in the 1st
Company. He was apparently made a prisoner in N.J. in 1777, as he
deserted from prisoner status at Lancaster, Pa., on 6 June 1778. He
had 5 yrs.' prior military experience in the Waldeck 1st Regiment.

BREY, Christoph   W200993
Sailed to America with the 1782 recruit shipment and was assigned
as private in the 5th Company. He died of illness on 4 January 1783.

BREY, Johann Henrich Daniel   W201116
Born in Fuerstenberg (W). Date and manner of joining the regiment
are uncertain. In 1777 he was a corporal in the 4th Company. He died
of illness on 14 August 1777.

BREYER, Anton   W200994
Sailed to America with the 1782 recruit shipment and was assigned
as private in the 5th Company. He returned to Germany with his unit
but deserted at Bremen on 30 September 1783.

BROCK, Konrad   W200849
Sailed to America with the 1781 recruit shipment and was assigned
as private in the 3rd Company. In July 1782 he was transferred to the
5th Company. He returned to Germany with the regiment and was
released at Korbach (W) on 23 October 1783.

BRUECKHAEUSER, Henrich   W200505
Born 1756 in Todtenhausen, Hesse. Evangelical. 5'7 1/4" tall.
Blacksmith by trade. Sailed to America with the regiment in 1776 as
corporal in the 5th Company. Taken prisoner at Amboy, New Jersey,
on 14 January 1777, he enlisted in the American army. Apparently he
later deserted back to his regiment, since he was released in America
on 6 September 1778 as an invalid. He returned to Europe on the *Echo*
on 8 October 1778 and arrived at Portsmouth on 1 January 1779. He
had 4 years and 2 months of previous military experience in the
Hessian army and 3 months' previous military experience in Holland,
probably in a Waldeck unit.

BRUEHNE, Carl Friedrich   W200135
Born 19 January 1756 in Helsen (W). Evangelical. Father – Johann
Christian B., master smith for the court; Mother – Maria Catherina,
nee Pampe. Sailed to America with the regiment in 1776 as corporal in
the 2nd Company. Taken prisoner on 5 January 1777 at Springfield,
New Jersey, he was sent from Lancaster to Philadelphia to be exchanged on 29 July 1778. He was transferred to the 4th Company in
December 1779 and promoted to captain at arms in April 1780. In June
of 1782 he was promoted to sergeant and transferred to the 5th Company. He apparently returned to Germany with the regiment in 1783. He
had 3 years' previous military experience in the Waldeck 2nd Regiment, and was probably a member of the 5th Waldeck Battalion serving Holland at the Cape of Good Hope from 1802 to 1806.

BRUEHNE, Otto   W200153
Born 1755 in Adorf (W). Evangelical. Sailed to America with the regiment in 1776 as private in the 2nd Company. Taken prisoner on the Amite River on 4 September 1779, he died of illness while in prisoner status at New Orleans on 23 January 1780.

BRUME, Gottfried   W200995
Sailed to America with the 1782 recruit shipment and was assigned as corporal in the 5th Company. He apparently returned to Germany with his unit in 1783.

BRUMHARD, Andreas Florentius Georg   W100017
Born 9 March 1758 in Nieder Wildungen (W). Father - Johann Philipp B., magistrate; Mother - Christiane Elisabeth, nee Frensdorff. Student in Giessen in 1775. Fathered an illegitimate child by Justine Paar of Reinhardshausen (W) in 1787. He died in Holland, a possible suicide, in September 1799. Sailed to America with the regiment in 1776 as ensign in the 5th Company. Promoted to 2nd lieutenant in 1776, he sailed up the Hudson River on 14 October 1777 in a force sent to relieve General Burgoyne, but came back down the river on 16 October and returned to Staten Island on the 21st. He was then promoted to 1st lieutenant (grenadier) on 14 April 1779. Taken prisoner at Baton Rouge on 21 September 1779, he may have returned to duty in May 1781, having been promoted 1st lieutenant while in prisoner status. By December 1781 he was assigned to the 1st Company, and returned to Germany with the regiment in 1783. He was a captain in the 5th Waldack Battalion when it entered Holland service in 1784. He received his promotion to major of the 5th Battalion (in Dutch service in Delft) on 1 April 1794, at the same time other senior officers of the battalion were promoted.

BUBENLEBER, Friedrich   W200996
Sailed to America with the 1782 recruit shipment and was assigned as private in the 5th Company. He apparently returned to Germany with his unit in 1783.

BUCHHOLTZ, Ludwig   W200850
Sailed to America with the 1781 recruit shipment and was assigned as private in the 3rd Company. In June 1782 he was transferred to the 5th Company. He returned to Germany with the regiment and was released at Korbach (W) on 16 October 1783.

BUDDE, Christoph   W200260S
Born 1742 in Fuerstenberg (W). Evangelical. Shoemaker by trade. Married with 1 child. Sailed to America with the regiment in 1776 as corporal in the 3rd Company. In April 1780 he was promoted to provost. He apparently returned to Germany with the regiment in 1783. He had 14 years' previous military experience in the Waldeck 2nd Regiment, and was apparently on his second enlistment, having last enlisted on 3 March 1768.

19

BUDDE, Friedrich W200154
Born 1753 in Hoerle (W). Evangelical. Sailed to America with the regiment in 1776 as private in the 2nd Company. Taken prisoner on the Amite River on 4 September 1779, he died of illness while in prisoner status at New Orleans on 9 September 1779.

BUDDE, Johannes W201171
Date and manner of joining the regiment are uncertain. By December 1781 he was a batman, probably in the 5th Company, as he was transferred to the 3rd Company in July 1782. He apparently returned to Germany with the regiment in 1783.

BUDELBACH, Johannes W200653
Date and manner of joining the regiment are uncertain. The only entry in the HETRINA indicates he was a Corporal in the 3rd Company in April 1779.

BUECHER, Adam W200654
Born in Engishausen. Sailed to America with the 1777 recruit shipment and was assigned as private in the 4th Company. After the capitulation of the Pensacola garrison he boarded the *Santa Rosalia* on 29 May 1779 for his return to New York. He was released from the regiment at Flatbush on 15 July 1783.

BUECKING, Wilhelm W200396
Born 1740 in Liggrechtrode, Hoehenstein. Records indicate both that he was Evangelical or Catholic. 5'5" tall. Married with 3 children. On a 3-year enlistment. Sailed to America with the regiment in 1776 as private in the 4th Company. Taken prisoner on 5 January 1777 at Springfield, New Jersey, after being wounded, he died in the hospital at Philadelphia on 19 September 1778 (possibly of his wounds).

BUEDDECKER, Bernhard Hermann W200521
Born 1759 in Wrexen (W). Evangelical. Sailed to America with the regiment in 1776 as private in the 5th Company. He was killed in the attack on Fort Washington on 16 November 1776.

BUEHLER, Johannes W200851
Born in Reutlingen. Sailed to America with the 1781 recruit shipment and was assigned as private in the 3rd Company. In July 1782 he was transferred to the 5th Company. He returned to Germany with the regiment and was released at Bremen on 19 September 1783.

BUEHLER, Sebastian W200852
Born in Degendorf. Sailed to America with the 1781 recruit shipment and was assigned to the 3rd Company. He returned to Germany with the regiment and was released at Bremen on 19 September 1783.

BULLE, Karl W200997
Sailed to America with the 1782 recruit shipment and was assigned as private in the 5th Company. He returned to Germany with his unit, but deserted at Bremen on 30 September 1783.

BUNSE, Konrad   W200397
Born 1758 in Stormbruch (W). Evangelical. Sailed to America with
the regiment in 1776 as private in the 4th Company. Taken prisoner at
Springfield, New Jersey, on 5 January 1777, he was sent from Lancaster to Philadelphia to be exchanged on 29 July 1778. During the siege
of Pensacola, he was wounded while serving at The Cliffs, an artillery
position. On 29 May 1779, he boarded the *Santa Rosalia* for his return
to New York after the capitulation of the Pensacola garrison. He
returned to Germany with the regiment and was released at Korbach
(W) on 20 October 1783.

BUNSE, Theodor   W200655
Born in Korbach (W). Sailed to America with the 1778 recruit
shipment and was assigned as private in the 3rd Company. He returned
to Germany with the regiment and was released at Korbach (W) on 20
October 1783.

BUNTROCK, Friedrich   W200275
Born 1756/57 in Elleringhausen (W). Evangelical. 5'4" tall. Sailed
to America with the regiment in 1776 as private in the 3rd Company.
He died of illness on 30 January 1778.

BURGHARD, Johannes   W200522
Born 1753 in Heringen, Schwarzburg. Evangelical. 5'3" tall. Sailed to
America with the regiment in 1776 as private in the 5th Company.
Taken prisoner at Amboy on 14 January 1777, he enlisted in the
American army. He apparently deserted back to his unit, as he was
taken prisoner again at Baton Rouge on 21 September 1779. While in
prisoner status at New Orleans, he deserted on 1 July 1780 and joined
the Spanish army.

BURGHARD, Michael   W200656
Sailed to America with the 1778 recruit shipment and was assigned
as private in the 2nd Company. In December 1779 he was transferred
to the 4th Company, and in June 1782 transferred back to the 2nd
Company. He returned to Germany with the regiment and was released
at Korbach (W) on 16 October 1783.

BURGHENN, Peter   W200853
Born in Bovenden. Sailed to America with the 1781 recruit shipment
and was assigned as private in the 3rd Company. In June 1782 he was
transferred to the 4th Company. He returned to Germany with the
regiment and was released "on the Weser" on 25 September 1783.

BURR, Johannes   W200657
Born in Zensenberg, Swabia. Sailed to America with the 1778 recruit
shipment and was sick upon his arrival. He was assigned as private
in the 5th Company. Taken prisoner at Baton Rouge on 21 September
1779, he died of illness while in prisoner status at New Orleans, on 26
February 1780.

BUSECK, Peter   W200658
Born in Braunfels. Sailed to America with the 1777 recruit shipment
and was assigned to the 1st Company. He deserted at Manchac On 7
August 1779.

BUTTERWECK, Jakob   W200398
Born 1757 in Elleringhausen (W). Evangelical. Sailed to America
with the regiment in 1776 as private in the 4th Company. He died of
fatigue on the march back to camp on 23 August 1777, after the regiment had participated in repulsing an American attack on Staten Island.

CANSTEIN, Bernhard von   W200046
Born 1750 in Canstein, Koeln. Catholic. Deserted on 5 May 1776 but
returned to duty on 15 May 1776, before the regiment departed for
America. Sailed to America with the regiment in 1776 as cadet in the
1st Company. Promoted to corporal in July 1779, he was then taken
prisoner at Baton Rouge on 21 September 1779. He died at Havana of
illness, while still in prisoner status, on 29 November 1780. He had 4
years' previous military experience in the Waldeck 2nd Regiment.

CANTZLER, Johann Georg   W200399
Born 1760 in Wetzlar. Evangelical. Sailed to America with the
regiment in 1776 as private in the 4th Company. Died of illness on 7
August 1777.

CARNISH, Josef   W200660
Born in Vienna. Sailed to America with the 1777 recruit shipment
and was assigned as private in the 2nd Company. He was taken prisoner on the Amite River on 4 September 1779. On 13 July 1780,
while in prisoner status, he deserted and joined the Spanish army.

CASPAR, Henrich   W201119
Born in Gross-Gerau. He sailed to America with the 1778 recruit
shipment and was sick upon arrival. He was assigned (as private?) in
the 2nd Company. He died of illness in the hospital at New York on 25
January 1779.

CASTNER, Georg   W201172
Date and manner of joining the regiment are uncertain. By December 1781 he was listed as a laborer with the regiment, and in June
1782 as a batman in the 1st Company. He apparently returned to
Germany with the regiment in 1783.

CHRISTENAU, Friedrich   W200857
Born in Riga. Sailed to America with the 1781 recruit shipment and
was assigned as private in the 3rd Company. He was transferred to the
1st Company in July 1782. He returned to Germany with the regiment,
but deserted on 18 September 1783 at Bremen.

CLEEMANN, Christoph   W200666
Born in Saxony. Date and manner of joining the regiment are uncertain. He may have been with the 1777 recruit shipment. By April 1779 he was private in the 4th Company. He was tried by court-martial on 10 July 1777 for desertion while on Staten Island. "He forgot he needed a boat," and was punished by running the gauntlet 12 times on 16 July 1777. He boarded the *Santa Rosalia* for the return to New York on 29 May 1781, after the capitulation of Pensacola, and died of illness on 10 October 1781 while in prisoner status.

CLEMENTZ, Johann Jakob   W200388
Born 26 April 1760 in Helsen (W). Evangelical. Father - Johannes C., drummer; Mother - Maria Christiana, nee Neuschaefer. While in the 5th Waldeck Battalion, in 1788 he married Maria Elizabeth Bauer, fathering a daughter, Catherina, born in 1788. He died 25 February 1805. Sailed to America with the regiment in 1776 as drummer in 4th Company. He boarded the *Santa Rosalia* for return to New York on 29 May 1781 after the capitulation of Pensacola. He served throughout the war in the 4th Company and apparently returned to Germany with the regiment in 1783.

COLLIG, Nikolaus   W200860
Sailed to America with the 1781 recruit shipment as a fifer in the 3rd Company. He apparently returned to Germany with the regiment in 1783.

CONET, Johannes   W200669
Born in Stuttgart. Sailed to America with the 1777 recruit shipment and was assigned as private in the 5th Company. Taken prisoner at Baton Rouge on 21 September 1779, he deserted from prisoner status at New Orleans on 19 July 1780.

CRAMER, Johann Franz Christian   W200048
Born 5 February 1751 in Landau (W). Evangelical. Father - Johann Ludwig C.; Mother - Elizabeth, nee Koester. Fourth of 7 children. Married. Sailed to America with the regiment in 1776 as private in the 1st Company. Taken prisoner on 4 January 1777 in New Jersey, he returned to duty in August 1778. Taken prisoner again at Baton Rouge on 21 September 1779, he deserted at Havana on 28 March 1782. He had 6 years' previous military experience in the Waldeck 2nd Regiment.

CRAMER, Klara Elizabeth (possible camp follower)
Born 14 February 1751 in Vasbeck (W). Had an illegitimate son, Johann Henrich Ludwig, born 4 March 1777, by the American soldier Georg Andreas Kuechler. She married Johann Henrich Eisenberg (see below) on 18 February 1784; they had 4 children. She died 10 September 1793. This seems to indicate that an advance party might have been sent to America by Waldeck in 1776.

CROLLPATH, Josef   W200675
Born in Eichstadt. Sailed to America with the 1778 recruit shipment and was assigned as private in the 4th Company. He boarded the *Santa Rosalia* on 29 May 1781, after the capitulation of Pensacola, for the return to New York. He returned to Germany with the regiment and was released at Bremen on 19 September 1783.

CUMMERO, Friedrich   W200677
Born in Koenigsberg. Sailed to America with the 1778 recruit shipment and was assigned as private in the 5th Company. In December 1779 he was transferred to the 3rd Company, and on 2 April 1781 he deserted at Pensacola.

DALWIGK, Ludwig Ferdinand Carl Georg von   W100002S
Born 5 April 1739 in Campff (W), the 15th generation of the family name. Evangelical. Father - Wilhelm Friedrich Ludwig von D., high bailiff and court advisor; Mother - Johanne Henriette Louise, nee von Rudesheim. He fathered a natural daughter, Luise Friedericke Dalwigk, born 27 April 1773, and a natural son, Johann Heinrich Christian August Dalwigk, born 12 October 1785 in Helsen (W). The mother of these children was Catharine Johanna Hofmann. He died at Helsen (W) as a colonel on 14/15 October 1788. Sailed to America with the regiment in 1776 as major, second in command of the regiment, and nominal commander of the 2nd Company. After being promoted to lieutenant colonel, he was released from the regiment in America (apparently due to poor health). On 4 November 1776 he sailed from West Chester to New York where he remained until his return to Germany in late June 1777. He had 20 years' previous military experience with the Waldeck 2nd Regiment and the forces of Creys. In 1763, during the Seven Years War, as a Waldeck ensign in Dutch service, he had been made a prisoner of war by the Prussians and held for a long time in Magdeburg. He was promoted to captain in 1773.

DANTZ, Johann Thomas   W200053
Born 1752 in Bergfreiheit (W). Evangelical. 5'5 1/4" tall. Sailed to America with the regiment in 1776 as private in the 1st Company. Taken prisoner at Baton Rouge on 21 September 1779, he apparently rejoined the regiment at a later date and returned to Germany in 1783.

DANTZ, Jost   W200164
Born 1757 in Bergfreiheit (W). Evangelical. Sailed to America with the regiment in 1776 as private in the 2nd Company. Taken prisoner at Springfield, New Jersey, on 5 January 1777. He enlisted in the American army on 21 March 1777. He apparently deserted back to the regiment as he was again taken prisoner on the Amite River on 4 September 1779. He died of illness at New Orleans, while still in prisoner status, on 8 December 1779.

DANTZER, Martin Wilhelm   W200680
Sailed to America with the 1778 recruit shipment and was sick upon
arrival. He was assigned as private in the 5th Company. In December
1779 he was transferred to the 3rd Company, and in July 1782 transferred back to the 5th Company. He returned to Germany with the
regiment and was released at Korbach (W) on 16 October 1783.

DAUDENBERG, Georg   W201011
Sailed to America with the 1782 recruit shipment and was assigned
as private in the 5th Company. Apparently returned to Germany with
his unit in 1783.

DECKER, Johannes   W201129
Born 1727/28 in Helmighausen (or Helmingen), Hanau. Sailed to
America with the 1777 recruit shipment and was assigned as private in
the 4th Company. He was released in America as an invalid on 30
June 1778. He returned to Europe on the *Echo* on 8 October 1778,
arriving at Portsmouth on 1 January 1779.

DECKER, Philipp   W200681
Born in Giessen. Sailed to America with the 1777 recruit shipment
and was assigned as private in the 2nd Company. Taken prisoner on
the Amite River on 4 September 1779, he deserted from prisoner status
on 9 July 1780 and joined the Spanish army.

DEEGE, Johannes   W200868
Sailed to America with the 1781 recruit shipment and was assigned
as private in the 3rd Company. In July 1782 he was transferred to the
1st Company, and apparently returned to Germany with the regiment in
1783.

DEHM, Georg   W200682
Born in Buschberg, Bamberg. Sailed to America with the 1777 recruit shipment and was assigned as private in the 2nd Company. In
December 1779 he was transferred to the 4th Company. On 17 May
1781, following the surrender at Pensacola, he deserted from prisoner
status and may have joined the Spanish army.

DEIERLEIN, Friedrich   W200683
Born in Reta. Sailed to America with the 1777 recruit shipment and
was assigned as private in the 5th Company. Taken prisoner at Baton
Rouge on 21 September 1779, he deserted from prisoner status at New
Orleans on 14 July 1780.

DEILINGER, Josef   W200165
Born 1758 in Braunschweig. Catholic. Sailed to America with the
regiment in 1776 as private in the 2nd Company. He was transferred to
the 4th Company in December 1779, and back to the 2nd Company in
June 1782. On 15 July 1783 he was released from the regiment at
Flatbush.

DEMMER, Johann Hermann   W200409
Born 26 April 1753 in Berndorf (W). Evangelical. 5'5" tall. Father
- Johann Arend Dammer [sic]; Mother - Ann-Engel Catharina, nee
Meinhard. Married Johanna Henriette Catherina Grothe on 19 November
1784. Four children: Johann Carl, born 7 March 1785; Johann Henrich
Christian, born 31 July 1790; Johann Friedrich, born 16 March 1797;
and Johannette Catherina Friederica, born 29 May 1801. Sailed to
America with the regiment in 1776 as private in the 4th Company. He
boarded the *Santa Rosalia* on 29 May 1781 for return to New York after
the capitulation of Pensacola. Served throughout the war in the 4th
Company, and apparently returned to Germany with the regiment in
1783.

DEMUTH, Valentin   W200527
Born 1752 in Homburg, Zweibruecken. Catholic. 5'4" tall. Sailed to
America with the regiment in 1776 as private in the 5th Company. He
deserted on 9 August 1777.

DENDER, Solomon   W200684
Born in Niemandshausen, Darmstadt. Sailed to America with the
1778 recruit shipment and was assigned as private in the 4th Company. He deserted at Pensacola on 16 April 1781.

DENGEL, Friedrich   W201012
Sailed to America with the 1782 recruit shipment and was assigned
as private in the 5th Company. He returned to Germany with his unit
and was released at Korbach (W) on 22 October 1783.

DEPMEIER, Henrich   W300003
Born in Hameln. Evangelical. 5'8" tall. Sailed to America with the
regiment in 1776 as cannoneer in the artillery section. Transferred to
the 3rd Company in June 1781. After the regiment lost its cannon, he
was apparently transferred again to the 5th Company in December
1782. He returned to Germany with the regiment and was released at
Korbach (W) on 16 October 1783.

DETTENDALER, Georg   W200685
Born in Duerrwangen. Sailed to America with the 1778 recruit
shipment and was assigned as private in the 4th Company. He boarded
the *Santa Rosalia* on 29 May 1781 for return to New York after the
capitulation of Pensacola. He returned to Germany with the regiment
and was released at Bremen on 19 September 1783.

DIAMOR, Leonhard   W200288
Born 1758 in Wetzlar. Catholic. 5'2 3/4" tall. Sailed to America
with the regiment in 1776 as private in the 3rd Company. He died of
illness at Pensacola on 9 August 1780.

DICKE, Jakob   W201013
Sailed to America with the 1782 recruit shipment and was assigned as
private in the 5th Company. He returned to Germany with his unit and
was released at Korbach (W) on 23 October 1783.

DICKE, Johann Henrich   W200289
Born in Anraff (W), and baptized on 13 March 1753. Evangelical.
Father - Jakob D.; Mother - Elizabeth. Sailed to America with the
regiment in 1776 as private in the 3rd Company. Taken prisoner on 8
January 1777 at Elizabethtown, New Jersey, he enlisted in the American army on 19 March 1777. He apparently deserted back to the
regiment as he died of illness at Baton Rouge on 12 September 1779.

DIEDRICH, Friedrich   W200870
Born in Oberelsungen. Sailed to America with the 1781 recruit shipment and was assigned as private in the 3rd Company. In July 1782 he
was transferred to the 1st Company, and on 5 May 1783 deserted at
Flatbush.

DIETRICH, Sebastian   W201014
Sailed to America with the 1782 recruit shipment and was assigned as
private in the 5th Company. Died of illness at Halifax on 11 Apr. 1783.

DIETZ, Christian   W200621
Born 1738 in Wildungen (W). Evangelical. 5'6" tall. Cabinet maker
by trade. Married with 3 children. Sailed to America with the regiment
in 1776 as private in the 2nd Company. Transferred to the 4th Company in December 1779. On 22 April 1781 he was shot and killed by
Indians in the woods near Pensacola. He had 7 1/2 years' previous
military experience in the service of Creyss, from which he deserted,
and 12 years' previous military experience in Waldeck service.

DIETZ, Daniel   W200166
Born 1760/61 in Braunau (W). Evangelical. 5'6" tall. Sailed to
America with the regiment in 1776 as private in the 2nd Company.
Taken prisoner on the Amite River on 4 September 1779, he died of
illness while in prisoner status at New Orleans on 2 January 1780.

DIETZ, Stephan   W200167
Born 1736 in Kleinern (W). Evangelical. Tailor by trade. Married with
1 child. Sailed to America with the regiment in 1776 as private in the
2nd Company. He died of fatigue on the march back to camp, on 23
August 1777, after the regiment had participated in repulsing an
American attack on Staten Island.

DIOR, Jakob (or Jean) de la   W200869
Born in Augsburg. Sailed to America with the 1781 recruit shipment
and was assigned as private in the 3rd Company. He was transferred to
the 2nd Company in July 1782, and deserted on the 16th of that same
month on Long Island.

DISTE, Christian   W200144
Born 1760 in Volkenmissen, Koeln. Catholic. Sailed to America with
the regiment in 1776 as drummer in the 2nd Company. Listed as private by April 1779, he was taken prisoner on the Amite River on 4
September 1779, and deserted from prisoner status at New Orleans on
18 July 1780.

DOEDECKE, Friedrich   W200410
Born 1753 in Hameln. Evangelical. Sailed to America with the regiment in 1776 as private in the 4th Company. He boarded the *Santa
Rosalia* on 29 May 1781 for return to New York after the Pensacola
capitulation. He was released from the regiment and transferred back
to Germany as an invalid in December 1782.

DRESCHLER, Johannes   W201015
Sailed to America with the 1782 recruit shipment and was assigned as
private in the 5th Company. He returned to Germany with his unit and
was released at Korbach (W) on 22 October 1783.

DREWES, Johann Jost   W200168
Born 25 December 1756 in Bringhausen (W). Evangelical. Father –
Henrich D., collier; Mother – Anna Margarete, nee Iselke. Second of 5
children. Sailed to America with the regiment in 1776 as private in the
2nd Company. Taken prisoner on the Amite River on 4 September
1779, he deserted on 14 April 1782, while still in prisoner status, at
Havana.

DRUBE, Adam   W200054
Born 1729/30 in Langenfeld, Hesse. Reformed. 5'6 1/2" tall.
Married. Sailed to America with the regiment in 1776 as private in the
1st Company. Taken prisoner in January 1777 in New Jersey, he deserted from prisoner status at Lancaster, Pennsylvania, on 6 June
1778. He had 5 years' previous military experience in the Waldeck
2nd Regiment.

DUCKENBERG, Johann Henrich   W200169
Born 1757 in Ober Urff, Hesse. Reformed. 5'5 1/4" tall. Sailed to
America with the regiment in 1776 as private in the 2nd Company. He
was transferred to the 4th Company in December 1779. On 17 May
1781, after the fall of Pensacola, he deserted from prisoner status and
may have joined the Spanish army. He had 3 years' previous military
experience in the Waldeck 1st Regiment.

DUESSE, Philipp   W200528
Born in Boehne (W), and baptized on 17 November 1758. Evangelical.
Father – Johann Michael D.; Mother – Clara. Sailed to America with
the regiment in 1776 as private in the 5th Company. Taken prisoner at
Baton Rouge on 21 September 1779. He deserted at Havana on 24
March 1782 while still in prisoner status.

DULLMANN, Christian   W200290
Born 1758 in Helminghausen (W). Evangelical. Sailed to America
with the regiment in 1776 as private in the 3rd Company, after having
originally enlisted as a fifer. Served throughout the war in the 3rd
Company and apparently returned to Germany with the regiment in
1783.

DURST, Johannes W200529
Born 1752 in Oranienburg. Reformed. Sailed to America with the regiment in 1776 as private in the 5th Company. Taken prisoner at Baton Rouge on 21 September 1779, he deserted from prisoner status at New Orleans on 20 July 1780. There is a possibility that Durst and two fellow Waldeckers may have gone up the Mississippi River to the Illinois Country.

EBE, Philipp W200622
Born 9 January 1755 in Twiste (W). Evangelical. Father Friedrich Wilhelm Ewe, wool spinner; Mother - Marie Magdalene, nee Goebel. Third of 6 children. Sailed to America with the regiment in 1776 as batman in the 1st Company. By December 1780 he was a private in the 5th Company, and was transferred that month to the 3rd Company. In July 1782 he was transferred back to the 5th Company. He apparently returned to Germany with the regiment in 1783.

EBERSBACH, Henrich W200055
Born 1750 in Sachsenhausen (W). Evangelical. Shoemaker by trade. Married with 1 child. Sailed to America with the regiment in 1776 as private in the 1st Company. Taken prisoner at Baton Rouge on 21 September 1779, he returned to duty in January 1782. He apparently returned to Germany with the regiment in 1783. He had 7 years 3 months' previous military experience with the Waldeck 2nd Regiment.

ECKHARD, Georg W200686
Born in Braunfels. Sailed to America with the 1777 recruit shipment and was assigned as private in the 4th Company. He boarded the *Santa Rosalia* on 29 May 1781 for return to New York after the capitulation of Pensacola. He was released from the regiment on 15 July 1783 at Flatbush.

EFFE, Kaspar W300004
Born in Schmalkalden. Date and manner of joining the regiment are uncertain. May have been with the 1777 recruit shipment, but by April 1779 he was cannoneer with the artillery section. In June 1781, after the regiment lost its cannon at Pensacola, he was transferred to the 3rd Company. By December 1782 he was transferred to the 5th Company. He was released from the regiment at Flatbush on 15 July 1783.

EICHINGER, Andreas W200687
Sailed to America with the 1777 recruit shipment as private in the 1st Company. Taken prisoner at Baton Rouge on 21 September 1779, he was returned to duty in January 1782. He returned to Germany with the regiment and was released at Korbach (W) on 16 October 1783.

EISEN, Johann Franz W200411
Born 1755 in Koenigshagen (W). Evangelical. 5'5 1/2" tall. Sailed to America with the regiment in 1776 as private in the 4th Company. He deserted at Manchac on 18 August 1779. He had 8 years' previous military experience in Holland, probably in a Waldeck unit.

EISENBERG, Christian   W200170
Born 22 August 1754 in Vasbeck (W). Evangelical. 5'5 1/4" tall.
Father - Johann Konrad E., shepherd; Mother - Katharina Elizabeth,
nee Pistorius. Seventh of 7 children and brother of Johann Henrich
Eisenberg (W200133). He married Klara Elizabeth, nee Kelter on 13
January 1786 and they had 5 children: Engel Katharina, born 1786;
Johann Friedrich, born 6 June 1789; Katharina Margarete, born 19
November 1791; Johann Christian Ludwig, born 23 January 1796; and
Johann Ludwig, born 19 February 1797. Christian Eisenberg died 21
May 1830. Sailed to America with the regiment in 1776 as private in
the 2nd Company. By April 1779 he was in the 1st Company. Taken
prisoner at Baton Rouge on 21 September 1779, he returned to duty in
January 1782. He returned to Germany with the regiment in 1783.

EISENBERG, Henrich   W200133
Born 19 July 1740 in Vasbeck (W). Evangelical. Father - Johann
Konrad E.; Mother - Katharina Elizabeth, nee Pistorius. First of 7
children and brother of Christian E. (W200170). He married Maria
Magdalina Kamm on 13 January 1784. Sailed to America with the
regiment in 1776 as quartermaster sergeant in the 2nd Company. In
December 1779 he was transferred to the 4th Company, and transferred
back to the 2nd Company in June 1782. The same month he was
promoted to sergeant. He apparently returned to Germany with the
regiment in 1783. He had 4 years' previous military experience with
the Hessian army and 4 years with the Waldeck 2nd Regiment, having
joined the Waldeck service on 4 October 1765.

EISENBERG, (Johann) Henrich   W200171
Born 2 March 1759 in Vasbeck (W). Evangelical. 5'5" tall. Father -
Johann Henrich E. Second of 2 children. Brother of Johann Christian E.
(W200172). On 18 February 1784 he married Klara Elizabeth Cramer
(see above) with whom he had 4 children: Susanne Marie, born 2
September 1784, died 19 March 1853; Maria Wilhelmine Christine,
born 1787; a daughter who died at birth on 21 March 1790; and a son
who also died at birth on 30 August 1793. His first wife died 10
September 1793. On 14 February 1794 he married Maria Elizabeth
Pincke, born 4 March 1762, died 19 February 1803, with whom he had
5 children: Henrich Christian, born 28 March 1795; a daughter who
died at birth on 12 May 1797; Johann Henrich, born 1798; Katherina
Elizabeth, born 1800; and Maria Elizabeth, born about 1802, died 8
January 1804. On 8 June 1803 he then married Maria Christine
Wiegand, born 13 December 1761, died 26 May 1818. They had no
children. He had become a swineherd in 1794, and he died 5 November 1828. Sailed to America with the regiment in 1776 as private in the
2nd Company. In December 1779 he was transferred to the 4th Company. On 7 January 1781 he was wounded in the attack on The Village,
near present-day Mobile, Alabama. Transferred back to the 2nd
Company in June 1782, he apparently returned to Germany with the
regiment in 1783.

EISENBERG, Johann Christian W200172
Baptized 26 December 1750 in Vasbeck (W). Evangelical. 5'3" tall.
Father – Johann Henrich E. Brother of (Johann) Henrich E.
(W200171). Married Katharina Elizabeth Wax on 9 January 1784. They
had 9 children, of whom only 2 lived beyond infancy: Maria Katherina
Margarete, born 1792, and Katharina Elizabeth born 1799. He was a
swineherd in 1786 and a farmhand in 1800. Johann Christian died on 5
April 1819. Sailed to America with the regiment in 1776 as private in
the 2nd regiment. He was transferred to the 4th Company in December
1779 and back to the 2nd Company in June 1782. He returned to
Germany with the regiment and was released at Korbach (W) on 24
October 1783.

EMBDE, Christoph W200130
Born 1744 in Goldhausen (W). Evangelical. Married with 2 children.
Sailed to America with the regiment in 1776 as sergeant in the 2nd
Company. In December 1779 he was transferred to the 4th Company.
He was wounded in the attack on The Village on 7 January 1781, and
transferred back to the 2nd Company in June 1781. He apparently
returned to Germany with the regiment in 1783. He had 4.5 years'
previous military experience with the Hannoverian army.

EMBDE, Johannes W200056
Born 4 September 1756 in Muehlhausen (W) and confirmed 1769.
Evangelical. 5'6" tall. Father – Johann Henrich E. from Langefeld;
Mother – Marie Margarete, nee Grothe. Second of 4 children. Sailed to
America with the regiment in 1776 as private in the 1st Company.
Taken prisoner at Baton Rouge on 21 September 1779, he returned to
duty in January 1782. He apparently returned to Germany with the
regiment in 1783.

EMDE, Friedrich W200773
Born in Goldhausen (W). Date and manner of joining the regiment are
uncertain, but he is listed in the HETRINA as a batman in 1781. He
died of illness on 10 December 1781.

ENGELHARD, Henrich W200871
Born 1765 in Nieder Werbe (W). Lutheran. 5' tall. Sailed to America
with the 1781 recruit shipment and was assigned as private in the 3rd
Company. He died of illness at Newtown, Long Island, on 12 December 1781.

ENGELHARD, Jakob Christoph W200530
Born 1753 in Wirmighausen (W). Evangelical. 5'4" tall. Sailed to
America with the regiment in 1776 as private in the 5th Company.
Taken prisoner at Baton Rouge on 21 September 1779, he returned to
duty in January 1782. He apparently returned to Germany with the
regiment in 1783. He had 2 years' previous military experience in a
Waldeck unit, probably in Holland.

ENGELHARD, Johann Georg   W200412
Born 1732 in Immighausen (W). Reformed. 5'7" tall. Sailed to America with the regiment in 1776 as private in the 4th Company. He died of illness on 9 December 1780. He had 12 years' previous military experience in the Hessian army.

ENSLIN, Ludwig   W201130
Sailed to America with the 1778 recruit shipment and was assigned as private in the 3rd Company. He died of illness on 12 September 1778.

ERB, Christian   W200872
Born in Sondershausen, Alsace. Sailed to America in the 1781 recruit shipment and was assigned as private in the 3rd Company. He died of illness at Newtown, Long Island, on 3 November 1781.

ERHARD, Peter   W200531
Born 1756 in Odewald, Erbach. Evangelical. Sailed to America with the regiment in 1776 as private in the 5th Company. Taken prisoner on 8 January 1777 at Elizabethtown, New Jersey, he deserted from prisoner status at York Point on 5 August 1778, possibly while on way to being exchanged.

ERLE, Michael   W200688
Born 1742/43 in Sibrechtsshausen, Wuerzburg. Sailed to America with the 1777 recruit shipment and was assigned as private in the 3rd Company. Taken prisoner at Baton Rouge on 21 September 1779, he died of illness while in prisoner status, on 3 November 1779.

ERNST, Peter   W200689
Sailed to America with the 1777 recruit shipment and was assigned as private in the 1st Company. Taken prisoner at Baton Rouge on 21 September 1779, he returned to duty in January 1782. In June of that year he was promoted to corporal and apparently returned to Germany with the regiment in 1783.

FASS, Alisius   W200690
Born in Dannhausen. Sailed to America with the 1778 recruit shipment and was assigned as private in the 3rd Company. He was released from the regiment at Flatbush on 15 July 1783.

FASSHAUER, Johannes   W201016
Sailed to America with the 1782 recruit shipment and was assigned as private in the 5th Company. He returned to Germany with his unit and was released from the regiment at Korbach (W) on 22 October 1783.

FAUSER, Jakob   W200691
Sailed to America with the 1777 recruit shipment and was assigned as private in the 3rd Company. He returned to Germany with the regiment and was released at Korbach on 16 October 1783.

FAUST, Johannes   W200057
Born 1748 in Neukirchen (W). Evangelical. Married. The HETRINA
lists his wife and child as having died in 1779. During the siege of
Baton Rouge the wives and children of the soldiers had been sent into
the forests for safety. Indians found and massacred all of them.
Faust's family may have been among them. Sailed to America with
the regiment in 1776 as private in the 1st Company. He died of illness
at Baton Rouge on 12 September 1779. He had 8 1/2 years' previous
military experience in the Waldeck army.

FERST, Johann Adam   W200532
Baptized 13 October 1757 in Bringhausen (W). Evangelical. Father –
Johann Wilhelm F.; Mother – Sybille Margarete, nee Kahlhoeber.
Second of 5 children. Sailed to America with the regiment in 1776 as
private in the 5th Company. He was taken prisoner on 27 October 1776
at Maroneok and was in prisoner status throughout the war. Listed as
a deserter at Elizabethtown, New Jersey, on 15 July 1783, he may
have deserted as early as 1777.

FICHTNER, Gottlieb   W200692
Born in Waltersdorf. Sailed to America with the 1778 recruit shipment
and was assigned as private in the 1st Company. Taken prisoner at
Baton Rouge on 21 September 1779, he died of illness while in prisoner status at New Orleans on 21 March 1780.

FIEBERLING, Jakob   W200874
Sailed to America with the 1781 recruit shipment and was assigned as
private in the 3rd Company. He was transferred to the 5th Company in
June 1782. He returned to Germany with the regiment and was released at Korbach (W) on 18 October 1783.

FIEGER, Johannes   W200875
Born in Eichstadt. Sailed to America with the 1781 recruit shipment
and was assigned as private in the 3rd Company. He was transferred to
the 5th Company in June 1782. He returned to Germany with the
regiment and was released at Bremen on 19 September 1783.

FIGGE, Bernhard   W200413
Born 1756 in Adorf (W). Evangelical. Sailed to America with the
regiment in 1776 as private in the 4th Company. He boarded the *Santa
Rosalia* on 21 May 1781 to return to New York after the capitulation at
Pensacola. He served in the 4th Company throughout the war and
apparently returned to Germany with the regiment in 1783.

FIGGE, Christian   W200291
Born 1756 in Elleringhausen (W). Evangelical. Sailed to America
with the regiment in 1776 as private in the 3rd Company. Taken prisoner at Baton Rouge on 21 September 1779, he deserted at Havana on
24 March 1782, while still in prisoner status.

FIGGE, Henrich   W200173
Born 1740 in Ober Waroldern (W). Evangelical. 5'8" tall. Sailed to
America with the regiment in 1776 as private in the 2nd Company. In
December 1779 he was transferred to the 4th Company, and died of
illness at Pensacola on 7 August 1780.

FIGGE, Johann Wilhelm   W200292
Born in Mengeringhausen (W), and baptized 16 November 1746. Evangelical. 5'6" tall. Miller by trade. Married. Father - Henrich F.;
Mother - Philippina. Sailed to America with the regiment in 1776 as
private in the 3rd Company. Served throughout the war in the 3rd
Company, and returned to Germany with the regiment. He was released at Korbach (W) on 20 October 1783.

FINGERHUT, Johann Friedrich   W200174
Born 15 December 1758 in Gembeck (W). Evangelical. 5'3" tall.
Teamster by trade. Father - Johann Christian; Mother - Anna Marga-
rete, nee Weber. Eleventh of 11 children. Cousin of Johann Christian
Bickmann (W200516). Sailed to America with the regiment in 1776 as
private in the 2nd Company. He was transferred to the 4th Company in
December 1779 and back to the 2nd Company in June 1782. He appar-
ently returned to Germany with the regiment in 1783.

FISCHER, Adam   W200693
Born in Fueretenau. Sailed to America with the 1778 recruit shipment
and was sick upon arrival. He was assigned as private in the 2nd
Company. He was transferred to the 4th Company in December 1779
and back to the 2nd Company in June 1782. He was released from the
regiment at Flatbush on 15 July 1783. An Adam Fischer is listed in
the 1790 census as living in the West Ward of New York City in a
household with one adult male, two males under sixteen years of age,
and one female.

FISCHER, Anton   W200533
Born in Holzhausen, Pyrmont, he was baptized as Johann Henrich
Anton Fischer on 25 July 1756. Evangelical. 5'4 1/2" tall. Father -
Johann Christoph F. On 6-year enlistment. Sailed to America with the
regiment in 1776 as private in the 5th Company. Carried on the rolls
as of December 1781, possibly his enlistment had expired, as a labor-
er and then from June 1782 as a batman. He apparently returned to
Germany with the regiment in 1783.

FISCHER Friedrich   W200695
Born in Nuernberg. Sailed to America with the 1778 recruit shipment
and was assigned as private in the 1st Company. He deserted at
Manchac on 12 August 1779.

FISCHER, Henrich   W200175
Born 1758 in Ammenhausen (W). Evangelical. Sailed to America with
the regiment in 1776 as private in the 2nd Company. Taken prisoner on
the Amite River on 4 September 1779, he deserted from prisoner status
at Havana on 2 April 1782.

FISCHER, Henrich   W200876
Born in Ammenhausen (W). Sailed to America with the 1781 recruit shipment and was assigned to the 3rd Company. He was transferred to the 5th Company in July 1782, and returned to Germany with the regiment and was released at Korbach (W) on 18 October 1783.

FISCHER, Johannes   W201131
Born in Braendel, Mainz. Sailed to America with the 1777 recruit shipment and was assigned as private in the 3rd Company. He died of illness on 11 August 1777.

FISCHER, Jost   W200058
Born 1758/59 in Luetersheim (W). Evangelical. Sailed to America with the regiment in 1776 as private in the 1st Company. Taken prisoner at Baton Rouge on 21 September 1779, he died of illness while in prisoner status at New Orleans on 31 October 1779.

FISCHER, Konrad   W200059
Born 1753 in Braunau (W). Evangelical. Sailed to America with the regiment in 1776 as private in the 1st Company. He died of illness in the hospital at Manchac on 8 August 1779. He had 6 years 10 months of previous military experience in the Waldeck army.

FISCHER, Ludwig   W200877
Sailed to America with the 1781 recruit shipment and was assigned as private in the 3rd Company. In July 1782 he was transferred to the 5th Comp., and apparently returned to Germany with the regiment in 1783.

FLAMME, Henrich   W200822
Born 1762/63 in Rhenegge (W). Sailed to America with the 1779 recruit shipment and was assigned as private in the 3rd Company. He was transferred to the 5th Company in July 1782, and deserted at Flatbush on 5 May 1783.

FLAMME, Henrich   W201124
Born 1762/63 in Schmillinghausen (W). Sailed to America with the 1779 recruit shipment and was assigned as private in the 4th Company. He was transferred to the 2nd Company in June 1782, and returned to Germany with the regiment and was released at Korbach (W) on 24 October 1783.

FLAMME, Henrich   W201176
Born in Twiste (W). Date and manner of joining the regiment are uncertain, but he was a batman with the 2nd Company by August 1779. He may have been Lieutenant Leonhardi's servant. He drowned on the Amite River on 12 August 1779.

FLAMME, Johannes   W200060
Born 24 December 1751 in Twiste. Evangelical. 5'5" tall. Father – Johann Wilhelm F.; Mother - Anna Elisabeth, nee Schneider. Sailed to America with the regiment in 1776 as private in the 1st Company. Died of illness in the hospital at Manchac on 5 August 1779.

FLAMME, Johannes (Henrich)   W200385
Born 1761 in Sudeck (W). Evangelical. Sailed to America with the
regiment in 1776 as fifer in the 4th Company. He boarded the *Santa
Rosalia* on 29 May 1781 for return to New York after the capitulation of
Pensacola. In late 1779 or early 1780 he was promoted to private. He
deserted at Flatbush on 5 May 1783.

FLAMME, Matthias   W200293
Born 1754 in Rhenegge (W). Evangelical. 5'5" tall. Sailed to America with the regiment in 1776 as private in the 3rd Company. Taken
prisoner on 5 January 1777 at Springfield, New Jersey, he was sent to
Philadelphia for exchange on 18 June 1778. He was again taken prisoner at Baton Rouge on 21 September 1779, and returned to duty in
January 1782. In December 1779 he was transferred to the 5th Company, and transferred back to the 3rd Company in July 1782. On 5 May
1783 he deserted at Flatbush. A Matthew Flam is listed in the 1790
census as living in East Portion, Cumberland County, Pennsylvania,
in a household with one adult male, one male under sixteen years of
age, and two females.

FLECK, Paul   W200534
Born 1751 in Neukircken (W). Evangelical. 5'4" tall. Shoemaker by
trade. Sailed to America with the regiment in 1776 as private in the
5th Company. He was killed in the attack on Fort Washington on 16
November 1776. He had 4 years' previous military experience in the
Waldeck 1st regiment.

FLEISCHHUT, Wilhelm   W200294
Born 1753 in Friedewald, Hesse. Reformed. Sailed to America with
the regiment in 1776 as private in the 3rd Company, having joined the
regiment at Beverungen on 22 May, on its march to the port. As a
member of the 2nd Company, he was released from the regiment in
America on 18 November 1776. He had 2 years' previous military
experience as a captain at arms with the Hessian army, from which he
had deserted.

FLINSCHBACH, Jakob   W201017
Sailed to America with the 1782 recruit shipment and was assigned as
private in the 5th Company. He returned to Germany with his unit and
was released at Korbach (W) on 22 October 1783.

FOCKESEN, Henrich   W201177
Date and manner of joining the regiment are uncertain. By December
1782 he was a batman in the 3rd Company. He apparently returned to
Germany with the regiment in 1783.

FRANCKE, Christian   W200295
Born 1756 in Mengeringhausen (W). Evangelical. Sailed to America
with the regiment in 1776 as private in the 3rd Company. He was
promoted to corporal in Apr. 1780 and reduced to private in Apr. 1783.
He deserted 14 June 1783 at Flatbush. He had 3 years' previous military experience in the Waldeck army, having joined on 13 March 1773.

FRANCKE, Christian   W200386
Born 1757 in Helsen (W). Evangelical. Sailed to America with the
regiment in 1776 as drummer in the 4th Company. By April 1779 he
was a private in the 4th Company. He boarded the *Santa Rosalia* on 29
May 1781 for the return to New York after the Pensacola capitulation.
He apparently returned to Germany with the regiment in 1783.

FRANCKE, Henrich   W200535
Born 1737/38 in Hannover. Evangelical. 5'2 1/2" tall. Tobacco
worker by trade. Married with 1 child. Taken prisoner at Baton Rouge
on 21 September 1779, he returned to duty in January 1782. He returned
to Germany with the regiment and was released at Korbach (W) on 19
October 1783. He had 6 years' previous military experience in the
Hannoverian army.

FRANCKE, Johannes   W201132
Born in Malsfeld. Sailed to America with the 1778 recruit shipment
and was assigned as private in the 1st Company. He did not sail to
West Florida with the regiment in 1778 but died of illness in the
hospital at New York on 2 January 1779.

FRANCKE, Sebastian   W200878
Born in Nuernberg. Sailed to America with the 1781 recruit shipment
and was assigned as private in the 3rd Company. In June 1782 he was
transferred to the 2nd Company. He returned to Germany with the
regiment and was released at Bremen on 19 September 1783.

FRANTZ, Georg   W200696
Born 1751/52 in Geislingen. Sailed to America with the 1778 recruit
shipment and was assigned as private in the 5th Company. Taken
prisoner at Baton Rouge on 21 September 1779, he died in November.

FRANTZ, Johannes   W200296
Born 1759 in Wellen (W). Evangelical. Sailed to America with the
regiment in 1776 as private in the 3rd Company. He died of illness in
the hospital at Manchac on 2 September 1779.

FRANTZER, Jakob   W201178
Date and manner of joining the regiment are uncertain, but he was a
batman in the 5th Company by August 1782. He may have returned to
Germany with the regiment in 1783.

FREDE, Dietrich Theodor   W200176
Born 13 January 1757 in Grossenberg, Pyrmont, and baptized on 16
January. Evangelical. 5' 3 1/4" tall. Father - Johann Konrad P.;
Mother - Anna Margarete. Shoemaker by trade. On 6-year enlistment.
Sailed to America with the regiment in 1776 as private in the 2nd
Company. He was wounded in the attack on Fort Washington on 16
November 1776. Transferred to the 4th Company in December 1779, he
was transferred back to the 2nd Company in June 1782. He apparently
returned to Germany with the regiment in 1783.

FREDE, Johann Barthold   W200061
Born 31 March 1750 in Grossenberg, Pyrmont. Evangelical. 5' 5 1/4"
tall. Married Anna Katharina Klenke from Eichenborn. Sailed to
America with the regiment in 1776 as private in the 1st Company. On
6-year enlistment. He deserted on 13 January 1777.

FREESE, Christoph   W200697
Born in Collstadt (or Golste). Sailed to America with the 1778 recruit
shipment and was assigned as private in the 1st Company. He did not
sail to West Florida with the regiment in 1778 but died of illness in
the hospital at New York on 20 May 1779.

FRESE, Christian   W200414
Born 1758 in Wetterburg (W). Evangelical. 5'3" tall. Sailed to
America with the regiment in 1776 as private in the 4th Company. He
died in November 1780.

FRESE, Franz Christoph   W200494
Born 29 April 1721 in Oesdorf, Pyrmont (listed in the HETRINA as
Holzhausen), and baptized on 4 May. Evangelical. Father - Christoph
F. Married with 6 children. Sailed to America with the regiment in
1776 as sergeant in the 5th Company. Taken prisoner at Baton Rouge
on 21 September 1779, he died of illness while a prisoner at New
Orleans on 10 October 1779. He had 18 years' previous military expe-
rience in Holland.

FRESE, Friedrich Christian   W200536
Born 14 May 1757 in Vasbeck (W). Evangelical. 5'4 1/4" tall. Father
- Johann Jakob F.; Mother - Anna Catharine, nee Gerhard. Sixth of 8
children. Sailed to America with the regiment in 1776 as private in
the 5th Company. Taken prisoner at Elizabethtown, New Jersey, on 8
January 1777, he enlisted in the American army. He apparently deserted back to his regiment, as he was again taken prisoner at Baton
Rouge on 21 September 1779. He died of illness while in prisoner
status at New Orleans on 18 November 1779.

FRESE, Johann Philipp   W200498
Born 1754 in Sudeck (W). He is also listed on documents as having
been born in Mengeringhausen and Wildungen. Evangelical. Hunter by
trade. Sailed to America with the regiment in 1776 as quartermaster
sergeant in the 5th Company. There is considerable confusion as to
what happened to him during the war. He is listed in the HETRINA as
having died in 1779, and being transferred to the 3rd Company, as
being restationed to Europe in 1780, and as being released in America
on 24 February 1781. He was sent back to Germany on the *Echo* on 8
October 1778 on recruiting duty, arriving at Portsmouth on 1 January
1779. He was stricken from the regimental records in 1781 as not
returning to America. He had 6 years' previous military experience in
the Waldeck army.

FREYSE, August   W200879
Born in Hannover. Sailed to America with the 1781 recruit shipment
and was assigned as private in the 3rd Company. He died of illness on
16 October 1781.

FRICKE, Anton   W200880
Sailed to America with the 1781 recruit shipment and was assigned as
drummer in the 3rd Company. In June 1782 he was transferred to the
2nd Company, and apparently returned to Germany with the regiment in
1783.

FRIEDEBORN, Georg   W200177
Born 1756 in Usseln (W). Evangelical. Shoemaker by trade. Sailed to
America with the regiment in 1776 as private in the 2nd Company.
Taken prisoner on the Amite river on 4 September 1779, he deserted at
Havana on 4 March 1782 while still in prisoner status.

FRIEDINGER, Sebastian   W200698
Born in Grunertshofen. Sailed to America with the 1778 recruit shipment and was assigned as private in the 3rd Company. He deserted on
15 May 1781 after the fall of Pensacola and may have joined the
Spanish army.

FUEHRER, Georg   W200699
Sailed to America with the 1777 recruit shipment and was assigned as
private in the 3rd Company. He returned to Germany with the regiment
and was released at Korbach (W) on 16 Ootober 1783.

GABELAENDFR, Peter   W201133
Born in Hassfurth. Sailed to America with the 1778 recruit shipment
and was sick upon arrival. He was assigned as private in the 4th
Company. He died of illness aboard the transport *Crawford*, at Port
Royal on 9 December 1778.

GANS, Johann Philipp   W200537
Born in 1749 in Wrexen (W). Evangelical. 5'8" tall. Sailed to America with the regiment in 1776 as private in the 5th Company. Taken
prisoner at Baton Rouge on 21 September 1779, he died of illness
while in prisoner status at New Orleans on 24 October 1779. He had 6
years' previous military experience in the Waldeck Regiment.

GEITZ, Adam   W200297
Born 1758 in Hemfurth (W). Evangelical. 5'4" tall. Linen weaver by
trade. Sailed to America with the regiment in 1776 as private in the
3rd Company. He served in the 3rd Company throughout the war and
apparently returned to Germany with the regiment in 1783.

GEITZ, Johann Georg   W200538
Born 12 February 1758 in Bringhausen (W), and baptized 15 February.
Evangelical. 5'7" tall. Father – Damian; Mother – Anna Elisabeth, nee
Uspruch. Fifth of 7 children. Sailed to America with the regiment in
1776 as private in the 5th Company. Taken prisoner on 5 January 1777
at Springfield, New Jersey, he was sent to Philadelphia for exchange
on 18 June 1778. He was taken prisoner again on 21 September 1779
at Baton Rouge, and returned to duty in January 1782. He apparently
returned to Germany with the regiment in 1783.

GENUIT, Franz Henrich   W200415
Born 1758 in Usseln (or Nieder Waroldern) (W). Evangelical. Sailed
to America with the regiment in 1776 as private in the 4th Company.
He boarded the *Santa Rosalia* on 29 May 1781 for return to New York
after the capitulation of Pensacola. He served in the 4th Company
throughout the war and apparently returned to Germany with the regiment in 1783.

GENUIT, Henrich   W200178
Born 1750 in Twiste (W). Evangelical. Married with 1 child. Sailed to
America with the regiment in 1776 as private in the 2nd Company. He
was transferred to the 4th Company in December 1779, and died of
illness at Pensacola on 6 August 1780. He had 4 years' previous military experience in the Waldeck 2nd Regiment.

GERGER, Johannes   W200881
Born in Sulz. Sailed to America with the 1781 recruit shipment and
was assigned as private in the 3rd Company. In July 1782 he was
transferred to the 1st Company. He was released at Flatbush on 15
July 1783, and may have gone to Nova Scotia as a Turger (probably
Gerger) of the Waldeck Regiment listed by DeMarce as having received a land grant for one man, one woman, and one child in 1784.

GERHARD, Georg   W200298
Born 1759 in Willingen (W). Evangelical. Sailed to America with the
regiment in 1776 as private in the 3rd Company. He died of illness on
26 February 1777.

GERHARD, Henrich   W200179
Born 1759 in Willingen (W). Evangelical. Sailed to America with the
regiment in 1776 as private in the 2nd Company. Taken prisoner at
Springfield, New Jersey, on 5 January 1777, he enlisted in the American army on 2 February 1777. He apparently deserted back to his
regiment as he was transferred to the 4th Company in December 1779.
He was transferred back to the 2nd Company in June 1782 and apparently returned to Germany with the regiment in 1783.

GERHARD, Karl   W200882
Born in Dinkelsbuehl. Sailed to America with the 1781 recruit shipment and was assigned to the 3rd Company. He returned to Germany
with the regiment and was released at Bremen on 19 October 1783.

GERLACH, Moritz   W200299
Born 1736 in Gellershausen (W). Evangelical. 5'7 1/2" tall. Married
with 1 child. Sailed to America with the regiment in 1776 as private in
the 3rd Company. In December 1782 he was transferred back to
Germany as an invalid. He had 16 years' previous military service in
the armies of Prussia and Bavaria.

GIEBEL, Johann Christian   W200883
Born 1766 in Baarsen, Pyrmont. Lutheran. 5'1" tall. Sailed to America with the 1781 recruit shipment and was assigned as private in the
3rd Company. He died of illness at Newtown on 30 January 1782.

GIEDE, David (or Daniel)   W200416
Born 1756 in Boehne (W). Evangelical. Sailed to America with the
regiment in 1776 as private in the 4th Company. He boarded the *Santa
Rosalia* on 29 May 1781 to return to New York after the capitulation of
Pensacola. Served throughout the war in the 4th Company and appar-
ently returned to Germany with the regiment in 1783.

GIER, Georg Ludwig   W200539
Born 1736 in Eutin, Holstein. Evangelical. 5'5" tall. On 4-year enlistment. Sailed to America with the regiment in 1776 as private in the
5th Company. Taken prisoner on 5 January 1777 at Springfield, New
Jersey, he was sent to Philadelphia to be exchanged on 18 June 1778.
However, on 5 August 1778, prior to rejoining the regiment, he deserted at York Point. He rejoined the regiment in December 1782, and
returned to Germany with the regiment. On 19 September 1783 he was
released at Bremen. He had 2 years' previous military experience in
the armies of Holstein and Kiel.

GIESENSCHLAEGER, Georg   W200417
Born 1745/46 in Berleberg, Prussia. Evangelical. 5'2" tall. Shoemaker by trade. On a 4-year enlistment. Sailed to America with the
regiment in 1776 as private in the 4th Company. Taken prisoner on 5
January 1777, at Springfield, New Jersey, he was sent to Philadelphia
to be exchanged on 21 June 1778. He died of illness on 3 March 1780.

GIESING, Henrich   W200062
Born 1751 in Berndorf (W). Evangelical. Sailed to America with the
regiment in 1776 as private in the 1st Company. He was wounded in
the attack on Fort Washington on 16 November 1776, and died of his
wounds on 5 December 1776.

GIESSEL, Christian   W200884
Born in Datum, Ansbach. Sailed to America with the 1781 recruit
shipment and was assigned as private in the 3rd Company. In December 1779 he was transferred to the 4th Company, and on 15 July 1783
he was released from the regiment at Flatbush.

GLAENTZER, Christoph   W400001
Born in Mengeringhausen (W). Evangelical. 5' 6" tall. Married with 1
child. Sailed to America with the regiment in 1776 as regimental
drummer on the staff. Served as regimental drummer throughout the
war and apparently returned to Germany with the regiment in 1783.

GLAENTZER, Konrad   W400002
Born 1723/24 in Freienhagen (W). Sailed to America with the regiment
in 1776 as provost on the staff. Died of illness in camp at Fort George
(Pensacola) on 17 April 1779.

GLEICHER, Franz   W200418
Born 1747/48 in Neusaal, Hungary. Catholic. 5'2 1/2" tall. Married
with 2 children. On 4-year enlistment. Sailed to America with the
regiment in 1776 as private in the 4th Company. Reportedly taken
prisoner on 5 January 1777 in New Jersey, according to the Waldeck
newspaper of that time. It seems unlikely, as his capture is not noted
in other records. He was released as an invalid, in America, on 30
June 1778, and returned to Europe on the *Echo*, sailing on 8 October
1778 and arriving at Portsmouth on 1 January 1779.

GOCKEL, Henrich   W200136
Born in 1748 in Lelbach (W). Evangelical. Sailed to America with the
regiment in 1776 as corporal in the 2nd Company. Taken prisoner on
the Amite River on 4 September 1779, he returned to duty in January
1782. He apparently returned to Germany with the regiment in 1783.
He had 8 years' previous military experience, having enlisted in the
Waldeck army on 27 April 1768.

GOCKEL, Johannes   W200180
Born 1750 in Kleinern (W). Evangelical. 5'4" tall. Tailor by trade.
Married with 2 children. Sailed to America with the regiment in 1776
as private in the 2nd Regiment. Taken prisoner on the Amite River on
4 September 1779, he returned to duty in January 1782. He apparently
returned to Germany with the regiment in 1783.

GOEBEL, Christian   W200063
Possibly born 10 June 1743 in Meineringhausen (W). Evangelical.
5'5" tall. Father - Daniel G. Third of 4 children. Sailed to America
with the regiment in 1776 as private in the 1st Company. There are
indications that he was taken prisoner on 31 December 1776, and
immediately released, then taken prisoner again in early January
1777. On 18 June 1778 he was sent to Philadelphia to be exchanged.
By December 1779 he was in the 2nd Company, and was then transferred to the 4th Company. In June 1782 he was transferred back to
the 2nd Company. He returned to Germany with the regiment and was
released at Korbach (W) on 21 October 1783.

GOEBEL, Henrich   W200181
Born 1752/53 in Willingen (W). Evangelical. 5'7" tall. Sailed to
America with the regiment in 1776 as private in the 2nd Company. He
died of illness on 19 January 1777.

GOEBEL, Johannes   W200300
Born 1759 in Willingen (W). Evangelical. Sailed to America with the regiment in 1776 as private in the 3rd Company. Taken prisoner at Baton Rouge on 21 September 1779, he deserted from prisoner status at Havana on 25 March 1782.

GOEBEL, Johannes   W200419
Born 1756 in Landau (W). Evangelical. 5'3" tall. Father - Johann Christian G.; Mother - Anna Elisabeth, nee Behr. Linen weaver by trade. Married Susanna Margaretha Oxenius on 27 March 1788, and they had 1 child. Sailed to America with the regiment in 1776 as private in the 4th Company. He boarded the *Santa Rosalia* on 29 May 1781 to return to New York after the capitulation of Pensacola. He served in the 4th Company throughout the war and apparently returned to Germany with the regiment in 1783.

GOBBEL, Johannes   W200420
Born 1752 in Rattlar (W). Evangelical. 5'4 1/2" tall. Sailed to America with the regiment in 1776 as private in the 4th Company. He was killed in action on 4 October 1777.

GOEBEL, Johannes   W200540
Born 1752/53 in Rattlar (W). Evangelical. 5'2" tall. Sailed to America with the regiment in 1776 as private in the 5th Company. Taken prisoner at Baton Rouge on 21 September 1779, he returned to duty in January 1782. He apparently returned to Germany with the regiment in 1783.

GOEBEL, Michael   W200701
Born in Gellershausen (W). Sailed to America with the 1778 recruit shipment and was assigned as private in the 3rd Company. He was wounded in the attack on The Village on 7 January 1781. He returned to Germany with the regiment and was released at Korbach (W) on 23 October 1783.

GOEBERT, Lorenz   W200064
Born 1750 in Braunau (W). Evangelical. 5'4" tall. Sailed to America with the regiment in 1776 as private in the 1st Company. Taken prisoner at Baton Rouge on 21 September 1779, he died of illness while a prisoner at New Orleans on 31 October 1779. He may have become a batman while in prisoner status, as at the time of his death he is listed as such.

GOECKE, Henrich   W300005
Born in Pyrmont. A Johann Henrich Goecke of Oesdorf, Pyrmont, was the father of a daughter, Johanna Christine, baptized on 13 March 1757. Sailed to America with the regiment in 1776 as cannoneer in the artillery section. Died of illness on 3 September 1777.

43

GOEDECKE, Johann Christian   W200541
Born 7 October 1758 in Vasbeck (W). Evangelical. Father - Johann
Justus G., shepherd; Mother - Anna Katharina, nee Pincke. Second of
3 children. He married Anna Elisabeth Schaefer, born 1753 in Helsen
(W), and they had 1 child, Johannette Sofie Friedrike, born 27 May
1792. At the time of the marriage he was a musketeer at Mengeringhausen (W). Sailed to America with the regiment in 1776 as private in
the 5th Company. Taken prisoner at Baton Rouge on 21 September
1779, he returned to duty in January 1782. He apparently returned to
Germany with the regiment in 1783.

GOEDELING, Johann Stephan Wilhelm   W200702
Born in Sachsenhausen (W), and baptized on 5 September 1753.
Father - Johannes G. Sailed to America with the 1777 recruit shipment
and was assigned as sergeant in the 1st Company. He died of illness
in the hospital at Manchac on 26 July 1779.

GOERCKE, Georg   W200885
Sailed to America with the 1781 recruit shipment and was assigned as
corporal in the 3rd Company. In July 1782 he was transferred to the 1st
Company, and apparently returned to Germany with the regiment in
1783.

GOETTE, Christian   W200703
Born in Korbach (W). Sailed to America in the 1778 recruit shipment
and was assigned as corporal in the 2nd Company. He died of illness
at Pensacola on 19 October 1779.

GOETTE, Johann Christian Ludwig   W200382
Born 1751 in Korbach (W), and baptized on 5 March 1752.
Evangelical. 5'6" tall. Father - Henrich Justig G. Johann Christian
Ludwig Goette died in 1792. Sailed to America with the regiment in
1776 as corporal in the 4th Company. He boarded the *Santa Rosalia* on
29 May 1781 to return to New York after the capitulation of Pensacola.
He served throughout the war in the 4th Company and apparently returned to Germany with the regiment in 1783. He had 9 years' previous
military experience in Holland, probably in a Waldeck unit.

GOETTE, Johann Friedrich   W200421
Born in Rhoden (W), and baptized on 15 January 1758. Confirmed in
1772. Evangelical. Father - Jakob Friedrich G. Sailed to America
with the regiment in 1776 as private in the 4th Company. He died of
illness on 11 October 1777.

GOSE, Johann Joachim   W200704
Born 1749/50 in Wehrstadt. Date and manner of joining the regiment
are uncertain. By April 1779 he was a private in the 5th Company.
Taken prisoner at Baton Rouge on 21 September 1779, he died of illness while still a prisoner, on 13 January 1780.

GOSSMANN, Johann Philipp   W200182
Born 1752/53 in Wetterberg (W). Evangelical. 5'4" tall. Father –
Johann G. Second of 3 children. Sailed to America with the regiment in
1776 as private in the 2nd Company. In December 1779 he was trans-
ferred to the 4th Company. On 22 April 1781 he was shot and killed by
Indians in the forests near Pensacola.

GOTTLIEB, Georg   W201018
Sailed to America with the 1782 recruit shipment. He deserted at
Halifax on 6 August 1783.

GRAEBE, Friedrich   W200301
Born 1753 in Mengeringhausen (W). Evangelical. 5'5 3/4" tall. Married. Sailed to America with the regiment in 1776 as private in the 3rd
Company. Served throughout the war in the 3rd Company, but deserted at Flatbush on 2 July 1783. He had 2 years' previous military
experience in the Waldeck 2nd Regiment. A John Frederick Grabe is
listed in the 1790 census as living in Northern Liberty Town, Philadelphia County, Pennsylvania, in a household with one adult male, one
male under sixteen years of age, and three females.

GRAEBE, Jakob   W300006
Born 1743 in Kassel. Evangelical. 5'3" tall. Sailed to America with
the regiment in 1776 as cannoneer in the artillery section. Transferred
to the 3rd Company in June 1781 after the regiment lost its guns at
Pensacola, and then in December 1782 to the 5th Company. He returned to Germany with the regiment and was released at Korbach (W)
on 16 October 1783.

GRAEBE, Jakob Henrich   W200251
Born 1741 in Rhoden (W). Evangelical. Married with 1 child in 1776.
He died on 16 January 1810 at the age of 69 of consumption. A retired
sergeant of the Waldeck 5th Battalion, he was survived by his wife
and 2 grown children. Sailed to America with the regiment in 1776 as
sergeant in the 3rd Company. He served throughout the war in the 3rd
Company, being wounded by friendly fire from Fort George (part of the
Pensacola defenses) on 12 April 1781. He returned to Germany with
the regiment in 1783. He had 13 years' previous military experience in
the Waldeck 2nd Regiment, having enlisted on 23 June 1763.

GRAEBE, Johannes   W200422
Born 1756 in Berndorf (W). Evangelical. Sailed to America with the
regiment in 1776 as private in the 4th Company. Taken prisoner at
Elizabethtown, New Jersey, on 8 January 1777, he was sent to Philadelphia to be exchanged on 13 July 1778. He boarded the *Santa Rosalia* on 29 May 1781 to return to New York after the capitulation of
Pensacola. He apparently returned to Germany with the regiment in
1783.

GRAEBER, Georg   W200924
Sailed to America with the 1782 recruit shipment and was assigned as
private in the 5th Company. He died of illness on 3 January 1783.

GRAEBES, Christoph W200705
Born in Doellnitz. Sailed to America with the 1778 recruit shipment and was assigned as private in the 1st Company. He deserted from Manchac on 8 August 1779.

GRAEBING, Johann Henrich W200302
Born 1756 in Freienhagen (W). Evangelical. Sailed to America with the regiment in 1776 as private in the 3rd Company. Taken prisoner on 8 January 1777 at Elizabethtown, N.J., he was listed as a prisoner throughout the war and then as a deserter at Elizabethtown on 15 July 1783. He probably deserted shortly after being made a prisoner.

GREIF, Henrich W201019
Sailed to America with the 1782 recruit shipment and was assigned as private in the 5th Company. He apparently returned to Germany with his unit in 1783.

GREISER, August W200375
Born 1756 in Unna, Prussia. Evangelical. 5'7" tall. Sailed to America with the regiment in 1776 as captain at arms in the 4th Company. He was promoted to quartermaster sergeant in April 1779 and to sergeant in April 1780. He served throughout the war in the 4th Company and was then released at Flatbush on 15 July 1783. He had 5 years' previous military experience in Holland, probably in a Waldeck unit. In June 1784 he was given a land grant in Nova Scotia for one man and one woman.

GRIESHEIM, Georg W200706
Born in Meisdorf. Sailed to America with the 1778 recruit shipment and was assigned as private in the 3rd Company. He deserted on 15 May 1781, after the fall of Pensacola, and may have joined the Spanish army.

GRIMM, Philipp W200183
Born 1757 in Zweibruecken. Evangelical. 5' 2" tall. Sailor by trade. Sailed to America with the regiment in 1776 as private in the 2nd Company. Transferred to the 4th Company in December 1779, he deserted on 29 May 1781, after the fall of Pensacola. He may have joined the Spanish army.

GROB, Johannes W200065
Born 1754 in Lintefels, Kurpfalz. Catholic. Sailed to America with the regiment in 1776 as private in the 1st Company. He died of illness on 14 May 1777.

GRUBERT, Georg W200066
Born 1725/26 in Bertrueck, Bateb. Catholic. Married with 4 children. Sailed to America with the regiment in 1776 as private in the 1st Company, having joined during the march to Bremerlehe. He deserted on 6 January 1777, probably after having been taken prisoner. He had 9 years' previous military experience in the Braunschweig army.

GRUBERT, Johannes   W200886
Born in Ederheim. Sailed to America with the 1781 recruit shipment
and was assigned as private in the 3rd Company. He apparently returned to Germany with the regiment in 1783.

GUENTHER, Ernst Christian   W200707
Born 1742/43 in Clausthal. Sailed to America with the 1778 recruit
shipment and was assigned as private in the 4th Company. He died of
illness in January 1780.

GUENTHER, Konrad   W201020
Sailed to America with the 1782 recruit shipment and was assigned as
private in the 5th Company. He returned to Germany with his unit and
was released at Korbach (W) on 22 October 1783.

GUERGEL, Andreas   W200303
Born 1754 in Fulda. Catholic. 5'2" tall. On 6-year enlistment. Sailed
to America with the regiment in 1776 as private in the 3rd Company.
He deserted on 3 April 1777.

GUNSTMANN, Johann Friedrich   W200423
Born 1756 in Kohlgrund (W). Evangelical. Sailed to America with the
regiment in 1776 as private in the 4th Company. He boarded the *Santa
Rosalia* on 29 May 1781 to return to New York after the capitulation of
Pensacola. He served throughout the war in the 4th Company. He
returned to Germany with the regiment and was released at Korbach
(W) on 20 October 1783.

GUTHMANN, Konrad   W201134
Born in Schoenberg, Pfalz. Sailed to America with the 1777 recruit
shipment and was assigned as private in the 1st Company. He died of
illness on 25 July 1777.

GUTTERMILCH, Johann Erdmann   W200424
Born 1752 in Danzig. Evangelical. Pewter smith. Sailed to America
with the regiment in 1776 as private in the 4th Company. He boarded
the *Santa Rosalia* on 29 May 1781 to return to New York after the
capitulation of Pensacola. Served in the 4th Company throughout the
war and then deserted at Flatbush on 5 May 1783.

HAACKE, Friedrich   W300007
Born in Hoya. Sailed to America with the regiment in 1776 as cannoneer in the artillery section. Died of illness on 20 May 1777.

HAACKE, Georg Ludwig Ferdinand von   W100006
Born about 1745 in Laas, Witgenstein, he was 25 years old in 1773.
Protestant. He spoke German, Dutch, and French prior to going to
America, and apparently learned English while serving there as he
wrote an entry in Commissary Marc's autograph book in English. He
died on 19 December 1811 at Arolsen (W). Sailed to America with the
regiment in 1776 as captain (date of rank of 19 April 1776) and
commanding officer of the 5th Company. Taken prisoner in New Jersey

on 5 January 1777, he visited Bethlehem, Pennsylvania, on 3 April 1777. He was released from prisoner of war status on 9 July 1778 and returned to camp the afternoon of 12 July. In August 1778 he was transferred to the 1st Company as commander. On 21 September 1779 he was taken prisoner at Baton Rouge. He was apparently exchanged in 1781 and promoted to major. Possibly he did not return to duty until March 1782. He returned to Germany with the regiment in 1783. He was stationed in Nijmegen, Holland, in 1773 with the 2nd Waldeck Regiment, and on 1 January 1775 was at Brielle, Holland. At that time he had been 27 months as an ensign and 106 months as a lieutenant. On 3 March 1785 he marched out of Waldeck, into Dutch service, as lieutenant colonel of the 5th Waldeck Battalion, and returned to Waldeck with the battalion on 16 February 1786. He later saw service in the 5th Battalion in Dutch service, and eventually became a general.

HAACKE, Simon   W300008
Born in Griessen. Sailed to America with the regiment in 1776 as cannoneer in the artillery section. He died of illness on 5 August 1777.

HAAG, Christoph   W200887
Sailed to America with the 1781 recruit shipment and was assigned as private in the 3rd Company. In July 1782 he was transferred to the 5th Company, and apparently returned to Germany with the regiment in 1783.

HAAG, Henrich   W200888
Born in Zimmersrode. Sailed to America with the 1781 recruit shipment and was assigned as private in the 3rd Company. He died of illness on Long Island on 30 May 1782.

HAASE, Christian   W200265
Born 1760 in Mengeringhausen (W). Evangelical. Sailed to America with the regiment in 1776 as drummer in the 3rd Company. Served in the 3rd Company throughout the war and apparently returned to Germany with the regiment in 1783.

HAASE, Jakob   W200542
Born 1739 in Sachsenhausen (W). Evangelical. Shoemaker by trade. Married with 1 child. Sailed to America with the regiment in 1776 as private in the 5th Company. Wounded in action in December 1776, he died of illness at Baton Rouge on 18 September 1779.

HAGEL, Jakob   W200889
Born in Prickingen, Limburg. Sailed to America with the 1781 recruit shipment and was assigned as private in the 3rd Company. He died of illness at New York on 22 November 1781.

HAGEMEYER, Kaspar   W200543
Born 1756 in Alraft (W). Evangelical. 5'4 1/2" tall. Sailed to America with the regiment in 1776 as private in the 5th Company. He was killed in action near Springfield, New Jersey, on 4 January 1777.

HAGENER, Jakob   W200708
Born in Oberbiel. Sailed to America with the 1777 recruit shipment and was assigned as private in the 3rd Company. He deserted at Pensacola on 2 April 1781. A Jacob Hagener is listed in the 1790 census as living in North Liberty Town, Philadelphia County, Pennsylvania, in a household with one adult male and three females.

HAHNE, Ernst   W200184
Born 1751 in Adorf (W). Evangelical. 5'4" tall. Smith by trade. Sailed to America with the regiment in 1776 as private in the 2nd Company. Taken prisoner on the Amite River on 4 September 1779, he deserted at Havana on 31 August 1781 while still in prisoner status. He had 6 years' previous military experience in the Waldeck 2nd Regiment.

HAHNE, Georg   W200067
Born 1753 in Pyrmont. Evangelical. 5'6" tall. On a 6-year enlistment. (A Frantz Henrich Georg Hahn was baptized at Oesdorf, Pyrmont, on 21 July 1755. His father was Johann Friedrich H.). Sailed to America with the regiment in 1776 as private in the 1st Company. He was killed in action at Baton Rouge on 21 September 1779. He had 9 months' previous military experience in the Waldeck 2nd regiment.

HAHNE, Karl Friedrich   W200709
Born 1751/52 in Bosenfeld, Hannover. Sailed to America with the 1778 recruit shipment and was assigned as private in the 4th Company. He died of illness on 14 March 1780.

HAHNEFELD, Andreas   W201021
Sailed to America with the 1782 recruit shipment and was assigned as private in the 5th Company. He apparently returned to Germany with his unit in 1783.

HAMEL, Johann Philipp   W200068
Born 17 June 1753 in Meineringhausen (W). Evangelical. 5'4" tall. Father - Johann Henrich H; Mother - Marie Elisabeth, nee Tent. Married Christine Benkner, widow from Dorfitter on 13 November 1804. Sailed to America with the regiment in 1776 as private in the 1st Company. Taken prisoner at Baton Rouge on 21 September 1779, he returned to duty in January 1782. He apparently returned to Germany with the regiment in 1783.

HAMEL, Wilhelm   W201022
Sailed to America with the 1782 recruit shipment and was assigned as private in the 5th Company. He returned to Germany with his unit and was released at Korbach (W) on 14 October 1783.

HAMM, Peter   W200890
Born in Aulenbach. Sailed to America with the 1781 recruit shipment and was assigned as private in the 3rd Company. In July 1782 he was transferred to the 5th Company, and on 15 July 1783 he was released from the regiment at Flatbush. He then settled in Nova Scotia.

HAMMERSDORF, Johannes   W200185
Born 1746 in Heidelberg. Reformed. 5'5" tall. Mason by trade. Sailed
to America with the regiment in 1776 as private in the 2nd Company.
He did not sail to West Florida with the regiment in 1778, but died of
illness in the hospital at New York on 2 May 1779.

HANCKE, Ludwig   W200425
Born 1753 in Stephenhasen, Mecklenburg. Evangelical. 5'3" tall. Baker
by trade. On 4-year enlistment. Sailed to America with the regiment in
1776 as private in the 4th Company. He deserted on 17 May 1781, after
the fall of Pensacola, and may have joined the Spanish army.

HANSMANN, Christian   W200544
Born 1758 in Ziegenhain, Hesse. Reformed. Tailor by trade. Sailed to
America with the regiment in 1776 as private in the 5th Company. He
was wounded in action and taken prisoner at Baton Rouge on 21
September 1779. He deserted from prisoner status at New Orleans on 1
July 1780 and joined the Spanish army.

HANSTEIN, Johann Friedrich   W200007
Born 1730 in Wildungen (W). Evangelical. Married with 2 children.
Sailed to America with the regiment in 1776 as corporal in the 1st
Company. He died of illness in the hospital on 21 October 1776, the
1st Waldeck soldier to die in America. He had 21 years' previous mili-
tary experience in the Waldeck 2nd Regiment.

HANXLEDEN, Johann Ludwig Wilhelm von   W100001S
Born in Gershausen (W). Evangelical. Father – Johann Wilhelm
v.H.; Mother – Charlotte Wilhelmine. First of 5 children. Father of
Wilhelm von Hanxleden (W200371). Sailed to America with the regiment in 1776 as lieutenant colonel commanding the regiment and
commanding officer of the 3rd Company. He was promoted to colonel
in 1776. He was killed leading the attack on The Village on 7 January
1781.

HANXLEDEN, Wilhelm von   W200371
Born 1746 in Gershausen (W). Evangelical. Father – Johann Ludwig
Wilhelm v.H. (W100001S). Sailed to America with the regiment in
1776 as cadet in the 3rd Company. Listed as a private in the 3rd
Company after April 1779, he was released from the regiment at
Pensacola on 25 April 1781, and apparently returned to Germany.

HAPPE, Henrich   W201023
Sailed to America with the 1782 recruit shipment and was assigned as
private in the 5th Company. He apparently returned to Germany with
his unit in 1783.

HAPPE, Peter   W200069
Born 1742 in Odershausen (W). Evangelical. Sailed to America with
the regiment in 1776 as private in the 1st Company. He died of illness
at Harlem on 5 December 1776. He had 20 years' previous military
experience in the Waldeck army.

HAPPEL, Daniel   W201024
Sailed to America with the 1782 recruit shipment and was assigned as
private in the 5th Company. He returned to Germany with his unit and
was released at Korbach (W) on 23 October 1783.

HARTEL, Alexander   W200710
Born in Unteroewisheim. Sailed to America with the 1778 recruit
shipment and was sick upon arrival. He was assigned as private in
the 3rd Company. He deserted at Pensacola on 5 April 1781.

HARTIG, Albrecht   W200891
Sailed to America with the 1781 recruit shipment and was assigned as
private in the 3rd Company. In July 1782 he was transferred to the 5th
Company. He returned to Germany with the regiment and was released
at Korbach (W) on 16 October 1783.

HARTMANN, Adam   W200545
Born 1756/57 in Reinhardshausen (W). Evangelical. Sailed to America with the regiment in 1776 as private in the 5th Company. Taken
prisoner on 21 September 1779 at Baton Rouge, he died of illness
while in prisoner status on 13 January 1780.

HARTMANN, Anton   W200892
Born in Ronsberg. Sailed to America with the 1781 recruit shipment
and was assigned as private in the 3rd Company. He was released
from the regiment at Flatbush on 15 July 1783, and then settled in
Nova Scotia.

HARTMANN, Daniel   W200070
Born 1753 in Reinhardshausen (W). Evangelical. Sailed to America
with the regiment in 1776 as private in the 1st Company. Taken prisoner at Baton Rouge on 21 September 1779, he returned to duty in
January 1782. He apparently returned to Germany with the regiment in
1783.

HARTMANN, Daniel   W201179
Date and manner of joining the regiment are uncertain, but by December 1781 he was a laborer in the 1st Company. In June 1782 he was a
batman in the 1st Company, and apparently returned to Germany with
the regiment in 1783.

HARTMANN, Johannes   W200546
Born 1756/57 in Welda, Paderborn. Catholic. 5'1" tall. Sailed to
America with the regiment in 1776 as private in the 5th Company.
Taken prisoner on 21 September 1779, he died of illness while in
prisoner status on 14 November 1779.

HARTMANN, Thomas   W201025
Sailed to America with the 1782 recruit shipment and was assigned as
private in the 5th Company. He apparently returned to Germany with
his unit in 1783.

HARTMANN, Ulrich   W200893
Sailed to America with the 1781 recruit shipment and was assigned as private in the 3rd Company. He was transferred to the 5th Company in July 1782. He returned to Germany with the regiment and was released at Korbach (W) on 17 October 1783.

HAUSCHILD, Matthias   W200186
Born 1759 in Waldeck (W). Evangelical. 5'3" tall. Sailed to America with the regiment in 1776 as private in the 2nd Company. He died of illness on 6 September 1777.

HAUSCHILD, Philipp   W201189
Born 1765 in Waldeck (W). Lutheran. 5'1" tall. Weaver by trade. Sailed to America with the 1781 recruit shipment and was assigned as drumner in the 3rd Company. He died of illness at Newtown on 11 December 1781.

HAUSER, Peter   W200894
Sailed to America with the 1781 recruit shipment and was assigned as private in the 3rd Company. He was transferred to the 5th Company in July 1782. He returned to Germany with the regiment and was released at Korbach (W) on 16 October 1783.

HEBERLEIN, Leonhard   W200895
Born 1763 in Obernzenn. Lutheran. 5'2" tall. Sailed to America with the 1781 recruit shipment and was assigned as private in the 3rd Company. He died of illness at Newtown on 31 January 1781.

HECK, Jakob   W200896
Born in Endersbach. Sailed to America with the 1781 recruit shipment and was assigned as private in the 3rd Company. In June 1782 he was transferred to the 5th Company. He returned to Germany with the regiment, but deserted "on the Weser" on 22 September 1783.

HECKENROTH, Andreas   W201135
Born in Blankenberg, Hesse. Sailed to America with the 1778 recruit shipment and was assigned (as private?) in the 4th Company. He did not sail to West Florida with the regiment in 1778 but died of illness in the hospital at New York on 16 January 1779.

HECKMANN, Johann Henrich   W200374
Born 6 July 1742 in Bringhausen (W), and baptized on 22 July. Lutheran. Father - Michael Ulrich, born in Frebershausen; Mother - Anna Catharina, nee Fornin. Sailed to America with the regiment in 1776 as sergeant in the 4th Company. He boarded the *Santa Rosalia* on 29 May 1781 to return to New York after the capitulatlon of Pensacola. He served throughout the war in the 4th Company, and apparently returned to Germany with the regiment in 1783. He had 17 years' previous military experience in Holland.

HEIDORN, Martin   W300009
Born 1737 in Pyrmont. Evangelical. 5'2" tall. Married with 2 children.
A locksmith, Johann Martin Heidorn was the father of a son, Johann
Friedrich H., baptized on 25 August 1765 in Bad Pyrmont. The mother
of the child was Maria Elisabeth, nee Geissler. Sailed to America with
the regiment in 1776 as bombardier in the artillery section. In June
1781, after the regiment lost its guns, he was transferred to the 3rd
Company, and in December 1782 he was transferred to the 5th Company. He returned to Germany with the regiment and was released at
Korbach (W) on 16 October 1783. He had 3 years' previous military
experience in the Wuerttemberg army.

HEILIG, Johannes   W200711
Born in Clausthal. Sailed to America with the 1778 recruit shipment
and was assigned as private in the 3rd Company. He deserted at
Pensacola on 2 April 1781.

HEINECKE, Gottlieb   W201026
Sailed to America with the 1782 recruit shipment and was assigned as
private in the 5th Company. He apparently returned to Germany with
his unit in 1783.

HEINECKE, Henrich   W200547
Born 1757 in Stewels, Eisenach. Evangelical. Paper maker by trade.
Sailed to America with the regiment in 1776 as private in the 5th
Company. Taken prisoner at Baton Rouge on 21 September 1779, he
returned to duty in January 1782. He apparently returned to Germany
with the regiment in 1783.

HEINEMANN, Jakob (Konrad)   W200387
Born 1759 in Boehne (W). Evangelical. 5'3" tall (in 1804). As a
soldier in the 5th Waldeck Battalion at Mengeringhausen he married
Dorothea Elisabeth Kuehne from Waldeck (W) on 24 March 1793. They
had more than the 1 child, Henriette Christine born 11 April 1790.
The others were born at Waldeck. He died 23 July 1813 at Waldeck.
Sailed to America with the regiment in 1776 as drummer in the 4th
Company. Taken prisoner on 5 January 1777 at Springfield, New Jersey, he was sent to Philadelphia to be exchanged on 21 June 1778. He
was promoted to private in the 4th Company in May 1780, and returned
to Germany with the regiment in 1783. He served in the 5th Waldeck
Battalion in Dutch service at the Cape of Good Hope from 1802 to
1806.

HEINEMANN, Philipp   W200304
Born 1758 in Boehne (W). Evangelical. 5'2" tall. Sailed to America
with the regiment in 1776 as private in the 3rd Company. Served
throughout the war in the 3rd Company. He returned to Germany with
the regiment and was released at Korbach (W) on 20 October 1783.

HEINSCHEL, Johann Balthasar   W200305
Born 1741 in Lippersdorf, Silesia. Evangelical. 5'3" tall. Sailed to America with the regiment in 1776 as private in the 3rd Company. Served throughout the war in the 3rd Company. He returned to Germany with the regiment and was released at Korbach (W) on 17 October 1783.

HEINTZ, Christoph   W201027
Sailed to America with the 1782 recruit shipment and was assigned as private in the 5th Company. Returned to Germany with his unit and was released at Korbach (W) on 22 October 1783.

HELDRING, Gerhard Henrich   W100014
Born in Rinteln, Schaumberg. Twenty-one years old in 1773. Lutheran. Single. Spoke German, Dutch, and French. Sailed to America with the regiment in 1776 as 1st lieutenant in the 4th Company with a date of rank of 6 March 1776. He was taken prisoner on 5 January 1777 in New Jersey; he visited Bethlehem, Pennsylvania, on 3 April 1777. He returned to duty on 9 July 1778. He was on leave in October 1779 and may have served the English as an engineer at this time. He was promoted to captain lieutenant on 25 April 1780, after being offered a captaincy in the English 60th Regiment. During the period of the regiment's stay at Pensacola he served as the post engineer and drew several maps of the Pensacola area. He boarded the *San Pedro and San Pablo* on 29 May 1781 to return to New York after the capitulation of Pensacola. He returned to Germany with the regiment in 1783. In 1773 he was a supernumery ensign with the 1st Waldeck Regiment at Bommel, Holland, and had the same rank on 1 January 1775, with 63 months in grade, when stationed at Dendermunde, Holland. During 1785 and 1786 he was the major of the 5th Waldeck Battalion which was then in Dutch service. At a later period, with the 5th Battalion at Delft in Holland, he was promoted to lieutenant colonel on 27 January 1794 and to colonel on 1 April 1794. When the 5th Battalion was preparing to sail for the Cape of Good Hope, he was transferred to the 1st Waldeck Battalion.

HELLER, Johann Daniel   W200426
Born in Anraff (W), and baptized on 31 August 1755. Evangelical. 5' 6 1/2" tall. Father – Christoph H. Sailed to America with the regiment in 1776 as private in the 4th Company. He boarded the *Santa Rosalia* on 29 May 1781 to return to New York after the capitulation of Pensacola. He served throughout the war in the 4th Company, and apparently returned to Germany with the regiment in 1783.

HEMMERLING, Amandus   W200712
Date and manner of joining the regiment are uncertain. By April 1779 he was a sergeant in the 3rd Company. He was restationed to Germany in April 1781 on recruiting duty.

HENCKELER, Franz   W200497
Born 1748 in Korbach (W). Evangelical. 5' 6 1/2" tall. Sailed to
America with the regiment in 1776 as captain at arms in the 5th
Company. Taken prisoner at Baton Rouge on 21 September 1779, he
returned to duty in January 1782. In June 1782 he was promoted to
sergeant and apparently returned to Germany with the regiment in
1783. He had 10 years and 6 months of previous military experience
in Holland.

HENCKELMANN, Johann Henrich   W200427
Born 1756 in Wethen (W). Evangelical. 5"1" tall. Herdsman. Married
Luise Vahle on 24 November 1784, and fathered 1 child. He died on
20 July 1788 at about 30 years of age. Sailed to America with the
regiment in 1776 as private in the 4th Company. Taken prisoner on 5
January 1777 at Springfield, New Jersey, he was sent to Philadelphia
to be exchanged on 18 June 1778. He boarded the *Santa Rosalia* on 29
May 1781 to return to New York after the capitulation of Pensacola.
He returned to Germany with the regiment and was released at Korbach
(W) on 20 October 1783.

HENDEL, Konrad   W200548
Born 1746 in Sudeck (W). Evangelical. 5'5" tall. Sailed to America
with the regiment in 1776 as private in the 5th Company. Taken prisoner at Baton Rouge on 21 September 1779, he returned to duty in
January 1782. He was promoted to corporal in June 1782, and apparently returned to Germany with the regiment in 1783. He had 14 years'
previous military experience in the Waldeck 1st Regiment.

HENRICH, Johann Philipp   W200306
Born in Giflitz (W), and baptized on 2 December 1752. Evangelical.
Linen weaver by trade. Father – Wilhelm Christian H. Sailed to
America with the regiment in 1776 as private in the 3rd Company.
Taken prisoner at Baton Rouge on 21 September 1779, he returned to
duty in January 1782. He apparently returned to Germany with the
regiment in 1783. He had 1 year of previous military experience in the
Waldeck 1st Regiment.

HENTZE, Gottfried   W300010
Born in Hameln. Sailed to America with the regiment in 1776 as
cannoneer in the artillery section. He died of illness on 5 August 1777.

HENTZE, Philipp Henrich   W200187
Born 1757 in Wrexen (W). Evangelical. Sailed to America with the
regiment in 1776 as private in the 2nd Company. Taken prisoner on 5
January 1777 at Springfield, New Jersey, he was sent to Philadelphia
to be exchanged on 18 June 1778. In December 1779 he was transferred to the 4th Company, and in June 1782 transferred back to the
2nd Company. He apparently returned to Germany with the regiment in
1783.

HERBOLD, Johann Henrich   W200071
Born in Helmscheid (W) and lived in Rhoden (W). Was baptized on 13
April 1746, and confirmed in 1757. Evangelical. Father - Johann Henrich H. Married Anna Rosina Elisabeth Boehme on 23 August 1771
and had a daughter, Anna Katherina, born 29 October 1772. His wife
was buried 10 November 1772. Sailed to America with the regiment in
1776 as private in the 1st Company. Taken prisoner at Baton Rouge on
21 September 1779, he returned to duty on January 1782. In December
1782 he was released in America as an invalid, and transferred back to
Germany.

HERBST, Andreas   W200188
Born 1758 in Sebecksen, Hannover. Evangelical. 5'4" tall. Sailed to
America with the regiment in 1776 as private in the 2nd Company. In
December 1779 he was transferred to the 4th Company, and in   June
1782 transferred back to the 2nd Company. On 15 July 1783 he was
released from the regiment at Flatbush.

HERDES, Jost   W200549
Born 25 April 1753 in Buehle (W). Evangelical. Father - Andreas H.;
Mother - Maria Regina, nee Kinolt, midwife. Second child, a twin
brother, Johann Jakob, died prior to his first birthday. Sailed to America with the regiment in 1776 as private in the 5th Company. Taken
prisoner at Baton Rouge on 21 September 1779, he died of illness
while a prisoner at New Orleans on 25 September 1779.

HERING, Johann Henrich   W200307
Born 4 February 1753 in Frebershausen (W). Evangelical. 5'4 1/2"
tall. Father - Johannes H.; Mother - Elisabeth Gerdrut, nee Geitz.
Sailed to America with the regiment in 1776 as private in the 3rd
Company. He served in the 3rd Company throughout the war, and
apparently returned to Germany with the regiment in 1783.

HERMANN, Georg   W200713
Born in Philippstein. Sailed to America with the 1777 recruit shipment
and was assigned as private in the 4th Company. He boarded the *Santa
Rosalia* on 29 May 1781 to return to New York after the capitulation of
Pensacola. He returned to Germany with the regiment and was re-
leased at Bremen on 19 September 1783.

HEROLD, Konrad   W200714
Born in Nuernberg. Sailed to America with the 1778 recruit shipment
and was assigned as private in the 1st Company. He deserted at
Manchac on 9 July 1779.

HERTER, Andreas   W200072
Born 1742/43 in Heystrey, Wuerzburg. Evangelical (also listed as
Catholic). 5'5" tall. Butcher by trade. On 4-year enlistment. Sailed to
America with the regiment in 1776 as private in the 1st Company. He
deserted on 13 January 1777. He had 10 years' previous military expe-
rience in the Wuerzburg army.

HERTZIG, Peter   W201028
Sailed to America with the 1782 recruit shipment and was assigned as
private in the 5th Company. He apparently returned to Germany with
his unit in 1783.

HERTZOG, Friedrich   W200898
Sailed to America with the 1781 recruit shipment and was assigned as
private in the 3rd Company. In July 1782 he was transferred to the 5th
Company, and apparently returned to Germany with the regiment in
1783.

HERTZOG, Stephan   W200308
Born 1743/44 in Wellen (W). Evangelical. Sailed to America with the
regiment in 1776 as private in the 3rd Company. He was promoted to
corporal in April 1779, and to captain at arms in June 1782. He apparently returned to Germany with the regiment in 1783. He had 16 years'
previous military experience in the Waldeck 2nd Regiment, having
joined on 28 December 1760.

HESSE, Johannes   W200309
Born 1758 in Luetersheim (W). Evangelical. 5'3" tall. Sailed to
America with the regiment in 1776 as private in the 3rd Company. He
served in the 3rd Company throughout the war, and apparently returned
to Germany with the regiment in 1783.

HESSE, Kaspar   W200715
Born 1749/50 in Saalbach. Sailed to America with the 1778 recruit
shipment and was sick upon arrival. He was assigned as private in
the 3rd Company. He died of illness on 26 February 1780.

HEUSTER, Andreas   W201029
Sailed to America with the 1782 recruit shipment and was assigned as
private in the 5th Company. He apparently returned to Germany with
his unit in 1783.

HILLEBRAND, Johann Jost   W200899
Born in Flechtdorf (W). Sailed to America with the 1781 recruit
shipment and was assigned as private in the 3rd Company. He died of
illness in the hospital at Newtown on 1 October 1781.

HIMMELMANN, Wilhelm   W200823
Born 1760/61 in Schmillinghausen (W). Sailed to America with the
1779 recruit shipment and was assigned as private in the 4th Company. He transferred to the 2nd Company in June 1782, and apparently returned to Germany with the regiment in 1783.

HINTENBERGER, Franz   W200824
Born 1763/64 in Ochsenfurt. Sailed to America with the 1779 recruit
shipment and was assigned as private in the 3rd Company. In May
1780 he was made a cadet in the 3rd Company, and in August 1780 he
was promoted to corporal. He deserted at Pensacola on 1 April 1781.

HINTERTHUER, Dietrich   W200716
Born in Goettingen. Sailed to America with the 1777 recruit shipment
and was assigned as private in the 2nd Company. Taken prisoner on
the Amite River on 4 September 1779, he deserted from prisoner status
at New Orleans on 12 July 1780 and joined the Spanish army.

HOEHLE, Georg   W200189
Born 14 December 1757 in Bringhausen (W). Evangelical. 5'7 1/2"
tall. Father - Johann Jeremiah H.; Mother - Anna Elisabeth, nee
Muench. Fifth of 5 children. Married Anna Elisabeth Hoehle on 25
January 1791. Two children: Katherina Wilhelmine, born 3 November
1791; and Johannes, born 18 June 1795. Sailed to America with the
regiment in 1776 as private in the 2nd Company. In December 1779 he
was transferred to the 4th Company and in June 1782 he was transferred back to the 2nd Company. He apparently returned to Germany
with the regiment in 1783.

HOEHLE, Michael   W200550
Born 1759 in Koenigshagen (W). Evangelical. Sailed to America with
the regiment in 1776 as private in the 5th Company. He died of illness
at Manchac on 5 September 1779.

HOELSCHER, Henrich Friedrich   W200310
Born in Holzhausen, Pyrmont, and baptized on 2 January 1757.
Evangelical. 5'3 1/4" tall. Father - Johann Henrich H.; On 6-year
enlistment. Sailed to America with the regiment in 1776 as private in
the 3rd Company. Taken prisoner at Baton Rouge on 21 September
1779, he returned to duty in January 1782. In December 1779 he was
transferred to the 5th Company, and transferred back to the 3rd
Company in July 1782. He apparently returned to Germany with the
regiment in 1783.

HOFFMANN, Daniel   W201030
Sailed to America with the 1782 recruit shipment and was assigned as
corporal in the 5th Company. He died of illness on 10 January 1783.

HOFFMANN, Georg   W201031
Sailed to America with the 1782 recruit shipment and was assigned as
private in the 5th Company. He returned to Germany with his unit and
was released at Korbach (W) on 23 October 1783.

HOFFMANN, Henrich (Konrad)   W200717
Born in Nuernberg. Sailed to America with the 1778 recruit shipment
and was assigned as private in the 2nd Company. He was transferred
to the 4th Company in December 1779, and back to the 2nd Company
in June 1782. He was released from the regiment at Flatbush on 15
July 1783.

HOFFMANN, Johann Henrich   W200428
Born 1756/57 in Gellershausen (W). Evangelical. 5'5" tall. Sailed to
America with the regiment in 1776 as private in the 4th Company. He
boarded the *Santa Rosalia* on 29 May 1781 to return to New York after

the capitulation of Pensacola. He served throughout the war in the 4th Company and returned to Germany with the regiment. He was released at Korbach (W) on 20 October 1783.

HOFFMEISTER, Johann Henrich   W200377
Born 1752 in Blanckenburg. Lutheran. Sailed to America with the regiment in 1776 as medic in the 4th Company. He boarded the *Santa Rosalia* on 29 May 1781 to return to New York after the capitulation of Pensacola. He served throughout the war in the 4th Company and apparently returned to Germany with the regiment in 1783.

HOFMANN, Christoph   W201192
Born in Sindringen. Date and manner of joining the regiment are uncertain, but by October 1778 he was apparently a private in the 4th Company. He died of illness on the transport *Crawford* on 28 November 1778, when the regiment was en route to West Florida.

HOFMANN, Johannes   W201032
Sailed to America with the 1782 recruit shipment and was assigned as private in the 5th Company. He apparently returned to Germany with his unit in 1783.

HOFMANN, Wolrath   W201033
Sailed to America with the 1782 recruit shipment and was assigned as private in the 5th Company. He apparently returned to Germany with his unit in 1783.

HOHMANN, Adam   W200190
Born 1753 in Hueddingen (W). Evangelical. 5'4" tall. Sailed to America with the regiment in 1776 as private in the 2nd Company. He was transferred to the 4th Company in December 1779 and back to the 2nd Company in June 1782. He returned to Germany with the regiment and was released at Korbach (W) on 19 October 1783.

HOHMANN, August Wilhelm   W200500C
Born in Bergheim (W), and baptized on 16 April 1759. Evangelical. Father - Lieutenant (Karl Christoph) Hohmann (W100015). Sailed to America with the regiment in 1776 as free corporal in the 5th Company. He was commissioned as an ensign in July 1779, but apparently taken prisoner at Baton Rouge on 21 September 1779 while still serving as a free corporal. He died of illness in December 1779, probably without ever knowing of his having been commissioned. He had 3 years' previous military experience in Holland, probably in a Waldeck unit.

HOHMANN, Christoph   W201199
Sailed to America with the 1778 recruit shipment and was sick upon arrival. He was assigned as private in the 4th Company, and then disappears from the records.

HOHMANN, Karl Christoph   W100015
Born in Bergheim (W). He was married in Bergheim (W) in 1756 and
was the father of August Wilhelm Hohmann (W200500C), who was
baptized on 16 April 1759. Sailed to America with the regiment in 1776
as ensign in the 4th Company. He boarded the *Santa Rosalia* with his
batman on 29 May 1781 to return to New York after the capitulation of
Pensacola. He served in the 4th Company throughout the war, being
promoted to 2nd lieutenant on 25 April 1780. He apparently returned to
Germany with the regiment in 1783.

HOHMANN, Kaspar   W200718
Born 1754/55 in Starfeld, Heese. Sailed to America with the 1778
recruit shipment and was sick upon arrival. He was assigned as private in the 3rd Company. He died of illness at Pensacola on 28 May
1779.

HOHMANN, Konrad   W200191
Born 1743 in Giflitz (W). Evangelical. Married with 2 children.
Sailed to America with the regiment in 1776 as private in the 2nd
Company. In December 1779 he was transferred to the 4th Company,
and in June 1782 transferred back to the 2nd Company. He returned to
Germany with the regiment and was released at Korbach (W) on 21
October 1783.

HOLTZAPPEL, Johannes   W200311
Born 1759 in Bergfreiheit (W). Evangelical. Sailed to America with
the regiment in 1776 as private in the 3rd Company. By April 1779 he
had been promoted to corporal. Taken prisoner at Baton Rouge on 21
September 1779, he died of illness while still a prisoner at New Orleans on 11 October 1779. He had 8 years' previous military experience in the Waldeck 2nd Regiment.

HOMBERGER, Andreas   W200719
Born 1760/61 in Frankfurt. Sailed to America with the 1778 recruit
shipment and was sick upon arrival. He was assigned as private in
the 3rd Company. He died of illness at Pensacola on 8 June 1779.

HOPPE, Johannes   W200900
Sailed to America with the 1781 recruit shipment and was assigned as
private in the 3rd Company. In July 1782 he was transferred to the 5th
Company, and apparently returned to Germany with the regiment in
1783.

HORN, Karl von   W100020
Father - Konrad Albrecht von Horn (W100003S). Sailed to America
with the 1779 recruit shipment and was assigned as ensign in the
5th Company. He died of illness at Pensacola on 19 July 1780, and
was buried next day.

HORN, Konrad Albrecht von   W100003S
Father of Karl von Horn (W100020). Sailed to America with the regiment in 1776 as captain commanding the 1st Company. He was
promoted to major, probably in early 1777. On 14 October he
sailed up the Hudson on the *Klenehorn*, part of the relief force
sent toward General Burgoyne, which then returned down river on 16
October and to Staten Island on the 21st. In August 1778 he was transferred to the 5th Company, and sailed back to Germany on the *Echo*,
departing New York on 8 October 1778 and arriving at Portsmouth on 1
January 1779. Promoted to lieutenant colonel on 14 April 1779, he led
the 1779 recruit shipment back to America, finally arriving at Pensacola on 6 April 1780. He boarded the *San Pedro and San Pablo* on 29
May 1781 to return to New York after the capitulation of Pensacola.
On the regiment's return to Germany, von Horn was the commanding
officer. When the 5th Waldeck Battalion entered Dutch service in
1785, he was the colonel commanding the battalion.

HORN, Stephan (Christoph)   W200312
Born 1759 in Neudorf (W). Evangelical. Sailed to America with the
regiment in 1776 as private in the 3rd Company. Taken prisoner at
Baton Rouge on 21 September 1779, he was transferred to the 5th
Company in December 1779. He died of illness at Havana, while still
in prisoner status, on 16 December 1780.

HORNSBERGER, Philipp Henrich   W200552
Born 1758 in Rhoden (W), and confirmed in 1770. Evangelical. Sailed
to America with the regiment in 1776 as private in the 5th Company.
In December 1779 he was transferred to the 3rd Company. He
deserted on 17 May 1781, after the fall of Pensacola, and may have
joined the Spanish army.

HUEBSCH, Wilhelm   W300011
Born 1745/46 in Hameln. Evangelical. 5'5" tall. Sailed to America
with the regiment in 1776 as cannoneer in the artillery section. In June
1781, after the regiment lost its guns, he was transferred to the 3rd
Company, and in December 1782 he was transferred to the 5th Company. He returned to Germany with the regiment and was released at
Korbach (W) on 16 October 1783. He had 12 years' previous military
experience in the Hannover army.

HUFEISEN, Henrich   W200720
Born in Ober Werbe (W). Possibly the Johann Henrich Hufeisen baptized at Sachsenhausen (W) on 8 December 1748. Father – David H.
Sailed to America with the 1778 recruit shipment and was assigned as
private in the 1st Company. He deserted at Manchac on 19 Aug. 1779.

HUFEISEN, Henrich   W201180S
Born 1746 in Voehl, Darmstadt. Evangelical. 5'4" tall. Date and
manner of joining the regiment are uncertain, but in 1777 he was a
laborer in the regiment. He served as laborer, batman, wagon servant,
and even servant for the military chest. He returned to Germany with
the regiment and was released at Korbach (W) on 16 October 1783.

HUGEN, Johann Peter   W200192
Born 1742 in Elberfeld, Kurpfalz. Reformed. 5'3" tall. Wig maker by
trade. Sailed to America with the Regiment in 1776 as private in the
2nd Company. In December 1779 he was transferred to the 4th Company. He died of illness at Newtown on 6 December 1781.

HUMBRACHT, Franz   W200193
Born 1753 in Anraff (W). Evangelical. Teamster by trade. Sailed to
America with the regiment in 1776 as private in the 2nd Company. In
December 1779 he was transferred to the 4th Company, and transferred
back to the 2nd Company in June 1782. He apparently returned to
Germany with the regiment in 1783.

HUNDERTMARCK, Hermann   W200721
Born 1742/43 in Tallensen. Sailed to America with the 1778 recruit
shipment and was sick upon arrival. He was assigned as private in
the 4th Company. He died of illness at Pensacola on 21 May 1779.

HUNECKE, Johann Henrich Bernhard   W200429
Born 1730 in Hagen, Pyrmont. Evangelical. 5'5" tall. Married with 2
children. On 6-year enlistment. A Johann Henrich Christoph Hunecke
was born 19 July 1730 in Hagen, and baptized on 22 July. Father –
Johann Christoph H. One of his godparents was a Henrich Berend
Kukuk. Sailed to America with the regiment in 1776 as private in the
4th Company. After being declared an invalid in September 1778, he
next appears in the HETRINA as a batman in February 1779. He died
of illness at Pensacola on 9 August 1780.

HUNOLD, Peter   W200901
Born in Medebach. Sailed to America with the 1781 recruit shipment
and was assigned as private in the 3rd Company. He was transferred to
the 2nd Company in June 1782. He returned to Germany with the
regiment and was released at Bremen on 19 September 1783.

HUTH, Hermann   W200553
Born 1759 in Bremen. Reformed. Wig maker by trade. Sailed to
America with the regiment in 1776 as private in the 5th Company,
having joined on the march to Bremerlehe. Taken prisoner at Baton
Rouge on 21 September 1779, he deserted from prisoner status at New
Orleans on 2 July 1780 and joined the Spanish army.

HUTHMAN, Christian   W200507
Born 1758 in Mengeringhausen (W). Evangelical. Sailed to America
with the regiment in 1776 as drummer in the 5th Company. Taken
prisoner in New Jersey on 5 January 1777, he was listed as a prisoner
throughout the war and as a deserter at Elizabethtown, New Jersey, on
15 July 1783. In all probability he deserted much earlier, possibly as
early as 1777.

HUTHMANN, David   W200722
Born in Mengeringhausen (W). Sailed to America with the 1778 recruit
shipment and was assigned as private in the 1st Company. Taken
prisoner at Baton Rouge on 21 September 1779, he deserted from
prisoner status on 3 July 1780. He then joined the Spanish army.

HUTHMANN, Wilhelm   W200902
Born 1765 in Mengeringhausen (W). Lutheran. 5'1" tall. Sailed to
America with the 1781 recruit shipment and was assigned as private in
the 3rd Company. He died of illness in the hospital at New York on 3
December 1781.

INDENKAUFF, Jakob   W201034
Sailed to America with the 1782 recruit shipment and was assigned as
private in the 5th Company. He returned to Germany with his unit but
deserted at Bremen on 30 September 1783.

INGENTRON, Josef   W201035
Sailed to America with the 1782 recruit shipment and was assigned as
private in the 5th Company. He apparently returned to Germany with
his unit in 1783.

ITZMANN, Josef   W200554
Born 1747 in Langensalz, Saxony. Evangelical. Cloth maker by trade.
Sailed to America with the regiment in 1776 as private in the 5th
Company. Taken prisoner at Baton Rouge on 21 September 1779, he
committed suicide by jumping overboard, probably from the *El Cayman*, and drowning on 4 August 1780 while being transported to Havana
as a prisoner.

JAEGER, Barthold   W200555
Born 1746 in Rattlar (W). Evangelical. Sailed to America with the
regiment in 1776 as private in the 5th Company. Taken prisoner at
Baton Rouge on 21 September 1779, he returned to duty in January
1782. He apparently returned to Germany with the regiment in 1783.
He had 4 years' previous military experience in the Waldeck army.

JAEGER, (Johann) Friedrich   W200194
Baptized 10 November 1755 in Oesdorf, Pyrmont. Evangelical. 5'1"
tall. Father was a pharmacist. On 6-year enlistment. Sailed to
America with the regiment in 1776 as private in the 2nd Company. He
was transferred to the 4th Company in December 1779, and died of
illness on Long Island 21 May 1782.

JAEGER, Johannes   W200430
Born 1755 in Usseln (W). Evangelical. Sailed to America with the
regiment in 1776 as private in the 4th Company. He boarded the *Santa
Rosalia* with his wife and child on 29 May 1781 to return to New York
after the capitulation of Pensacola. He served in the 4th Company
throughout the war and apparently returned to Germany with the regiment in 1783.

JAKOB, Johann Adam   W200431
Born 1733 in Lispenhausen, Hesse. Reformed. Married with 4 children.
Sailed to America with the regiment in 1776 as private in the 4th
Company. He deserted on 17 April 1777. He had 7 years' previous
military service in the Hessian army.

JONAS, Martin   W200903
Born in Luxembourg. Sailed to America with the 1781 recruit shipment
and was assigned as private in the 3rd Company. He returned to
Germany with the regiment and was released at Bremen on 19 September 1783.

JOST, Johann Georg   W200313
Born 1755 in Ulrichstein, Darmstadt. Evangelical. 5' 8 3/4" tall.
Shoemaker by trade. Sailed to America with the regiment in 1776 as
private in the 3rd Company. Taken prisoner on 5 January 1777 at
Springfield, New Jersey, he was sent to Philadelphia from Lancaster
to be exchanged on 21 July 1778. He was wounded in the attack on The
Village on 7 January 1781 and released from the regiment at Flatbush
on 15 July 1783. He had one year of previous military experience in
the Waldeck 1st Regiment. A George Yost is listed in the 1790 census
as living in Hoosick, Albany County, New York, in a household with
one adult male and six females.

JUNCKER, Ludwig   W201191
Born in Holzhausen, Darmstadt. Sailed to America with the 1777 recruit shipment and was assigned as private in the 1st Company. He
died of illness on 5 August 1777.

JUNCKERMANN, Carl Henrich Friedrich   W200556
Born in Mengeringhausen (W) and baptized 26 February 1747. Evangelical. 5' 6 1/2" tall. Father - Philipp J.; Mother - Emma, nee
Hartwig. Saddlemaker by trade. Sailed to America with the regiment in
1776 as private in the 5th Company. Taken prisoner at Baton Rouge on
21 September 1779, he died of illness at Vera Cruz, Mexico, while in
prisoner status, on 16 August 1780. He had 5 1/2 years' previous
military experience in the Holland Guard Dragoons.

JUNG, Ernst Johann Christian   W200011
Born 1748 in Rosdorf, Hanau. Evangelical. 5' 5" tall. Sailed to
America with the regiment in 1776 as corporal in the 1st Company. He
apparently committed suicide on 27 April 1777. He had 12 years'
previous military experience in the Hanau militia.

JUTLEIN, Johann Josef   W201036
Sailed to America with the 1782 recruit shipment and was assigned as
private in the 5th Company. He died of illness at Halifax, Nova Scotia,
on 16 July 1783.

KABEL, Henrich   W201118
Born in Klingelbach, Darmstadt. Sailed to America with the 1778
recruit shipment and was sick upon arrival. He was assigned (as
private?) in the 2nd Company. He died of illness in the hospital at
New York on 11 January 1779.

KABEL, Leonhard   W200155
Born 1758 in Erbach, Oderwald. Evangelical. Linen weaver by trade.
Sailed to America with the regiment in 1776 as private in the 2nd
Company. Taken prisoner on the Amite River on 4 September 1779, he
died of illness at New Orleans, while in prisoner status, on 8 July
1780.

KAESEMEYER, Georg   W200276
Born 1732 in Holzhausen, Pyrmont. Reformed. 5'9 1/2" tall. Married
with 3 children. A Johann Georg Kessenmeier (apparently the same
individual) is listed in the Holzhausen Kirchenbuch as being the father
of a daughter born in 1762, and of a son who died at birth on 23 August
1764. His wife was Margarete Elisabeth, nee Foerster. Sailed to
America with the regiment in 1776 as private in the 3rd Company. He
died of illness on 6 May 1778. He had 13 years' previous military
experience in the English army.

KAHLER, Jakob   W200659
Born 1757/58 in Altenlotheim. Sailed to America with the 1778 recruit
shipment and was assigned as private in the 5th Company. Taken
prisoner at Baton Rouge on 21 September 1779, he died of illness,
while in prisoner status, on 22 November 1779.

KALTWASSER, Balthasar   W200156
Born 1759 in Wetzlar. Catholic. 5' 4 1/4" tall. Linen weaver by trade.
Sailed to America with the regiment in 1776 as private in the 2nd
Company. Taken prisoner on the Amite River on 4 September 1779, he
deserted from prisoner status on 20 July 1780. It appears that he then
went up the Mississippi River with Ludwig Ruppert (W200756) and
joined the American army under George Rogers Clark. A John Coldwater (anglicized from Kaltwasser) joined Captain John Girault's
Company of the Illinois Regiment on 16 July 1781, for the duration of
the war, and served as a private until at least late 1783.

KAMPF, Ernst de la   W200998
Sailed to America with the 1782 recruit shipment and was assigned as
private in the 5th Company. He returned to Germany with his unit and
was released from the regiment at Korbach (W) on 22 October 1783.

KAMPF, Karl   W200854
Sailed to America with the 1782 recruit shipment and was assigned as
private in the 3rd Company. In July 1782 he was transferred to the 5th
Company. He returned to Germany with the regiment and was released
at Korbach (W) on 18 October 1783.

KANN, Adam   W200030
Born 1754 in Nieder Werbe (W). Evangelical. Sailed to America with
the regiment in 1776 as private in the 1st Company. Taken prisoner at
Baton Rouge on 21 September 1779, he deserted from prisoner status
at Havana on 14 April 1782.

KANN, Johannes   W200031
Born 24 July 1752 in Nieder Werbe (W), and baptized on 9 August.
Evangelical. 5'4" tall. Sailed to America with the regiment in 1776 as
private in the 1st Company. Taken prisoner at Baton Rouge on 21
September 1779, he returned to duty in January 1782. He apparently
returned to Germany with the regiment in 1783.

KANN, Wilhelm   W200032
Born in Giflitz (W), and baptized on 19 May 1754. Evangelical. 5'5"
tall. Father - Hermann K., a soldier. Sailed to America with the
regiment in 1776 as private in the 1st Company. Taken prisoner on 31
December 1776 (or possibly on 27 October 1776 at Maroneck, New
York), he was listed as a prisoner throughout the war, and then as a
deserter at Elizabethtown, New Jersey, on 15 July 1783. He probably
deserted much earlier, even as early as 1777.

KAUFFMANN, Johann Henrich   W200033
Born 29 February 1756 in Helsen (W). Evangelical. 5'6" tall. Father -
Johannes K., grenadier; Mother - Anna Johana, nee Mangel. Married
Johanne Marie Margarete Schaefer on 28 December 1785. They had 8
children. He died on 1 November 1815. Sailed to America with the
regiment in 1776 as private in the 1st Company. Taken prisoner on 31
December 1776, he returned to duty in July 1778. He was again taken
prisoner at Baton Rouge on 21 September 1779, and returned to duty in
January 1782. He apparently returned to Germany with the regiment in
1783.

KAUFMANN, Jost   W200999
Sailed to America with the 1782 recruit shipment and was assigned as
private in the 5th Company. He returned to Germany with his unit, but
deserted at Bremen on 30 September 1783.

KAUS, Peter   W200277
Born 1732 in Beckerswill, Hechingen. Catholic. 5'9" tall. Sailed to
America with the regiment in 1776 as private in the 3rd Company. He
served in the 3rd Company throughout the war and apparently returned
to Germany with the regiment in 1783. He had 27 years' previous
military experience in the Prussian army.

KEIPEL, Bernhard   W200855
Sailed to America with the 1781 recruit shipment and was assigned as
private in the 3rd Company. In July 1782 he was transferred to the 5th
Company. He returned to Germany with the regiment and was released
at Korbach (W) on 16 October 1783.

KEITEL, Johann Henrich   W200400
Born 17 April 1756 in Nieder Werbe (W), and baptized on 2 May.
Evangelical. 5'4" tall. Mason by trade. Sailed to America with the
regiment in 1776 as private in the 4th Company. He was wounded in
the attack on Fort Washington on 16 November 1776. He boarded the
Santa Rosalia on 29 May 1781 to return to New York after the capitulation of Pensacola. He served throughout the war in the 4th Company,
and apparently returned to Germany with the regiment in 1783. He had
1 year of previous military experience in Holland, probably in a
Waldeck unit.

KELFS, Henrich   W201000
Sailed to America with the 1782 recruit shipment and was assigned as
private in the 5th Company. He apparently returned to Germany with
his unit in 1783.

KELTER, Johann Friedrich   W200401
Born 1754 in Rhenegge (W). Evangelical. 5'3" tall. Sailed to America with the regiment in 1776 as private in the 4th Company. He boarded the *Santa Rosalia* on 29 May 1781 to return to New York after the
capitulation of Pensacola. He served in the 4th Company throughout
the war and apparently returned to Germany with the regiment in 1783.

KEPPEL, Wilhelm   W100010
Born 1755 in Gelnhausen, Hanau, and listed on a Waldeck roster of
1775 as 19 years old. Reformed. Single. Spoke only German. Sailed
to America with the regiment in 1776 as 1st lieutenant in the 2nd
Company with a date of rank of 7 March 1776. On 24 June 1776 he
transferred to the transport *Adamant* at Spithead, England, for the
ocean crossing. He was transferred to the 4th Company in December
1779 and to the 5th Company in August 1782. He returned to Germany
with the regiment in 1783. He had 1 year of previous military experience as a free corporal in the Hessian army, and 2 years as an ensign
in Holland, having been a supernumery ensign for 19 months in the 2nd
Battalion of the 1st Waldeck Regiment at Hertogenboech, Holland, as
of 1 January 1775.

KERN, Bernhard   W200661
Born 1748/49 in Schwasbisch Hall. Sailed to America with the 1778
recruit shipment and was sick upon arrival. He was assigned as private in the 5th Company. Taken prisoner at Baton Rouge on 21 September 1779, he died of illness while still a prisoner on 26 October
1779.

KESSLER, Gottlieb   W200856
Sailed to America with the 1781 recruit shipment and was assigned as
private in the 3rd Company. He was transferred to the 5th Company on
July 1782 and apparently returned to Germany with the regiment in
1783.

KESTANS, Johann Theodor W200034
Born 1747 in Mengeringhausen (W), and baptized on 18 October. Evangelical. Father - Philipp Henrich K., Mother - Emma Elisabeth, nee Cramer. Shoemaker by trade. Sailed to America with the regiment in 1776 as private in the 1st Company. He had deserted on 16 May 1776, before the march to the port, but rejoined on 31 May 1776. He was wounded in the attack on Fort Washington on 16 November 1776, and taken prisoner at Baton Rouge of 21 September 1779. He returned to duty in January 1782, and apparently returned to Germany with the regiment in 1783. He had 8 years' previous military experience in the Waldeck army.

KESTING, Andreas W201120
Born in Sachsenhausen (W). Sailed to America with the 1778 recruit shipment and was sick upon arrival. He was assigned as private in the 4th Company. He died of illness aboard the transport *Crawford* at Port Royal, Jamaica, on 10 December 1778, when the regiment was en route to West Florida.

KESTING, Emanuel Franziskus W200035
Born 11 November 1753 in Helsen (W). Evangelical. Father - Johann Wilhelm K., grenadier; Mother - Henriette Catherina, nee Roth. Brother of Moritz Kesting (W200402). Sailed to America with the regiment in 1776 as private in the 1st Company. Taken prisoner at Baton Rouge on 21 September 1779, he died of illness at Baton Rouge on 1 October 1779, while in prisoner status.

KESTING, Moritz Henrich W200402
Born 12 May 1756 in Helsen (W). Evangelical. 5' 1 1/2" tall. Brother of Emanuel Kesting (W200035). Sailed to America with the regiment in 1776 as private in the 4th Company. He died of illness on 26 September 1777.

KIEPE, Anton W201001
Sailed to America with the 1782 recruit shipment and was assigned as private in the 5th Company. He returned to Germany with his unit and was released from the regiment at Korbach (W) on 23 October 1783.

KINOLD, Henrich W200278
Born 1724 in Trendelburg, Hesse. Reformed. Married. Sailed to America with the regiment in 1776 as private in the 3rd Company. Taken prisoner at Springfield, New Jersey, on 5 January 1777, he was sent to Philadelphia to be exchanged on 18 June 1778. In December 1782 he was released in America and then transferred to Germany as an invalid. He may have been considered an invalid from the time of his return from prisoner status in 1778. He had 28 years' previous military experience in the Hessian army.

KINTZLER, Valentin W201002
Sailed to America with the 1782 recruit shipment and was assigned as private in the 5th Company. He apparently returned to Germany with his unit in 1783.

KIRSCHNER, Georg   W200662
Born in Obernett, Meiningen (or Oberellen). Sailed to America with the
1777 recruit shipment and was assigned as private in the 5th Company. He was transferred to the 4th Company in December 1779, and
wounded in the attack on The Village on 7 January 1781. In June 1782
he was transferred to the 2nd Company, and on 15 July 1783 he was
released from the regiment at Flatbush.

KIRSCHNER, Johannes   W200663
Born in Oberellen (or Obernett). Sailed to America with the 1777 recruit shipment and was assigned as private in the 4th Company. He
deserted at Pensacola on 2 April 1781.

KLAHOLD, Kaspar   W200280
Born 1750/51 in Reisebeck, Koeln. Catholic. 5'3" tall. Paper
maker by trade. Sailed to America with the regiment in 1776 as private
in the 3rd Company. He served throughout the war in the 3rd Company
and was released at Flatbush on 15 July 1783. He then went to Nova
Scotia.

KLAPP, Daniel   W200403
Born 24 February 1759 at Buehle (W). Evangelical. Father - Johann
Henrich K., stocking weaver; Mother - Anna Katharina Wilhelmina,
nee Missing. Third of 6 children. Sailed to America with the regiment
in 1776 as private in the 4th Company. Taken prisoner on 8 January
1777 at Elizabethtown, New Jersey, he enlisted in the American army.
Apparently he then deserted back to his regiment as he died of illness
on the transport *Crawford*, at Port Royal, Jamaica, on 5 December
1778. At that time the regiment was en route to West Florida.

KLAPP, Johann Henrich   W200281
Born 19 January 1756 in Sachsenhausen (W), and baptized on 25 Janu-
ary. Evangelical. Father Nicolaus K., lathe operator. Sailed to
America with the regiment in 1776 as private in the 3rd Company.
Taken prisoner on 8 January 1777 at Elizabethtown, New Jersey, he
joined the American army. He was carried on the regimental rolls as
a prisoner until 15 July 1783, at which time he was declared a desert-
er, at Elizabethtown. He obviously had deserted early in 1777. A Henry
Klapp is listed in the 1790 census as living in Northfield, Richmond
County, New York, in a household with one adult male, one male under
sixteen years of age, three females, and two other "free" persons.
A John Klapp is also listed in the 1790 census as living in Bern
Township, Berks County, Pennsylvania, in a household with one adult
male, three males under sixteen years of age, and three females.

KLAUS, Henrich   W200157
Born 1759 in Schmillinghausen (W). Evangelical. Sailed to America
with the regiment in 1776 as private in the 2nd Company. Taken prisoner at Springfield, New Jersey, on 5 January 1777, he was sent to
Philadelphia to be exchanged on 18 June 1778. He was taken prisoner
again on the Amite River on 4 Sept. 1779, and returned to duty in Jan.
1782. He apparently returned to Germany with the regiment in 1783.

KLAUS, Johann Philipp (Peter)   W200282
Born 1753 in Schmillinghausen (W). Evangelical. 5'7 3/4" tall.
Sailed to America with the regiment in 1776 as private in the 3rd
Company. He served throughout the war in the 3rd Company, and
apparently returned to Germany with the regiment in 1783. He had 5
years' previous military experience in the Waldeck 2nd Regiment.

KLEE, Christian   W200664
During his tour of duty in America, he received religious instruction
from Chaplain Waldeck and was confirmed on 3 December 1780.
Sailed to America with the 1778 recruit shipment and was assigned as
fifer in the 1st Company. He was transferred to the 3rd Company in
December 1779, and back to the 1st Company in July 1782. He apparently returned to Germany with the regiment in 1783.

KLEE, Henrich   W200665
Sailed to America with the 1778 recruit shipment and was assigned as
private in the 3rd Company. He served throughout the war in the 3rd
Company. He returned to Germany with the regiment and was released
at Korbach (W) on 20 October 1783.

KLEIMENHAGEN, Johann Henrich   W201121
Born in Ober Waroldern (W). Sailed to America with the regiment as
batman in the 4th Company. He deserted on 5 April 1777, but was
allowed to rejoin the regiment as a private in the 4th Company on 10
April 1777. He returned to Germany with the regiment and was released at Korbach (W) on 19 October 1783.

KLEIN(E), Karl Friedrich   W200283
Born 12 August 1755 in Bringhausen (W). Evangelical. Father -
Dietmar K., herdsman; Mother - Katherine Margarete. Sailed to
America with the regiment in 1776 as private in the 3rd Company.
Taken prisoner at Baton Rouge on 21 September 1779, he deserted at
Havana on 21 September 1782, while in prisoner status.

KLEINE, Konrad   W200036
Born 1754 in Reinhardshausen (W). Evangelical. Sailed to America
with the regiment in 1776 as private in the 1st Company. Taken prisoner at Baton Rouge on 21 September 1779, he died of illness at
New Orleans on 12 November 1779.

KLEINEISEN, Josef   W201122
Sailed to America with the 1778 recruit shipment and was assigned (as
private?) in the 5th Company. He died of illness in the hospital at New
York on 24 December 1778.

KLEMANN, Justus   W201004
Sailed to America with the 1782 recruit shipment and was assigned as
private in the 5th Company. He apparently returned to Germany with
his unit in 1783.

KLEUCKER, Johann Jost (Stephan)   W200037
Born in Korbach (W), and baptized 31 May 1752. Evangelical. Father –
Jacob K., Mother – Anna. Sailed to America with the regiment in 1776
as private in the 1st Company. Taken prisoner at Baton Rouge on 21
September 1779, he returned to duty in January 1782. He was promoted to corporal in June 1782, and apparently returned to Germany with
the regiment in 1783. He had 5 years' previous military experience in
the Waldeck 1st Regiment.

KLOPFER, Philipp   ·   W201123
Born in Buedingen. Sailed to America with the 1778 recruit shipment
and was assigned (as private?) in the 4th Company. He died of illness
on the transport *Crawford* on 31 October 1778, when the regiment was
en route to West Florida.

KLUCKER, Anton   W201005
Sailed to America with the 1782 recruit shipment and was assigned as
private in the 5th Company. He returned to Germany with his unit, but
deserted at Bremen on 30 September 1783.

KLUECKS, Friedrich   W200667
Born in Troeglitz. Sailed to America with the 1778 recruit shipment
and was sick upon arrival. Assigned as private in the 2nd Company.
Taken prisoner on the Amite River on 4 September 1779, he deserted
from prisoner status on 10 July 1780 and joined the Spanish army.

KLUNCK, Adam   W201006
Sailed to America with the 1782 recruit shipment and was assigned as
private in the 5th Company. He returned to Germany with his unit and
was released at Korbach (W) on 23 October 1783.

KLUS(S), Johann Georg   W200038
Born 2 March 1756 in Eichenborn, Pyrmont, and baptized on 7 March.
Evangelical. 5'8" tall. Father – Johann Georg K. Sailed to America
with the regiment in 1776 as private in the 1st Company. He died of
illness in the hospital at Manchac on 5 August 1779.

KNEES, Georg   W200858
Born in Reinerzhausen, Darnstadt. Sailed to America with the 1781
recruit shipment and was assigned as private in the 3rd Company. He
died of illness in the hospital at Newtown on 24 September 1781.

KNEILE, Daniel   W201007
Sailed to America with the 1782 recruit shipment and was assigned as
private in the 5th Company. He returned to Germany with his unit and
was released at Korbach (W) on 23 October 1783.

KNIES, Henrich   W200668
Born in Buedingen. Sailed to America with the 1778 recruit shipment
and was assigned as private in the 2nd Company. In December 1779 he
was transferred to the 4th Company. He died of illness at Newtown
on 10 October 1781.

KNIPP, Johann Christian August Daniel   W200158
Born 2 January 1757 in Goddelsheim (W). Evangelical (also listed as
Catholic). 5' tall. Father – Johann Christoph K.; Mother – Anna Elisa-
beth, nee Graessler (Kreisler, or Greisler). Only child. Sailed to
America with the regiment in 1776 as private in the 2nd Company. He
died of illness on 29 October 1777.

KNIPSCHILD, Friedrich, Jr.   W201125
Date and manner of joining the regiment are uncertain, but by July
1780 he was a private in the 4th Company. He boarded the *Santa Rosalia* on 29 May 1781 to return to New York after the capitulation of
Pensacola. He apparently returned to Germany with the regiment in
1783.

KNIPSCHILD, Henrich Jakob   W100013S
Born in Korbach (W). Evangelical. Sailed to America with the regiment in 1776 as ensign in the 3rd Company. He was promoted to 2nd
lieutenant in April 1779, and to 1st lieutenant with date of rank of 25
April 1780. Following the death of 2nd lieutenant Johann Henrich
Stierlein (W100018S) at The Village on 7 January 1781, Knipschild
was transferred to the staff as regimental adjutant. Released from the
regiment in America on 24 August 1783, he went to Nova Scotia where
he was given a land grant for one man, one woman, and two Negro
servants.

KNIPSCHILD, Johann Jakob   W200404
Born 1757 in Nieder Waroldern (W). Evangelical. Tailor by trade.
Sailed to America with the regiment in 1776 as private in the 4th
Company. He boarded the *Santa Rosalia* on 29 May 1781 to return to
New York after the capitulation of Pensacola. He served throughout
the war in the 4th Company, but deserted at Flatbush on 5 May 1783.

KNOCHE, Johann Henrich   W200523
Born 1759 in Itter, Darmstadt. Evangelical. Sailed to America with
the regiment in 1776 as private in the 5th Company. He was killed in
the attack on Fort Washington on 16 November 1776.

KNOECHEL, Barthold   W200159
Born 1754 in Mandern (W). Evangelical. Linen weaver by trade.
Sailed to America with the regiment in 1776 as private in the 2nd
Company. Taken prisoner on the Amite River on 4 September 1779, he
deserted at Havana on 21 March 1782, while in prisoner status.

KNOECHEL, Christian   W200279
Born 1757 in Albertshausen (W). Evangelical. 5'7" tall. Sailed to
America with the regiment in 1776 as private in the 3rd Company.
Taken prisoner at Springfield, New Jersey, on 5 January 1777, he was
sent to Philadelphia to be exchanged on 18 June 1778. He was killed
at Fort George, during the siege of Pensacola, on 12 April 1781.

KNOECHEL, Johannes   W200256
Born 1749/50 in Albertshausen. Evangelical (also listed as Lutheran).
5'10" tall. Sailed to America with the regiment in 1776 as corporal in
the 3rd Company. He may have been captured in late 1776 or early
1777 and released immediately, as a January 1777 HETRINA entry
lists him as a prisoner of war, but there is no return entry. He was
promoted to captain at arms in April 1779, and died of illness at
Newtown on 17 November 1782. He had 8 years' previous military
experience in the Waldeck army.

KNUEPPEL, Adam   W200017
Born 1760 in Odershausen (W). Evangelical. Sailed to America with
the regiment in 1776 as drummer in the 1st Company. He died of illness on 1 August 1777.

KNUEPPEL, Johannes   W200405
Born 1759 in Buhlen (W). Evangelical. 5'4" tall. Sailed to America
with the regiment in 1776 as private in the 4th Company. He drowned
while bathing in the ocean at Staten Island on 21 August 1778.

KNUEPPEL, Peter   W200406
Born 1755 in Odershausen (W). Evangelical. Sailed to America with
the regiment in 1776 as private in the 4th Company. Taken prisoner at
Elizabethtown, New Jersey, on 8 January 1777, he was sent to Philadelphia to be exchanged on 18 June 1778. He boarded the *Santa Rosalia* on 29 May 1781 to return to New York after the capitulation of
Pensacola. He died of illness at Newtown on 30 September 1781.

KNUST, Johann Philipp (Andreas, Anton)   W200039
Born 9 June 1757 in Meineringhausen (W). Evangelical (also listed as
Catholic). 4'10 1/2" tall. Father - Philipp K., tenant farmer; Mother -
Anna Margarete, nee Lamm. Fourth of 7 children. On 6-year enlist-
ment. Sailed to America with the regiment in 1776 as private in the
1st Company. He was killed in the fighting in the Springfield, New
Jersey, area on 5 January 1777.

KOBER, Friedrich   W200040
Born 1755 in Wrexen (W). Evangelical. Sailed to America with the
regiment in 1776 as private in the 1st Company. He died of illness at
Baton Rouge on 10 September 1779.

KOBERT, Johann Ernst   W200140
Born 15 February 1752 in Neersen, Pyrmont, and baptized on 20
February. Evangelical. Father - Johann Ernst K.; Mother Ilse Maria,
nee Spitzen. Sailed to America with the regiment in 1776 as corporal
in the 2nd Company. In December 1779 he was transferred to the 4th
Company, and in June 1782 transferred back to the 2nd Company. He
apparently returned to Germany with the regiment in 1783. He had 5
years' previous military experience in the Waldeck army, having
joined on 1 April 1771.

73

KOCH, Friedrich (Franz)   W200041
Born 1747/48 in Hanau. Evangelical (also listed as Reformed). 5'4"
tall. Married with 1 child. Sailed to America with the regiment in 1776
as private in the 1st Company. Taken prisoner on 9 January 1777, he
deserted from prisoner status at Lancaster, Pennsylvania, on 6 June
1778. He had 3 years' previous military experience in the Hessian
army.

KOCH, Georg Henrich   W200042
Born 1755 in Lich, Solms. Evangelical. 5'8 1/2" tall. Sailed to
America with the regiment in 1776 as private in the 1st Company. He
was wounded in the fighting in New Jersey in early 1777, taken prison-
er, and died of his wounds in the hospital at Philadelphia on 27
November 1777. He had 2 years' previous military experience in the
Waldeck 2nd Regiment.

KOCH, Johann Henrich   W200506
Born 1760 in Carlshaven, Hesse. Reformed. Shoemaker by trade.
Sailed to America with the regiment in 1776 as fifer in the 5th Compa-
ny. Taken prisoner at Baton Rouge on 21 September 1779, he deserted
from prisoner status at New Orleans on 2 July 1780, and joined the
Spanish army.

KOCH, Johannes   W200284
Born 22 January 1756 in Mehlen (W). Evangelical. Father - Johann
Adam K.; Mother - Anna Maria. Eighth of 9 children. Sailed to
America with the regiment in 1776 as private in the 3rd Company. He
was wounded in fighting on 27 October 1776 at Maroneck, New York,
and died of his wounds in the hospital on 2 November 1776.

KOCKE, Konrad   W200043
Born 1758 in Wrexen (W). Evangelical. Sailed to America with the
regiment in 1776 as private in the 1st Company. He died of illness on
27 March 1777.

KOEHLER, Johann Henrich   W200524
Born in Boehne (W), and baptized on 13 April 1753. Evangelical. 5'7"
tall. Father - Johannes K., carpenter by trade. Sailed to America with
the regiment in 1776 as private in the 5th Company. He was transferred to the 3rd Company in December 1779, and back to the 5th
Company in July 1782. He apparently returned to Germany with the
regiment in 1783.

KOEHLER, Johann Wilhelm   W200044
Born 17 November 1750 in Helmscheid (W). Evangelical. Father -
Johann Wilhelm K., merchant; Mother - Katharina Elisabeth, nee
Goette. Sailed to America with the regiment in 1776 as private in the
1st Company. He was transferred to the 5th Company by April 1779,
and taken prisoner at Baton Rouge on 21 September 1779. He died of
illness at New Orleans on 16 July 1780, while still a prisoner.

KOENIG, Konrad   W200045
Born 1746 in Korbach (W). Evangelical. 5'8 1/2" tall. Sailed to America with the regiment in 1776 as private in the 1st Company. He was taken prisoner in New Jersey on 5 January 1777 (listed as a prisoner under the name King [Koenig translates as King] on 20 January 1777 when he was sent to Pennsylvania). He apparently returned to duty in July or August 1778, as he died of illness in the hospital at Manchac on 1 August 1779.

KOHL, Lorenz   W200859
Sailed to America with the 1781 recruit shipment and was assigned as private in the 3rd Company. In July 1782 he was transferred to the 5th Company. He apparently returned to Germany with the regiment in 1783.

KOHL, Johann Nikolaus   W200407
Born 1756 in Frankfurt am Main. Evangelical. 5'3" tall. Baker by trade. Sailed to America with the regiment in 1776 as private in the 4th Company. Taken prisoner on 8 January 1777 at Elizabethtown, New Jersey, he deserted from prisoner status at Lancaster, Pennsylvania, on 4 May 1778.

KOHLBOERSCH, Ludwig   W201126
Born in Braunfels. Sailed to America with the 1777 recruit shipment and was assigned as private in the 5th Company. He died of illness on 16 August 1777.

KOPPE, Johann Christian   W200047
Born 30 October 1746 in Wetterburg (W). Evangelical. 5'4" tall. Father – Johann Christoph K.; Mother – Philippina Margaretha, nee Mayer. First of 5 children. Sailed to America with the regiment in 1776 as private in the 1st Company. Taken prisoner on 9 January 1777 in New Jersey, he was sent to Philadelphia to be exchanged on 18 June 1778. He died of illness in the hospital at Manchac on 13 August 1779.

KOPPENHOEFFER, Adam (Kaspar)   W201003
Sailed to America with the 1782 recruit shipment and was assigned as private in the 5th Company. He returned to Germany with his unit and was released from the regiment at Korbach (W) on 14 October 1783.

KORAL, Georg   W201127
Born in Duensbach. Sailed to America with the 1778 recruit shipment and was sick upon arrival. He was assigned as private in the 2nd Company. He died of illness on the transport *Britania* at Port Royal, Jamaica, on 7 December 1778, when the regiment was en route to West Florida.

KRAEMER, Georg   W201008
Sailed to America with the 1782 recruit shipment and was assigned as private in the 5th Company. He returned to Germany with his unit and was released at Korbach (W) on 23 October 1783.

KRAFT, Johannes   W200670
Born in Gnadenthal. Sailed to America with the 1777 recruit shipment
and was assigned as private in the 1st Company. Taken prisoner at
Baton Rouge on 21 September 1779, he deserted from prisoner status at
New Orleans on 2 July 1780 and joined the Spanish army.

KRAMER, Philipp (David)   W200285
Born 1728 in Wildungen (W). Evangelical. 5'5" tall. Married with 1
child. Sailed to America with the regiment in 1776 as private in the
3rd Company. He served in the 3rd Company until December 1782
when he was released from the regiment in America as an invalid and
transferred back to Germany.

KRAMER, Siegfried   W200671
Born in Strassburg. Sailed to America with the 1778 recruit shipment
and was assigned as private in the 5th Company. Taken prisoner at
Baton Rouge on 21 September 1779, he deserted from prisoner status
at New Orleans on 12 July 1780 and joined the Spanish army.

KRATZ, Johannes (Jakob)   W200049
Born 22 February 1754 in Wildungen (W), and confirmed in 1767.
Evangelical. Sailed to America with the regiment in 1776 as private in
the 1st Company. Taken prisoner at Baton Rouge on 21 September
1779, he died of illness at New Orleans on 16 December 1779.

KRAUSS, Georg   W200861
Born in Engolling. Sailed to America with the 1781 recruit shipment
and was assigned as private in the 3rd Company. In July 1782 he was
transferred to the 5th Company, and on 15 July 1783 he was released
from the regiment at Flatbush. He then went to Nova Scotia where he
had a land grant for one man.

KRELL, Bernhard   W201009
Sailed to America with the 1782 recruit shipment and was assigned as
private in the 5th Company. He apparently returned to Germany with
his unit in 1783.

KREMER, Peter   W200286
Born 1753 in Hemfurth (W). Evangelical. 5'4" tall. Sailed to America
with the regiment in 1776 as private in the 3rd Company. According to
newspaper accounts of the time, he was taken prisoner in New Jersey
in January 1777, and was probably exchanged in the summer of 1779.
Taken prisoner at Baton Rouge on 21 September 1779, he was transferred to the 5th Company in December 1779. He returned to duty in
January 1782 and was transferred back to the 3rd Company in July
1782. He apparently returned to Germany with the regiment in 1783.

KREUTZER, Balthasar Henrich   W200672
Born 1757/58 in Langenfeld. Sailed to America with the 1778 recruit
shipment and was assigned as private in the 3rd Company. Taken
prisoner at Baton Rouge on 21 September 1779, he died of illness
on 18 November 1779.

KREUTZER, Johann Adam   W200160
Born 1755 in Haddamar, Hanau. Reformed. 5'4 1/2" tall. Linen
weaver by trade. Sailed to America with the regiment in 1776 as private in the 2nd Company. He died of illness on 12 April 1778.
He had 3 years' previous military experience in the Waldeck 1st Regiment.

KREUTZER, Valentin   W200673
Born in Schlitz. Sailed to America with the 1778 recruit shipment and
was assigned as private in the 2nd Company. Taken prisoner on the
Amite River on 4 September 1779, he died of illness at New Orleans
on 5 October 1779.

KREYER, Karl   W200863
Sailed to America with the 1781 recruit shipment and was assigned as
private in the 3rd Company. In July 1782 he was transferred to the 4th
Company. He returned to Germany with the regiment and was released
at Korbach (W) on 17 October 1783.

KRIEGSMANN, Christian   W200105
Born in Mengeringhausen (W). Sailed to America with the regiment in
1776 as drummer in the 2nd Company, having joined on the first day of
the regiment's march to Bremerlehe. By April 1779 he was a private.
He was taken prisoner at Baton Rouge on 21 September 1779 and died
there of illness 3 days later.

KRIEGSMANN, Christian   W200864
Born in Mengeringhausen (or Kuelte) (W). Sailed to America with the
1781 recruit shipment and was assigned as private in the 3rd Company. He died of illness on 31 October 1781.

KRIEGSMANN, Friedrich   W200865
Sailed to America with the 1781 recruit shipment and was assigned as
drummer in the 3rd Company. He was transferred to the 4th Company
in July 1782, and apparently returned to Germany with the regiment in
1783.

KROLL, Christian   W200525
Born in Bergheim (W), and baptized on 31 August 1749.
Evangelical. Father - Jakob K., a miller. Married. Musician by
trade. Sailed to America with the regiment in 1776 as private in the
5th Company. By 8 September 1778, when he transferred to the English
army, he was a fifer in the 1st Company.

KRUHM, Georg   W200050
Born 1746 in Wichdorf, Hesse. Reformed. 5'7" tall. Sailed to America with the regiment in 1776 as private in the 1st Company. He was
reported as having been taken prisoner on 31 December 1776, as a
returned prisoner in January 1777, and as being sent to Philadelphia to
be exchanged on 18 June 1778. Therefore, he may have been taken
prisoner a second time, in early January 1777, in New Jersey. On
19 July 1779 he deserted at Manchac. He had 9 years' previous
service in the Waldeck 1st Regiment.

KRUSE, Johann Konrad W200526
Born 1757/58 in Wrexen (W). Evangelical. 5'4" tall. Sailed to America with the regiment in 1776 as private in the 5th Company. Taken prisoner at Baton Rouge on 21 September 1779, he died of illness at New Orleans on 24 November 1779.

KUECHER, Johannes W201010
Sailed to America with the 1782 recruit shipment and was assigned as private in the 5th Company. He returned to Germany with his unit and released from the regiment at Korbach (W) on 23 October 1783.

KUEHNE, Wilhelm W201174
Date and manner of joining the regiment are unknown, but by December 1781 he was a batman in the 4th Company. He apparently returned to Germany with the regiment in 1783.

KUEMPEL, Henrich W200676
Born in Lauterbach. Sailed to America with the 1777 recruit shipment and was assigned as private in the 4th Company. He died of illness at Pensacola on 20 December 1779.

KUESTER, Franz Henrich W200408
Born 12 August 1760 in Grossenberg, and baptized on 17 August. Evangelical. Father – Dietrich K. Sailed to America with the regiment in 1776 as private in the 4th Company. He boarded the *Santa Rosalia* on 29 May 1781 to return to New York after the capitulation of Pensacola. He served in the 4th Company throughout the war and apparently returned to Germany with the regiment in 1783.

KUESTER, Henrich Gottfried (Jakob) W200161
Born 5 June 1757 in Wildungen (W), and confirmed in 1770. Evangelical. 5'4" tall. Shoemaker by trade. Sailed to America with the regiment in 1776 as private in the 2nd Company. He was transferred to the 4th Company in December 1779, and back to the 2nd Company in June 1782. He apparently returned to Germany with the regiment in 1783.

KUESTER, Ludwig W200162
Born 1757/58 in Helsen (W). Evangelical. 5'3" tall. Shoemaker by trade. Sailed to America with the regiment in 1776 as private in the 2nd Company. Taken prisoner on the Amite River on 4 September 1779, he deserted from prisoner status at Havana on 5 October 1780.

KUETHE, Henrich W200163
Born in 1756 Basedorf, Darmstadt. Evangelical. 5'7" tall. Shoemaker by trade. Sailed to America with the regiment in 1776 as private in the 2nd Company. Taken prisoner on the Amite River on 4 September 1779, he deserted from prisoner status at Havana on 5 October 1780.

KUETHE, Henrich W200821
Born 1761/62 in Waroldern (W). Sailed to America with the 1779 recruit shipment and was assigned as private in the 3rd Company. He apparently returned to Germany with the regiment in 1783.

KUHLEMANN, Johann Josef   W201195
Born 1755 in Hermete, Paderborn. Catholic. Sailed to America with
the regiment in 1776 as private in the 1st Company. He deserted on 6
January 1777.

KUHN, Johannes   W200867
Born in Holzdorf, Hesse. Sailed to America with the 1781 recruit
shipment and was assigned as private in the 3rd Company. In July
1782 he was transferred to the 5th Company. He was separated at
Flatbush on 15 July 1783, and received a land grant in Nova Scotia in
June 1784 for one man.

KUNCKEL, Johannes   W200287
Born 1754/55 in Maasborn, Hanau. Evangelical. Sailed to America
with the regiment in 1776 as private in the 3rd Company. Taken prisoner on 8 January 1777 at Elizabethtown, New Jersey, he deserted on
24 July 1778 at York Point, apparently while being exchanged.

KUNTZMANN, Christoph   W201128
Born in Harburg. Sailed to America with the 1777 recruit shipment and
was assigned as private in the 2nd Company. He died of illness on 7
September 1777.

KUSSENBAUER, Christoph   W200678
Born 1761/62 in Unterriexingen. Sailed to America with the 1777 recruit shipment and was assigned as private in the 2nd Company. He
was transferred to the 4th Company in December 1779, and killed in
the attack on The Village on 7 January 1781.

LACOUR, Friedrich   W200195
Born 1752 in Copenhagen, Denmark. Evangelical. 5' 2" tall. Book
binder by trade. Sailed to America with the regiment in 1776 as private
in the 2nd Company. He deserted on 7 April 1777.

LAHME, Johannes   W200557
Born 1758/59 in Schweinsbuehl (W). Evangelical. 5' tall. Sailed to
America with the regiment in 1776 as private in the 5th Company,
after having been transferred from the 1st Company as a fifer on 29
May 1776. Taken prisoner at Baton Rouge on 21 September 1779, he
died of illness on 15 January 1780, while still a prisoner.

LAHR, Nikolaus   W200558
Born 1736 in Grebenstein, Hesse. Reformed. 5'7" tall. Shoemaker by
trade. Married with 1 child. Sailed to America with the regiment in
1776 as private in the 5th Company. Died of illness on 8 Sept. 1777.
He had 6 years' previous military experience in the Hessian army.

LANDSBERGER, Henrich   W200724
Born in Loeh. Date and manner of joining the regiment are uncertain, but by April 1779 he was a private in the 1st Company. Taken
prisoner at Baton Rouge on 21 September 1779, he died of illness at
New Orleans on 16 June 1780 while still a prisoner.

LANGE, Gottfried (Georg)   W201037
Sailed to America with the 1782 recruit shipment and was assigned as
private in the 5th Company. He returned to Germany with his unit and
was released from the regiment at Korbach (W) on 22 October 1783.

LANGE, Henrich   W200314
Born 1756 in Wirmighausen (W). Evangelical. Sailed to America with
the regiment in 1776 as private in the 3rd Company. He deserted on 5
April 1777, and returned to duty on 7 January 1778. He returned to
Germany with the regiment and was released at Korbach (W) on 18
October 1783, under other than honorable conditions.

LANGE, Philipp Henrich   W200196
Born 1757 in Wirmighausen (W). Evangelical. Sailed to America with
the regiment in 1776 as private in the 2nd Company. Listed in the
HETRINA as both a prisoner and a deserter in 1777, he returned to
duty in January 1778. He deserted again in August 1778.

LAUBACH, Philipp   W200904
Born in Kleinern (W). Sailed to America with the 1781 recruit shipment and was assigned as private in the 3rd Company. He had been a
member of the recruit shipment for 1779, but had been left in Germany
due to illness. In July 1782 he was transferred to the 1st Company,
and apparently returned to Germany with the regiment in 1783.

LAUE, Christian   W200905
Born in Arzen. Sailed to America with the 1781 recruit shipment and
was assigned as private in the 3rd Company. In July 1782 he was
transferred to the 5th Company. He returned to Germany with the
regiment and was released at Bremen on 19 September 1783.

LEESER, Johannes   W200315
Born 1760 in Fuerstenberg (W). Evangelical. Sailed to America with
the regiment in 1776 as private in the 3rd Company. Taken prisoner at
Baton Rouge on 21 September 1779, he died of illness at New Orleans on 28 October 1779.

LEIDNER, Kaspar   W201137
Born in Freiburg. Sailed to America with the 1778 recruit shipment and
was sick upon arrival. He was assigned as private in the 5th Company. He died of illness on the transport *Britannia* on 4 December 1778
at Port Royal, Jamaica, when the regiment was en route to West
Florida.

LEIMBACH, Bernhard   W200432
Born 1757 in Ober Niess, Fulda. Evangelical. 5'8 1/2" tall. Sailed to
America with the regiment in 1776 as private in the 4th Company. He
was promoted to corporal in April 1780. On 29 May 1781 he boarded
the *Santa Rosalia* to return to New York after the capitulation of
Pensacola. He died of illness on 16 December 1782. He had 2 years'
previous military experience in Holland, probably in a Waldeck unit.

LEMMERING, Henrich   W200559
Born 1741 in Waltzerode, Zell. Evangelical. Sailed to America with
the regiment in 1776 as private in the 5th Company, after having originally been assigned to the 3rd Company, then the 1st Company, and
finally to the 5th Company. He died of illness on 16 May 1777. He had
2 1/2 years' previous military experience in Braunschweig.

LENDE, Christoph   W201138
Born in Dilchen, Swabia. Date and manner of joining the regiment are
uncertain, but by February 1779 he was a private in the 4th Company.
He did not sail to West Florida with the reginent in 1778 but died of
illness in the hospital at New York on 7 February 1779.

LENGEL, Andreas   W201038
Sailed to America with the 1782 recruit shipment and was assigned as
private in the 5th Company. He returned to Germany with his unit, but
deserted at Bremen on 30 September 1783.

LENTZER, Adam   W200906
Sailed to America with the 1781 recruit shipment and was assigned as
private in the 3rd Company. He was transferred to the 5th Company in
July 1782. He returned to Germany with his unit and was released
from the regiment at Korbach (W) on 19 October 1783.

LEONHARDI, Johann Wilhelm   W100016
Born in Mengeringhausen (W), and baptized on 12 November 1747. On
a 1 January 1773 roster of the 1st Battalion of the 1st Waldeck
Regiment, he was listed as being 25 years old. Lutheran. Father -
Franz Adolf L.; Mother - Dorothea Johanna, nee Sudin. Single. Spoke
German, Dutch, and French. Sailed to America with the regiment in
1776 as 1st lieutenant in the 5th Company. Mistakenly reported as
killed in action at Fort Manchac, by von Eelking, he was wounded and
taken prisoner at Baton Rouge on 21 September 1779. He died 5 days
later, on the Mississippi River, while being taken to New Orleans. In
1773 he was listed as having served 46 months as a cadet and adjutant
and 2 months as an ensign and adjutant at Bommel, Holland, with the
1st Regiment. On a 1 January 1775 roster he had the same assignment and was stationed at Dendermonde, Holland.

LERCHER, Friedrich   W201039
Sailed to America with the 1782 recruit shipment and was assigned as
private in the 5th Company. He died of illness on 1 December 1782.

LESMANN, Bernhard   W201040
Sailed to America with the 1782 recruit shipment and was assigned as
private in the 5th Company. He returned to Germany with his unit and
was released from the regiment at Korbach (W) On 22 October 1783.

LEUGLING, Friedrich   W201041
Sailed to America with the 1782 recruit shipment and was assigned as
private in the 5th Company. He returned to Germany with his unit and
was released from the regiment at Korbach (W) on 14 October 1783.

LEUTMANN, Friedrich　　　　　　　　　　　　W200907
Born in Feuchtenau on the Ens. Sailed to America with the 1781 recruit shipment and was assigned as private in the 3rd Company. He
died of illness in the hospital at New York on 21 September 1781.

LEYDENBERG, Johann Georg Eberhard　　　　　W200073
Born 18 August 1744 in Hameln. Evangelical. 5'4" tall. Father –
Johann Georg L. Sailed to America with the regiment in 1776 as private in the 1st Company. He died of illness in the hospital at Pensacola on 10 July 1779.

LICHT, Peter　　　　　　　　　　　　　　　　W200725
Born in Felsen. Date and manner of joining the regiment are uncertain,
but by April 1779 he was a private in the 1st Company. He deserted at
Manchac on 8 August 1779.

LICHTNER, Johannes　　　　　　　　　　　　W200726
Sailed to America with the 1778 recruit shipment and was sick upon
arrival. He was assigned as private in the 3rd Company. He returned
to Germany with the regiment and was released at Korbach (W) on 16
October 1783.

LIMPERT, Henrich August　　　　　　　　　　W200560
Born 1753 in Korbach (W). Evangelical. 5'6" tall. Sailed to America
with the regiment in 1776 as private in the 5th Company. He was
killed in the fighting near Elizabethtown, New Jersey, on 9 January
1777.

LINCKER, Ludwig (Wilhelm)　　　　　　　　　W200316
Born 1754 in Affersleben, Prussia. Evangelical. 5'2" tall. Apothe-
cary by trade. On 3-year enlistment. Sailed to America with the
regiment in 1776 as private in the 3rd Company. He deserted on 15
May 1781, after the fall of Pensacola, and may have joined the Spanish army.

LINDAUER, Michael　　　　　　　　　　　　W200908
Sailed to America with the 1781 recruit shipment and was assigned as
private in the 3rd Company. In July 1782 he was transferred to the 5th
Company. He returned to Germany with the regiment and was released
at Korbach (W) on 16 October 1783.

LINDE(N), Johann Valentin　　　　　　　　　W200074
Born 4 January 1755 in Mehlen (W). Evangelical. Father – Andreas
L., Mother – Anna Gertrud, nee Wigand. Tenth of 10 children. Sailed
to America with the regiment in 1776 as private in the 1st Company.
He was wounded and taken prisoner at Baton Rouge on 21 September
1779, and deserted from prisoner status at New Orleans on 15 July
1780. He had 2 years and 4 months of previous military experience in
the Waldeck army.

LINDEMEYER, Franz   W200909
Born in Buchendorf. Sailed to America with the 1781 recruit shipment
and was assigned as private in the 3rd Company. He was transferred to
the 1st Company in July 1782. He returned to Germany with the regiment and was released at Bremen on 19 September 1783.

LINDENBORN, Henrich   W201042
Sailed to America with the 1782 recruit shipment and was assigned as
private in the 5th Company. He apparently returned to Germany with
his unit in 1783.

LINDIG, Johann Henrich   W200433
Born 1749 in Ramss, Saxony. Evangelical. 5'9" tall. Stone mason by
trade. Sailed to America with the regiment in 1776 as private in the
4th Company. He was promoted to corporal in April 1780, and died of
illness at Pensacola on 26 January 1781.

LINDNER, Karl Wilhelm   W200317
Born 2 October 1757 in Nordenbeck (W). Evangelical. 5'3" tall.
Father - Johann Christoph L.; Mother - Marie Anna Margarete, nee
Zimmermann. Married Charlotte Marie Schmidt on 3 May 1784. They
had 2 children. He died of an epileptic seizure on 6 October 1788. He
served in the 4th Company throughout the war and returned to Germany
with the regiment. He was released at Korbach (W) on 20 October
1783.

LINDNER, Konrad   W200434
Born 1748 in Usseln (W). Evangelical. Sailed to America with the
regiment in 1776 as private in the 4th Company. He boarded the *Santa
Rosalia* on 29 May 1781 to return to New York after the capitulation of
Pensacola. He served in the 4th Company throughout the war, and
apparently returned to Germany with the regiment in 1783.

LINDNER, Wilhelm   W200435
Born 1746 in Usseln (W). Evangelical. Sailed to America with the
regiment in 1776 as private in the 4th Company. He boarded the *Santa
Rosalia* on 29 May 1781 to return to New York after the capitulation of
Pensacola. He served in the 4th Company throughout the war. He
returned to Germany with the regiment and was released at Korbach
(W) on 20 October 1783. He had 6 years' previous military experience
in Holland, probably in a Waldeck unit.

LIOR, Jean (Johannes) de   W200723
Sailed to America with the 1778 recruit shipment and was assigned as
private in the 5th Company. Taken prisoner at Baton Rouge on 21
September 1779, he deserted from prisoner status on 4 July 1780 and
joined the Spanish army.

LITTLET, Wilhelm   W200197
Born 1757 in Libstadt, Prussia. Reformed. Sailed to America with the
regiment in 1776 as private in the 2nd Company. He was taken prisoner on 5 January 1777 and deserted from prisoner status on 1 August
1778. He had returned to duty by November 1780. In June 1782, as a
member of the 4th Company, he was transferred back to the 2nd
Company. He returned to Germany with the regiment and was released
at Korbach (W) on 24 October 1783.

LITZAU, Henrich   W300012
Born in Hameln (or Nienburg). Sailed to America with the regiment in
1776 as cannoneer in the artillery section. He was killed in The
Redoubt during the siege of Pensacola on 7 May 1781.

LOCK, Konrad   W200318
Born 1756 in Heimmershausen, Hesse. Reformed. 5'4 3/4" tall.
Sailed to America with the regiment in 1776 as private in the 3rd
Company. Wounded in the attack on Fort Washington on 16 November
1776, he died of his wounds on 7 December 1776. He had 3 years'
previous military experience in the Waldeck 1st Regiment.

LOEBLEIN, Jakob   W201043
Sailed to America with the 1782 recruit shipment and was assigned as
sergeant in the 5th Company. He returned to Germany with his unit and
was released from the regiment at Korbach (W) on 22 October 1783.

LOEFFLER, Johannes   W200727
Born in Wallersdorf. Sailed to America with the 1777 recruit shipment
and was assigned as private in the 2nd Company. Taken prisoner on
the Amite River on 4 September 1779, he deserted from prisoner status
at New Orleans on 15 July 1780.

LOHRMANN, David Johann Michael Friedrich   W200436
Born 1759 in Hamburg. Evangelical. 5'3" tall. On 6-year enlist-
ment. Sailed to America with the regiment in 1776 as private in the
4th Company, having been transferred from the 3rd Company on 30
May 1776. He boarded the *Santa Rosalia* on 29 May 1781 to return to
New York after the capitulation of Pensacola. He served in the 4th
Company throughout the war, and returned to Germany with the regi-
ment. He was released at Bremen on 19 September 1783.

LUECKEL, Henrich   W200198
Born 1751 in Bergfreiheit (W). Evangelical. 5'6" tall. Sailed to
America with the regiment in 1776 as private in the 2nd Company. He
was transferred to the 4th Company in December 1779, and back to the
2nd Company in June 1782. He returned to Germany with the regiment, and was released at Korbach (W) on 24 October 1783.

LUENERT, Philipp   W200561
Born 1757 in Waldeck (W), and confirmed in 1770. Evangelical. 5'
tall. Father - Johann Philipp L. Sailed to America with the regiment
in 1776 as private in the 5th Company. Taken prisoner at Baton Rouge
on 21 September 1779, he died of illness at Havana on 4 December
1780 while still in prisoner status.

LUTZ, Johannes   W200139
Born 1746 in Langscheid, Anhalt-Schaumburg. Reformed. 5'11" tall.
Sailed to America with the regiment in 1776 as corporal in the 2nd
Company. Taken prisoner on the Amite River on 4 September 1779, he
deserted from prisoner status at New Orleans on 12 July 1780 and
joined the Spanish army.

MAETSCH, Gottlieb   W201139
Born in Freudenstadt. Sailed to America with the 1778 recruit shipment and was sick upon arrival. He was assigned (as private?) in the
2nd Company. He died of illness on the transport *Britannia* off Staten
Island on 29 October 1778.

MALCHES, Valentin   W200319
Born 1756 in Fritzlar, Mainz. Catholic. 5'2" tall. Sailed to America
with the regiment in 1776 as private in the 3rd Company. Served
throughout the war in the 3rd Company. He was released from the
regiment at Flatbush on 15 July 1783.

MANGEL, Johann Franz   W200562
Born 12 March 1752 in Anraff (W). Evangelical. 5'4" tall. Father -
Stephan M., farmer and local official who married in Mehlen (W).
Third of 3 children. Sailed to America with the regiment in 1776 as
private in the 5th Company. Taken prisoner at Elizabethtown, New
Jersey, on 8 January 1777, he enlisted in the American army. He
apparently deserted back to his own regiment, as he was transferred to
the 3rd Company in December 1779. He was released in America in
December 1780, and then taken back into the regiment as a batman the
same month. By December 1782 he had been transferred to the 5th
Company, and apparently returned to Germany with the regiment.

MANN, Daniel   W201044
Sailed to America with the 1782 recruit shipment and was assigned as
private in the 5th Company. He apparently returned to Germany with
his unit in 1783.

MARC, Philipp   W400003
Born 1739 in Arolsen (W). Jewish. Father - Moritz M., court agent.
Died at Bamberg, in Germany, on 5 May 1801. Sailed to America with
the regiment in 1776 as auditor on the staff. This position seems to
have combined most staff support functions. He served in America
throughout the war, having gone from Pensacola to New Orleans under
a flag of truce from 3 February to 25 April 1780 to arrange financial
accounts for the prisoners of war. He boarded the *San Pedro and San
Pablo* on 29 May 1781 to return to New York after the capitulation of

Pensacola. He was released from the regiment at New York on 24 August 1783. A Philipp Mark is listed in the 1790 census as living in the East Ward of New York City in a household with 4 adult males, 1 female, and 1 slave. He worked as a salesman/merchant in New York for a time, and then was appointed the American consul at Bamberg. He maintained an autograph book during the war which contains entries made by many of the officers of the 3rd Regiment, as well as by English and Provincial officers, and civilians. The original is in the archives of the Waldeck Historical Society, in Arolsen, Germany.

MARCKERT, Friedrich   W200728
Born in Barchfeld. Sailed to America with the 1778 recruit shipment and was assigned as private in the 3rd Company. He died of illness at Pensacola on 29 September 1779.

MARTIN, Daniel   W200320
Born 1758 in Namur, Braband. Evangelical. 5'4 1/2" tall. Sailed to America with the regiment in 1776 as private in the 3rd Company. Served in the 3rd Company throughout the war, and then was released at Flatbush on 15 July 1783. He had 1 year of previous military experience in the Waldeck 1st Regiment.

MARTIN, Peter   W200321
Born 1757 in Wega (W). Evangelical. Sailed to America with the regiment in 1776 as private in the 3rd Company. Served in the 3rd Company throughout the war, and returned to Germany with the regiment. He was released at Korbach (W) on 20 October 1783.

MATERNS, Henrich   W201140
Date and manner of joining the regiment are uncertain, but by November 1782 he was a batman in the 1st Company. He apparently returned to Germany with the regiment in 1783.

MATTE, Johann Jakob   W200016
Born in Rhoden (W), and baptized on 10 November 1751. Evangelical. Father – Christoph M. Died 18 June 1805 of illness at Cape of Good Hope while serving in the 5th Waldeck Battalion. Sailed to America with the regiment in 1776 as drummer in the 1st Company. Taken prisoner at Baton Rouge on 21 September 1779, he returned to duty in January 1782. He returned to Germany with the regiment in 1783. He had 8 years' previous military experience in the Waldeck army. In 1802 he sailed to the Cape of Good Hope with the 5th Waldeck Battalion in the service of Holland.

MATTERN, Christian   W400004
Born 1745 in Mengeringhausen (W). Evangelical. Sailed to America with the regiment in 1776 as regimental surgeon on the staff. He sailed up the Hudson River on the *Klenehorn* on 14 October 1777 as part of General Clinton's effort to relieve General Burgoyne, but returned down river on 16 October and went to Staten Island on the 21st. He served throughout the war on the staff and apparently returned to Germany with the regiment in 1783.

MATTHIAS, Kaspar   W200729
Born in Ober Werbe (W). Sailed to America with the 1778 recruit shipment and was assigned as private in the 2nd Company. He was transferred to the 4th Company in December 1779, and died of illness at Pensacola on 8 August 1780.

MAUER, Peter   W200075
Born 1744 in Mandern (W). Evangelical. 5'6" tall. Sailed to America with the regiment in 1776 as private in the 1st Company. He died of illness on 2 October 1777.

MAURER, Valentin   W200322
Born 1748 in Maeckebach, Kurpfalz. Evangelical. 5'6" tall. Sailed to America with the regiment in 1776 as private in the 3rd Company. Died of illness on 11 July 1777.

MAY, Henrich   W200323
Born 1724/25 in Marburg, Hesse. Evangelical. 5" 4 1/2" tall. Shoemaker by trade. Sailed to America with the regiment in 1776 as private in the 3rd Company. Taken prisoner on 5 January 1777 at Springfield, New Jersey, he deserted on 24 July 1778 at York Point, apparently while being exchanged from prisoner status. He returned to duty in December 1782. He returned to Germany with the regiment and was released at Korbach (W) on 23 October 1783. He had previous military experience in the Prussian army.

MECHEL, Johann Daniel   W200324
Born 29 December 1756 in Buehle (W). Evangelical. Father - Johannes M.; Mother - Anna Dorothea, nee Oberburg. Fifth of 6 children. Sailed to America with the regiment in 1776 as private in the 3rd Company. Wounded and possibly taken prisoner in January 1777, he died of his wounds on 1 August 1777.

MECKEL, Georg   W200563
Born 1753 in Muenster, Hohen Solms. Evangelical. 5'4" tall. Linen weaver by trade. Sailed to America with the regiment in 1776 as private in the 5th Company. Taken prisoner at Springfield, New Jersey, on 5 January 1777, he was sent to Philadelphia to be exchanged on 18 June 1778. He was taken prisoner again at Baton Rouge on 21 September 1779, and died of illness while in prisoner status at New Orleans on 6 October 1779. He had 2 years' previous military experience in the Waldeck 1st Regiment.

MECKEL, Kaspar   W201141
Born in Goettingen. Sailed to America with the 1778 recruit shipment and was assigned as private in the 5th Company. Taken prisoner at Baton Rouge on 21 September 1779, he deserted from prisoner status at New Orleans on 1 July 1780 and joined the Spanish army.

MECKLER, Johann Friedrich   W200910
Born in Woltershausen. Sailed to America with the 1781 recruit
shipment and was assigned as private in the 3rd Company. He was
transferred to the 1st Company in July 1782. He returned to Germany
with the regiment and was released at Bremen on 19 September 1783.

MEIDT, Johannes   W200730
Sailed to America with the 1778 recruit shipment and was assigned as
private in the 4th Company. He boarded the *Santa Rosalia* on 29 May
1781 to return to New York after the capitulation of Pensacola. He
returned to Germany with the regiment and was released at Korbach
(W) on 18 October 1783.

MEIER, Christian   W200325
Born 1756 in Ober Waroldern (W). Evangelical. Furrier by trade.
Sailed to America with the regiment in 1776 as private in the 3rd
Company. Taken prisoner at Baton Rouge on 21 September 1779, he
was transferred to the 5th Company in December 1779. On 19 July
1780 he deserted from prisoner status at New Orleans. He had 3 years'
previous military experience in the Waldeck army.

MEIER, Zacharias Wilhelm   W200564
Born 31 July 1755 in Sachsenhausen (W), and baptized on 3 August.
Evangelical. 5'2 1/2" tall. Father - Johannes M. Sailed to America
with the regiment in 1776 as private in the 5th Company. Taken pris-
oner at Baton Rouge on 21 September 1779, he deserted at Havana on 5
October 1780.

MEINHARD, Wolrath   W201045
Sailed to America with the 1782 recruit shipment and was assigned as
private in the 5th Company. He apparently returned to Germany with
his unit in 1783.

MEISNER, Christian   W200825
Born 1764/65 in Ernshausen, Muenster. Sailed to America with the
1779 recruit shipment and was assigned as private in the 3rd Company. He was transferred to the 5th Company in July 1782. He returned
to Germany with the regiment and was released at Korbach (W) on 16
October 1783.

MEISNER, Johann Henrich   W200008
Born 1744/45 in Rhoden (W), and confirmed in 1756. Evangelical.
Sailed to America with the regiment in 1776 as corporal in the 1st
Company. Taken prisoner in New Jersey on 4 January 1777, he was
sent to Philadelphia to be exchanged on 18 June 1778. He was taken
prisoner again at Baton Rouge on 21 September 1779, and deserted at
Havana on 3 October 1780.

MEISTER, Georg Philipp   W200326
Born 21 April 1758 in Helsen (W). Evangelical. 5'4" tall. Father -
Emanuel M.; Mother - Catherina Elisabeth, nee Grass. Fourth of 6
children. Father of 6 children. Shoemaker by trade. Died 18 April 1829.
Sailed to America with the regiment in 1776 as private in the 3rd
Company. He was promoted to corporal in August 1780. On 25 April
1781 he was wounded at the Advanced Redoubt at Pensacola. He re-
turned to Germany with the regiment in 1783, and later served in the
Waldeck 5th Battalion.

MELCHER, Wilhelm (Philipp)   W200327
Born 1758 in Arolsen (W). Evangelical 5"4 1/2" tall. Tinker by trade.
Sailed to America with the regiment in 1776 as private in the 3rd
Company. During 1778 he was made a fifer and served as such until
the end of the war. He apparently returned to Germany with the regi-
ment in 1783. He had 1 year of previous military experience in the
Waldeck 2nd Regiment.

MELTZER, Ludwig   W200731
Born in Hannover Muenden. Sailed to America with the 1778 recruit
shipment and was assigned as private in the 5th Company. He died of
illness at Baton Rouge on 14 September 1779.

MENCKEL, Jost   W200199
Born 1758 in Altenlotheim. Evangelical. Sailed to America with the
regiment in 1776 as private in the 2nd Company. He was transferred to
the 4th Company in December 1779. He boarded the *Santa Rosalia* on
29 May 1781 to return to New York after the capitulation of Pensacola.
He transferred back to the 2nd Company in June 1782 and apparently
returned to Germany with the regiment in 1783.

MENGER, Adam   W201046
Sailed to America with the 1782 recruit shipment and was assigned as
private in the 5th Company. He returned to Germany with his unit, but
then deserted at Bremen on 30 September 1783.

MENGERINGHAUSEN, Bernhard   W200565
Born 1758 in Padberg, Koeln. Catholic. Sailed to America with the
regiment in 1776 as private in the 5th Company. Taken prisoner at
Baton Rouge on 21 September 1779, he returned to duty in January
1782. He returned to Germany with the regiment, and was released at
Korbach (W) on 19 October 1783.

MERCKER, Friedrich   W200732
Born in Berlin. Sailed to America with the 1776 recruit shipment and
was assigned as private in the 1st Company. He deserted from Manchac on 20 July 1779.

MERTZ, Johannes W200076
Born 1726 in Wildungen (W). Evangelical. 5'4 1/2" tall. Married. Sailed to America with the regiment in 1776 as private in the 1st Company. Taken prisoner on 5 January 1777, he was sent to Philadelphia to be exchanged on 18 June 1778. He boarded the *Santa Rosalia* on 29 May 1781 to return to New York after the capitulation of Pensacola. He died of illness on Long Island on 18 May 1782. He had 21 years previous military experience in the Waldeck 1st Regiment.

MERTZ, Ludwig W200911
Sailed to America with the 1781 recruit shipment and was assigned as private in the 3rd Company. He was transferred to the 5th Company in July 1782. He returned to Germany with the regiment and was released at Korbach (W) on 18 October 1783.

METTE, Jakob W200077
Born 1752 in Hueddingen (W). Evangelical. 5'6" tall. Sailed to America with the regiment in 1776 as private in the 1st Company. He died of illness on 29 September 1777.

MEUSER, Johann Bartholomeus W200328
Born in Anraff (W)), and baptized 16 April 1758. Evangelical. 5'5" tall. Father - Johannes M., farmer; Mother - Katherina Elisabeth, nee Melwig. Sailed to America with the regiment in 1776 as private in the 3rd Company. Taken prisoner in New Jersey on 5 January 1777, he returned to duty in August 1778. He was wounded in the attack on The Village on 7 January 1781, and apparently returned to Germany with the regiment in 1783.

MEUSKE, Adam W200329
Born 1730 in Landau (W). Evangelical. 5'3" tall. Married Elisabeth Cramer in November 1761. They had 2 children. Mason by trade. In the *Ortsippenbuch for Landau* (W), he is listed as a citizen and shopkeeper from Alt Wildungen (W), a widower who went to America with the regiment and died there. Sailed to America with the regiment in 1776 as private in the 3rd Company. He died of illness on 2 October 1777. He had 8 years' previous military experience in the Waldeck 1st Regiment.

MEUSCKE, Johannes W200330
Born 28 November 1754 in Wildungen (W), and baptized 1 December. Evangelical. 5'3 1/2" tall. Father - Moritz; Mother - Maria Catharina, nee Rudelbach. Sailed to America with the regiment in 1776 as private in the 3rd Company. Taken prisoner at Baton Rouge on 21 September 1779, he was transferred to the 5th Company in December 1779. He deserted at Havana on 24 March 1782 while still in prisoner of war status.

MEYBAUM, Johannes   W200200
Born 1756 in Volkmarsen, Koeln. Catholic. Sailed to America with the
regiment in 1776 as private in the 2nd Company. Taken prisoner at
Springfield, New Jersey, on 5 January 1777, he enlisted in the American army on 19 March 1777. He apparently deserted back to his
regiment as he was taken prisoner again on the Amite River on 4
September 1779. He returned to duty in January 1782, and apparently
returned to Germany with the regiment in 1783.

MEYER, Christoph   W200078
Born 1724/25 in Bruhne, Hesse. Reformed. 5'2" tall. Sailed to
America with the regiment in 1776 as private in the 1st Company. He
was transferred to the 4th Company in April 1779, and died at Pensacola of illness on 4 December 1779. He had 18 years' previous military experience in the Prussian army.

MEYER, Eberhard   W200499
Born 1745 in Ulm, Swabia. Evangelical. Sailed to America with the
regiment in 1776 as medic in the 5th Company. He was released in
America on 15 April 1779. He had 6 years' previous military experience in the French army.

MEYER, Franz   W200733
Sailed to America with the 1778 recruit shipment and was assigned as
private in the 5th Company. He deserted at Manchac on 2 September
1779.

MEYER, Georg   W201142
Born in Lehmingen. Sailed to America with the 1778 recruit shipment
and was sick upon arrival. He was assigned (as private?) in the 4th
Company. He died of illness on the transport *Crawford*, en route to
West Florida, on 5 November 1778.

MEYER, Henrich   W200201
Born 1748 in Netze (W). Evangelical. Sailed to America with the
regiment in 1776 as private in the 2nd Company. He was transferred to
the 4th Company in December 1779 and back to the 2nd Company in
June 1782. He apparently returned to Germany with the regiment in
1783. He had 12 years' previous military experience in the Waldeck
1st Regiment.

MEYER, Henrich   W200566
Born in Holzhausen, Pyrmont, and baptized on 17 April 1757.
Evangelical. Illegitimate. Father – supposed to be Johann Henrich
Meier; Mother – Anna Hedwig Duevelhaupt. Sailed to America with the
regiment in 1776 as private in the 5th Company. Taken prisoner on 5
January 1777 at Springfield, New Jersey, he was listed as a prisoner
on a 17 June 1778 exchange list, but scratched and then listed as a
prisoner throughout the war and as a deserter at Elizabethtown, New
Jersey, on 15 July 1783. He probably deserted much earlier, even as
early as 1777.

MEYER, Jakob   W200567
Born 1747/48 in Kleinern (W). Evangelical. 5'4" tall. Married Barbara
Meiers in Affoldern (W) on 14 November 1788. They had 1 child,
Johann Michael, born about 1790. Mason by trade. Jakob Meyer was
buried 6 July 1804. Sailed to America with the regiment in 1776 as
private in the 5th Company. Taken prisoner at Baton Rouge on 21
September 1779, he returned to duty in January 1782, and apparently
returned to Germany with the regiment in 1783.

MEYER, Johannes   W200912
Date and manner of joining the regiment are uncertain, but by April
1781 he was a private in the 4th Company. He was transferred to the
2nd Company in June 1782. He returned to Germany with the regiment
and was released at Korbach (W) on 16 October 1783.

MEYER, Johann Georg   W200128
Born 1753/54 in Langenscheid, Schaumburg. Reformed. 5'7 1/2"
tall. Sailed to America with the regiment in 1776 as private in the 1st
Company. Taken prisoner in New Jersey on 8 January 1777, he was
sent to Philadelphia to be exchanged on 18 June 1778. He died of
illness on 26 October 1779. He had 5 years' previous military experience in the Waldeck 1st Regiment.

MEYER, Johann Konrad   W200331
Born 1740 in Wildungen (W). Evangelical. 5'9 1/2" tall. Married
with 1 child. Sailed to America with the regiment in 1776 as private in
the 3rd Company. Taken prisoner at Elizabethtown, New Jersey, on 8
January 1777, he was sent to Philadelphia to be exchanged on 18 June
1778. He was taken prisoner again at Baton Rouge on 21 September
1779, and transferred to the 5th Company in December 1779. He died of
illness on Long Island on 12 July 1782, after having been exchanged
earlier in the year. He had 20 years' previous military experience in
the Waldeck 1st Regiment.

MEYER, Konrad   W200913
Born in Wildungen (W). Sailed to America with the 1781 recruit
shipment and was assigned as private in the 3rd Company. He returned
to Germany with the regiment and was released at Bremen on 19
September 1783.

MEYER, Thomas   W201047
Sailed to America with the 1782 recruit shipment and was assigned as
private in the 5th Company. He returned to Germany with his unit and
was released from the regiment at Korbach (W) on 22 October 1783.

MICHAEL, Georg   W200914
Born in Oberhausen (W). Sailed to America with the 1781 recruit
shipment and was assigned as private in the 3rd Company. In July
1782 he was transferred to the 5th Company. He returned to Germany
with the regiment, but deserted at Korbach (W) on 10 October 1783.

MICHEL, Daniel   W200438
Born 1760 in Reinhardshausen (W). Evangelical. Sailed to America
with the regiment in 1776 as private in the 4th Company. He boarded
the *Santa Rosalia* on 29 May 1781 to return to New York after the
capitulation of Pensacola. He served throughout the war in the 4th
Company, and apparently returned to Germany with the regiment in
1783.

MICHEL, Johannes   W200568
Born 1749 in Dehausen (W). Evangelical. Sailed to America with the
regiment in 1776 as private in the 5th Company. By April 1779 he had
been transferred to the 1st Company. Taken prisoner at Baton Rouge
on 21 September 1779, he deserted at Havana on 29 March 1782.

MEIDING, Johannes   W200569
Born 1744 in Wildungen (W). Evangelical. Sailed to America with
the regiment in 1776 as private in the 5th Company after having been
transferred from the 3rd Company to the 1st Company to the 5th
Company. Taken prisoner at Baton Rouge on 21 September 1779, he
deserted from prisoner status at New Orleans on 3 July 1780 and
joined the Spanish army. He had 6 years' previous military experience
in the Waldeck 1st Regiment.

MEILIG, Wilhelm   W200734
Born in Giessen. Sailed to America with the 1777 recruit shipment and
was assigned as private in the 1st Company. He deserted at Manchac
on 19 July 1779.

MINCKE, Georg Henrich   W200570
Born 1755 in Kirchberg, Hesse. Reformed. 5'5 1/2" tall. Sailed to
America with the regiment in 1776 as private in the 5th Company.
Taken prisoner at Amboy on 14 January 1777, he was sent to
Philadelphia to be exchanged on 18 June 1778. He died of illness at
Baton Rouge on 17 September 1779. He had 2 years' previous military
experience in Holland, probably in a Waldeck unit.

MISCO, Johannes   W200826
Born 1761/62 in Willingen (W). Lutheran. 5' 2 1/2" tall. Sailed to
America with the 1779 recruit shipment and was assigned as private in
the 4th Company. He died of illness at Newtown on 15 December 1781.

MITZE. Johannes   W200332
Born 17 April 1757 in Sachsenhausen (W), and baptized on 27 April.
Evangelical. 5' tall. Father - Hermann M. Sailed to America with the
regiment in 1776 as private in the 3rd Company. Taken prisoner at
Baton Rouge on 21 September 1779, he died of illness at New Or-
leans on 5 December 1779.

MOEHLEN, Philipp   W200439
Born 1758 in Wirmighausen (W). Tailor by trade. Sailed to America with the regiment in 1776 as private in the 4th Company. He did not sail to West Florida with the regiment in 1778 but died of illness in the hospital on 4 January 1779. He had 6 months' previous military experience in Holland, probably in a Waldeck unit.

MOER, Christoph   W200440
Born 1751 in Bringhausen, Hesse. Lutheran. 5'5" tall. Sailed to America with the regiment in 1776 as private in the 4th Company. Taken prisoner in late 1776 or early 1777, he deserted from prisoner status at Lancaster, Pennsylvania, on 4 May 1778. He had 2 years' previous military experience in the Waldeck 2nd Regiment.

MOEHRING, Johann Wilhelm   W200441
Born 12 July 1756 in Baarsen, Pyrmont, and baptized on 18 July. Evangelical. 5'3" tall. Father – Johann Wilhelm H.; Mother – Anna Marie, nee Koester. As a soldier he married Christine Oesterling at Mengeringhausen, date unknown, then Johanne Sophie Dorothee Helms on 30 July 1816, Marie Catharine Schwerd on 30 March 1819, and Anne Katherine Wiedbrock on 25 February 1820. Shoemaker by trade. He died 17 March 1820. Sailed to America with the regiment in 1776 as private in the 4th Company. He boarded the *Santa Rosalia* on 29 May 1781 to return to New York after the capitulation of Pensacola. He served in the 4th Company throughout the war, and returned to Germany with the regiment in 1783.

MOLLE. Friedrich   W200202
Born 1758 in Mengeringhausen (W). Evangelical. Butcher by trade. Sailed to America with the regiment in 1776 as private in the 2nd Company. He was transferred to the 4th Company in December 1779, and back to the 2nd Company in June 1782. He apparently returned to Germany with the regiment in 1783.

MOOCK, Johannes   W200079
Born 1750 in Wega (W). Evangelical. Married with 1 child. Sailed to America with the regiment in 1776 as private in the 1st Company. Taken prisoner at Baton Rouge on 21 September 1779, he returned to duty in January 1782. He apparently returned to Germany with the regiment in 1783. He had 3 years and 7 months of previous military experience in the Waldeck army.

MUELLER, Alexander   W200827
Born in Holzhausen, Pyrmont, and baptized on 29 May 1750. Father – Alexander M. Sailed to America with the 1779 recruit shipment and was assigned as private in the 4th Company. He deserted on 13 May 1781, after the fall of Pensacola, and may have joined the Spanish army.

MUELLER, Andreas   W201048
Sailed to America with the 1782 recruit shipment. Assigned as private
in the 5th Company. Apparently returned to Germany with unit in 1783.

MUELLER, August, Jr.   W100021
Sailed to America with the 1782 recruit shipment, having been com-
missioned an ensign in January 1782, and was assigned to the 5th
Company. He apparently returned to Germany with his unit in 1783.

MUELLER, Barthold   W200916
Sailed to America with the 1781 recruit shipment and was assigned as
private in the 3rd Company. In July 1782 he was transferred to the 5th
Company. He returned to Germany with the regiment and was released
at Korbach (W) on 18 October 1783.

MUELLER, Christian   W200571
Born 1753 in Muehlhausen (W). Evangelical. Smith by trade. Sailed
to America with the regiment in 1776 as private in the 5th Company.
Taken prisoner at Baton Rouge on 21 September 1779, he died of
illness at New Orleans on 28 October 1779. He had 4 years' previous
military experience in the Waldeck army.

MUELLER, Christian   W200645
Date and manner of joining the regiment are uncertain, but by April
1779 he was a private in the 1st Company. Taken prisoner at Baton
Rouge on 21 September 1779, he returned to duty in January 1782. He
apparently returned to Germany with the regiment in 1783.

MUELLER, Christian   W201162
Sailed to America with the 1781 recruit shipment and was assigned as
private in the 3rd Company. On 13 October 1781 he was taken prisoner
while on duty at Paulus Hook, New Jersey, and returned to duty in
August 1782. He returned to Germany with the regiment and was
released at Korbach (W) on 19 October 1783.

MUELLER, Christoph   W200081
Born 1751 in Mandern (W). Evangelical. 5'4 1/2" tall. Sailed to
America with the regiment in 1776 as private in the 1st Company. He
died of illness in the hospital at Manchac on 28 July 1779.

MUELLER, Christoph   W200333
Born 1759 in Helsen (W). Evangelical. Sailed to America .with the
regiment in 1776 as private in the 3rd Company. He died of illness on
2 September 1777.

MUELLER, Daniel   W200334
Born in 1760 in Armsfeld (W). Evangelical. Sailed to America with
the regiment in 1776 as private in the 3rd Company. Taken prisoner at
Baton Rouge on 21 September 1779, he transferred to the 5th Company
in December 1779. He returned to duty in January 1782, and was transferred back to the 3rd Company in July 1782. He apparently returned
to Germany with the regiment in 1783.

MUELLER, Daniel Christian   W200203

Born 1756 in Schorbuch, Hesse. Reformed. Married. Sailed to America with the regiment in 1776 as private in the 2nd Company. Taken prisoner at Springfield, N.J., on 5 January 1777, he was sent to Philadelphia to be exchanged on 21 June 1778. He was transferred to the 4th Company in December 1779, and back to the 2nd Company in August 1782. On 5 December 1782 he was transferred to the Hesse Cassel Knyphausen Regiment from which he had deserted in Germany in 1776.

MUELLER, Franz   W200572

Born 1761 in Reitzenhagen (W). Evangelical. Sailed to America with the regiment in 1776 as private in the 5th Company. Taken prisoner at Baton Rouge on 21 September 1779, he deserted from prisoner status at New Orleans on 11 July 1780 and joined the Spanish army. He then deserted back to his regiment on 10 April 1781, from the Spanish army besieging Pensacola. In July 1782 he was transferred to the 3rd Company, and apparently returned to Germany with the regiment in 1783.

MUELLER, Franz   W200918

Sailed to America with the 1781 recruit shipment and was assigned as medic in the 3rd Company. In July 1782 he was transferred to the 1st Company, and apparently returned to Germany with the regiment in 1783.

MUELLER, Friedrich   W200573

Born 1748 in Buedingen, Ysenburg. Evangelical (also listed as Reformed). 5'4 1/2" tall. Paper maker by trade. Sailed to America with the regiment in 1776 as private in the 5th Company. Apparently taken prisoner at Baton Rouge on 21 September 1779, he deserted from prisoner status at New Orleans on 24 June 1780. He had 3 years and 3 months of previous military experience with the Waldeck 1st Regiment.

MUELLER, Friedrich   W201049

Born 1766 in Arolsen (W). Sailed to America with the 1782 recruit shipment as a free corporal and was assigned to the 5th Company. He returned to Germany with the regiment in 1783. He sailed to the Cape of Good Hope as the captain commanding the 2nd Company of the 5th Waldeck Battalion, then in Dutch service, in 1802. He had served 1 year 10 months as a free corporal, 8 years 11 months as a 2nd lieutenant, and 8 years 1 month as a 1st lieutenant prior to his promotion to captain on 18 May 1802. Wounded during the Wars of the First Coalition in the late eighteenth century, he was wounded again in the fighting in South Africa.

MUELLER, Georg   W200919

Sailed to America with the 1781 recruit shipment and was assigned as private in the 3rd Company. He returned to Germany with the regiment and was released at Korbach (W) on 20 October 1783.

MUELLER, Henrich   W200204
Born 1756/57 in Sachsenhausen (W). Evangelical. 5'5" tall. Sailed to
America with the regiment in 1776 as private in the 2nd Company. He
was transferred to the 4th Company in December 1779, and back to the
2nd Company in June 1782. He apparently returned to Germany with
the regiment in 1783.

MUELLER, Henrich   W200442
Born 1753 in Katzenfort, Braunfels. Cabinet maker by trade. Sailed to
America with the regiment in 1776 as private in the 4th Company. He
was wounded in the attack on Fort Washington on 16 November 1776,
and deserted on 6 April 1777.

MUELLER, Henrich Karl Christian   W200080
Born 1753 in Korbach (W). Evangelical. Sailed to America with the
regiment in 1776 as volunteer in the 1st Company. On 2 December
1776 he was released from the regiment. He joined the 3rd Company of
the Hesse Cassel Donop Regiment as a free corporal in March 1777.
He was transferred to the 2nd Company of that regiment in May 1778,
and released in America in February 1779.

MUELLER, Johann Peter   W200443
Born 1755 in Ober Urff, Hesse. Evangelical. 5'3 3/4" tall. Sailed to
America with the regiment in 1776 as private in the 4th Company. By
April 1779 he had been promoted to corporal. He boarded the *Santa
Rosalia* on 29 May 1781 to return to New York after the capitulation of
Pensacola. He served throughout the war in the 4th Company, and was
released at Flatbush on 15 July 1783. He had 4 years' previous mili-
tary experience in Holland, probably in a Waldeck unit.

MUELLER, Johannes   W200205
Born 1753 in Schlitz, Goertz. Evangelical. Sailed to America with the
regiment in 1776 as private in the 2nd Company. Taken prisoner at
Springfield, New Jersey, on 5 January 1777, he deserted from prisoner
status on 1 August 1778.

MUELLER, Johannes   W200674
Born in Gemmingen. Date and manner of joining the regiment are
uncertain, but by April 1779 he was a private in the 3rd Company. He
deserted at Pensacola on 1 April 1781.

MUELLER, Karl   W200082
Born 1752 in Korbach (W). Evangelical. Sailed to America with the
regiment in 1776 as private in the 1st Company. He had deserted on
16 May 1776 but rejoined the regiment on 31 May. He was wounded in
the fighting in New Jersey in January 1777, and taken prisoner at
Baton Rouge on 21 September 1779. He died of illness, while in prisoner status, on 9 July 1780. He had 8 years' previous military experience in the Waldeck army.

MUELLER, Karl   W200378C
Born 1761 in Thalitter, Darmstadt, and according to an 1804 roster he
was then 45 years old. Evangelical. Sailed to America with the
regiment in 1776 as free corporal in the 4th Company. He was promoted to ensign with a date of rank of 15 April 1779, and continued to
serve throughout the war in the 4th Company. He returned to Germany
with the regiment in 1783. As a major, he was the godfather for Friedrich Wilmowsky's 2nd son in June 1802. He sailed to the Cape of
Good Hope as a lieutenant colonel in the 5th Waldeck Battalion, in
Dutch service, in 1802, and upon the death of Colonel Wilmowsky,
assumed command of the battalion. His service in the Waldeck army
included 4 years 1 month as a free corporal; 3 years 10 months as an
ensign; 9 1/2 months as a 2nd lieutenant; 9 years 1 month as a 1st
lieutenant; and 6 years 2 months in various roles of captain; 2 years 8
months as major; his date of rank as lieutenant colonel was 16 July
1802. In June 1806 he was a prisoner of war of the English forces in
South Africa. The 5th Battalion apparently departed from South Africa
in 1806. He had also served during the Wars of the First Coalition in
the mid-1790s.

MUELLER, Kaspar   W200335
Born 1755 in Haarbach, Darmstadt. Evangelical. 5'4 3/4" tall.
Sailed to America with the regiment in 1776 as private in the 3rd
Company. Taken prisoner at Baton Rouge on 21 September 1779, he
deserted from prisoner status at New Orleans on 15 July 1780. He had
2 years' previous military experience in the Waldeck 1st Regiment.

MUELLER, Konrad   W200083
Born 1751 in Armsfeld (W). Evangelical. Locksmith by trade. Sailed
to America with the regiment in 1776 as private in the 1st Company.
Taken prisoner at Baton Rouge on 21 September 1779, he deserted
from prisoner status at New Orleans on 20 July 1780. He had 4 years'
previous military experience in the Waldeck army.

MUELLER, Ludwig   W200679
Date and manner of joining the regiment are uncertain, but by April
1779 he was a private in the 4th Company. He boarded the *Santa Rosalia* on 29 May 1781 to return to New York after the capitulation of
Pensacola. He returned to Germany with the regiment and was released at Korbach (W) on 16 October 1783.

MUELLER, Nikolaus   W200206
Born 1744 in Ehrbach, Odenwald. Evangelical. Cooper by trade.
Married with 1 child. Sailed to America with the regiment in 1776 as
private in the 2nd Company. He was transferred to the 4th Company in
December 1779, and back to the 2nd Company in June 1782. He re-
turned to Germany with the regiment and was released at Korbach (W)
on 21 October 1783. He had 6 years' previous military experience in
Holland, probably in a Waldeck unit.

MUELLER, Nikolaus   W200694
Born in Eckenrad, Fulda. Sailed to America with the 1778 recruit
shipment and was assigned as private in the 1st Company. Taken
prisoner at Baton Rouge on 21 September 1779, he died of illness on
9 October 1779.

MUELLER, Philipp   W200084
Born 1746 in Billinghausen (W). Evangelical. Sailed to America with
the regiment in 1776 as private in the 1st Company. He was promoted
to corporal in 1777. Taken prisoner at Baton Rouge on 21 September
1779, he returned to duty in January 1782. He was promoted to captain
at arms in June 1782, and apparently returned to Germany with the
regiment in 1783.

MUENCH, Philipp Friedrich   W201143
Born in Ottlar (W). Date and manner of joining the regiment are uncertain, but by April 1779 he was a private in the 3rd Company. He deserted at Flatbush on 2 July 1783.

MUENCHEMEYER, Henrich   W200920
Born 1741 in Meelen, Braunschweig. Lutheran. 5'2" tall. Sailed to
America with the 1781 recruit shipment and was assigned as private in
the 3rd Company. He died of illness at Newtown on 26 January 1782.
He had 4 years' previous military experience in the Danish army.

MUENDER, Johannes   W201050
He fathered an illegitimate child of Anna Elisabeth Pistorius, Christian Friedrich Anton, born 4 June 1782 and died 10 December 1783.
Sailed to America with the 1782 recruit shipment and was assigned as
private in the 5th Company. He apparently returned to Germany with
his unit in 1783.

MUENSTER, Andreas   W200735
Born in Idstein. Sailed to America with the 1777 recruit shipment and
was assigned as private in the 4th Company. He boarded the *Santa
Rosalia* on 29 May 1781 to return to New York after the capitulation of
Pensacola. He returned to Germany with the regiment and was re-
leased at Bremen on 19 September 1783.

MUNDHENCKE(N), Henrich Anton   W200574
Born 1756 in Dahl, Pyrmont, and baptized on 21 March. Evangelical. Father - Franz Henrich. Sailed to America with the regiment in
1776 as private in the 5th Company. Taken prisoner at Baton Rouge on
21 September 1779, he died of illness at New Orleans on 8 October
1779.

MUNTERBACH, Jost (Justus)   W201051
Sailed to America with the 1782 recruit shipment and was assigned as
private in the 5th Company. He apparently returned to Germany with
his unit in 1783.

MUNTHENCK, Johann Bernd (Bernhard) W200207
Born 1755 in Hagen, Pyrmont, and baptized on 29 September. Evangelical. 5'3" tall. Father - Johann Hermann Munthenken. Sailed to America with the regiment in 1776 as private in the 2nd Company. Taken prisoner on the Amite River on 4 September 1779, he returned to duty in January 1782. He apparently returned to Germany with the regiment in 1783.

MUSS, Jakob W200575
Born 1752 in Wethen (W). Evangelical. Shoemaker by trade. Sailed to America with the regiment in 1776 as private in the 5th Company. He died of fatigue on the march back to camp after the regiment participated in repulsing an American attack on Staten Island on 23 August 1777.

MUSS, Johann Georg Henrich W200259
Born 6 October 1752 in Wildungen (W), and baptized on 9 October. Evangelical. Father - Johann Georg; Mother - Anna Maria. Married Luise Elisabeth Brust at Meineringhausen (W) on 3 December 1784 and they had 4 children: Joh. Katherina Elisabeth, born 25 July 1785; Joh. Maria Christian, born 4 April 1789; Joh. Christian Friedrich, born 27 September 1791; and Georg Ludwig, born 22 October 1797. Sailed to America with the regiment in 1776 as corporal in the 3rd Company and served in that company throughout the remainder of the war. He was promoted to quartermaster sergeant in April 1780, and apparently returned to Germany with the regiment in 1783. He had 11 years' previous military experience in the Waldeck 2nd Regiment.

MUSS, Henrich W200261
Born 1736 in Wethen (W). Evangelical. 5'6 1/2" tall. Married. Sailed to America with the regiment in 1776 as corporal in the 3rd Company. Taken prisoner at Elizabethtown, New Jersey, on 8 January 1777, he was sent to Philadelphia to be exchanged on 21 June 1778. He was demoted to private in April 1780, and promoted back to corporal in October of the same year. He apparently returned to Germany with the regiment in 1783. He had previous military experience in the French and Waldeck armies.

MUSS, Philipp Christoph W200009
Born 1 August 1753 in Helsen (W). Evangelical. 5'7 1/4" tall. Father - Karl Wilhelm M., road commissioner; Mother - Catherina Elisabeth, nee Goette. Fourth of 4 children. Sailed to America with the regiment in 1776 as corporal in the 1st Company. By April 1779 he had been transferred to the 5th Company. He was taken prisoner at Baton Rouge on 21 September 1779, and died of illness at New Orleans on 13 December 1779. He had 5 years' previous military experience in the Waldeck 2nd Regiment.

NAHM, Friedrich W201052
Sailed to America with the 1782 recruit shipment and was assigned as private in the 5th Company. He died of illness at Halifax on 3 May 1783.

100

NASEMANN, Barthold W200208
Born 1756 in Wildungen (W). Evangelical. Pants maker by trade. Sailed to America with the regiment in 1776 as private in the 2nd Company. Taken prisoner on the Amite River on 4 September 1779, he died of illness at Vera Cruz, Mexico, on 6 August 1780, while still in prisoner status.

NASER, Bernhard W201053
Sailed to America with the 1782 recruit shipment and was assigned as private in the 5th Company. He returned to Germany with his unit and was released from the regiment at Korbach (W) on 14 October 1783.

NASSLER, Andreas W200736
Born 1749/50 in Katzenstein. Date and manner of joining the regiment are uncertain, but by April 1779 he was a private in the 5th Company. Taken prisoner at Baton Rouge on 21 September 1779, he died of illness on 16 November 1779.

NEHM, Daniel von W200576
Born 1752/53 in Helmighausen (W). Evangelical. 5'3" tall. Married. Sailed to America with the regiment in 1776 as private in the 5th Company. Taken prisoner at Baton Rouge on 21 September 1779, he returned to duty in January 1782. He apparently returned to Germany with the regiment in 1783.

NEHM, Johann Kaspar von W200004
Born 1746 in Helmighausen (W). Evangelical. Sailed to America with the regiment in 1776 as corporal in the 1st Company. Taken prisoner on 8 January 1777 in New Jersey, he was exchanged in 1778. In September 1779 he was promoted to sergeant. Taken prisoner at Baton Rouge on 21 September 1779, he returned to duty in January 1782. He apparently returned to Germany with the regiment in 1783. He had more than 15 year's previous military experience in the Waldeck 1st Regiment.

NELLE, Johann Christian Friedrich W200381
Born 2 July 1747 in Wetterburg (W). Evangelical. Father – Hermann N.; Mother – Anna Catherina. Second of 4 children. Sailed to America with the regiment in 1776 as corporal in the 4th Company. He was captured with several privates at Maroneck, near West Chester, New York, on 27 October 1776 and apparently released. He was promoted to captain at arms in April 1780, and served throughout the war in the 4th Company. He apparently returned to Germany with the regiment in 1783. He had previous military experience in the Waldeck army.

NETTER, Johannes W200784
Born in Ansbach. Date and manner of joining the regiment are uncertain, but in April 1781 he was a private in the 4th Company. He is listed in the HETRINA as being released in America in April 1781 and as deserter the next month. A list of Waldeck deserters shows that he deserted at Pensacola on 9 May 1781, the day that the surrender of the garrison was signed.

NEUBAUER, Franz   W201054
Sailed to America with the 1782 recruit shipment and was assigned as
private in the 5th Company. He apparently returned to Germany with
his unit in 1783.

NEUBAUER, Wilhelm   W200737
Born in Halberstadt. Sailed to America with the 1778 recruit shipment
and was assigned as private in the 5th Company. Taken prisoner at
Baton Rouge on 21 September 1779, he returned to duty in January
1782. He returned to Germany with the regiment, but deserted at
Bremen on 19 September 1783.

NEUENDORF, Johann Friedrich Gottfried   W200444
Born 1753 in Herborn, Dillenburg. Evangelical. Shoemaker by trade.
Sailed to America with the regiment in 1776 as private in the 4th
Company. He boarded the *Santa Rosalia* on 29 May 1781 to return to
New York after the capitulation of Pensacola. He served in the 4th
Company throughout the war and then returned to Germany with the
regiment. He was released at Korbach (W) on 17 October 1783.

NEUMANN, Ferdinand   W200085
Born 1750 in Cuehte, Paderborn. Evangelical. 5'5" tall. Sailed to
America with the regiment in 1776 as private in the 1st Company.
Taken prisoner at Baton Rouge on 21 September 1779, he deserted
from prisoner status at New Orleans on 16 July 1780. He had 2 years'
previous military experience in the Waldeck 2nd regiment.

NEUMEIER, Ernst   W200922
Sailed to America with the 1781 recruit shipment and was assigned as
private in the 3rd Company. He was transferred to the 4th Company in
July 1782, and apparently returned to Germany with the regiment in
1783.

NEUMEYER, Johannes   W200086
Born 1759/60 in Herbsen (W). Evangelical. 5'3" tall. Sailed to
America with the regiment in 1776 as private in the 1st Company.
Taken prisoner at Baton Rouge on 21 September 1779, he died there of
illness on 17 October 1779.

NEUMEYER, Wilhelm (Henrich)   W200577
Born 1758 in Fuerstenberg (W). Evangelical. Miller by trade. Sailed
to America with the regiment in 1776 as private in the 5th Company.
He may have been captured on 27 October 1776 at Maroneck, near
West Chester, New York, and immediately released. Taken prisoner
at Elizabethtown, New Jersey, on 18 December 1776, he was listed as
a prisoner throughout the war, and as deserting at Elizabethtown on 15
July 1783. He probably deserted much earlier, even as early as 1778,
as his name was on an 18 June 1778 exchange list of prisoners of war
being sent to Philadelphia.

NEUSCHAEFER, Bernhard   W201168
Sailed to America with the 1782 recruit shipment and was assigned as
private in the 5th Company. He returned to Germany with his unit and
was released from the regiment at Korbach (W) on 23 October 1783.

NEUSCHAEFER, Friedrich Christian   W201181
Born in Kuelte (W). Date and manner of joining the regiment are
uncertain, but by 1777 he was a batman in the 3rd Company. He apparently returned to Germany with the regiment in 1783.

NEUSCHAEFFER, Henrich   W200087
Born 1733/34 in Helsen (W). Evangelical. 5'8 1/4" tall. Married with
3 children. Sailed to America with the regiment in 1776 as private in
the 1st Company. He died of illness in the hospital at Manchac on 20
August 1779. He had previous military experience in the Waldeck 2nd
Regiment.

NIKOLAUS, Gottfried   W200738
Born in Altenburg. Sailed to America with the 1777 recruit shipment
and was assigned as private in the 3rd Company. He served throughout
the war in the 3rd Company. He returned to Germany with the regiment, and was released at Bremen on 19 September 1783.

NOELTING, Johann Henrich Friedrich   W100011
Born 2 September 1744 in Pyrmont. He was baptized on 6 September
as Johann Friedrich, and confirmed in 1760 as Henrich Friedrich.
Evangelical. Father – Georg Friedrich N. Sailed to America with the
regiment in 1776 as ensign in the 2nd Company. On 24 June 1776 he
was transferred to the transport *Adamant* for the ocean crossing. He
was killed in the fighting on the Amite River on 4 September 1779, not
at Baton Rouge as mentioned by Max von Eelking. He had 4 years'
previous military experience as a sergeant in the Waldeck 2nd Regiment, having been promoted to ensign in March 1776.

NOLL, Friedrich Anton   W200088
Born 1756 in Rothenburg, Hesse. Reformed. 5'7" tall. Sailed to
America with the regiment in 1776 as private in the 1st Company.
Taken prisoner on 31 December 1776, he returned from prisoner status
in August 1778. Taken prisoner again on 21 September 1779 at Baton
Rouge, he deserted from prisoner status, probably at Havana, on 28
March 1782. He was reinducted into the regiment in May 1783, and
apparently returned to Germany with the regiment in 1783. He had 2
years' previous military service in the Waldeck 1st Regiment.

NOLLE, Paulus   W200089
Born 1752 in Bergfreiheit (W). Evangelical. Sailed to America with
the regiment in 1776 as private in the 1st Company. He died of illness
on 2 June 1777.

NOLT, Jakob Wilhelm   W200578
Born 1759 in Wetzlar. Evangelical. 5'3" tall. Butcher. On 4-year
enlistment. Sailed to America with the regiment in 1776 as private in
the 5th Company. Taken prisoner at Baton Rouge on 21 Sept. 1779, he
deserted from prisoner status at New Orleans on 14 July 1780.

NOLTE, Christian Philipp   W200090
(Possibly the Johann Christian Nolte) born 23 May 1757 in Buehle
(W). Evangelical. (if so) Father - Johann Franz N.; Mother - Marie
Magdalene. Sailed to America with regiment in 1776 as private in 1st
Company. Died of illness in the hospital at Pensacola on 7 July 1779.

NOLTE, Friedrich   W200579
Born 1760 in Herbsen (W). Evangelical. Sailed to America with the
regiment in 1776 as private in the 5th Company. Taken prisoner at
Baton Rouge on 21 September 1779, he deserted from prisoner status
at New Orleans on 7 July 1780 and joined the Spanish army.

NOLTE, Henrich   W200700
Sailed to America with the 1778 recruit shipment and was assigned as
private in the 4th Company. He boarded the *Santa Rosalia* on 29 May
1781 to return to New York after the capitulation of Pensacola. He
returned to Germany with the regiment, but deserted at Korbach (W) on
18 October 1783.

NOLTE, Johannes   W200445
Born 1755 in Buehle (W). Evangelical. 5'1" tall. Sailed to America
with the regiment in 1776 as private in the 4th Company. He died of
illness in the hospital at Pensacola on 30 May 1781.

OBACHER, Johannes   W201055
Sailed to America with the 1782 recruit shipment and was assigned as
private in the 5th Company. He apparently returned to Germany with
his unit in 1783.

OBERLAENDER, Paul   W200739
Born in Boemersheim. Sailed to America with the 1778 recruit shipment and was assigned as private in the 1st Company. He died of
illness at Baton Rouge on 15 September 1779.

OBERMANN, Henrich   W200923
Sailed to America with the 1781 recruit shipment and was assigned as
drummer in the 3rd Company. In July 1782 he was transferred to the
5th Company, and apparently returned to Germany with the regiment in
1783.

OBERMANN, Melchior   W200619
Born in Lauterbach. Date and manner of joining the regiment are
uncertain, but by April 1779 he was a private in the 4th Company. The
same entries are in the HETRINA for Obermann as for Netter, and he
was reported as deserting at Pensacola on 9 May 1781, the day the
surrender articles were signed at Pensacola.

OBKIRCHER, Thomas   W200925
Born in Bobingen. Sailed to America with the 1781 recruit shipment and was assigned as private in the 3rd Company. He returned to Germany with the regiment and was released at Bremen on 19 September 1783.

OCHSE, Matthias   W200580
Born 1758 in Mandern (W). Evangelical. 5' 4 1/2" tall. Linen weaver by trade. Sailed to America with the regiment in 1776 as private in the 5th Company. He died of illness on 25 April 1777.

OEHL, Henrich   W200740
Born 1753/54 in Berndorf (W). Sailed to America with the 1778 recruit shipment and was assigned as private in the 5th Company. Taken prisoner at Baton Rouge on 21 September 1779, he died of illness at New Orleans on 2 December 1779.

OHMS, Hermann   W200091
Born 1751 in Ortenstein. Braunschweig. Evangelical. 5'6" tall. Sailed to America with the regiment in 1776 as private in the 1st Company. He did not sail to West Florida with the regiment but died of illness in the hospital at New York on 27 April 1779. He had 6 years' previous military experience in the Braunschweig army.

OHNGEFOCHTEN, Daniel   W201056
Sailed to America with the 1782 recruit shipment and was assigned as private in the 5th Company. He returned to Germany with his unit and was released from the regiment at Korbach (W) on 23 October 1783.

OLHABER, Matthias   W200741
Date and manner of joining the regiment are uncertain, but by April 1779 he was a private in the 3rd Company. He returned to Germany with the regiment and was released at Korbach (W) on 17 October 1783.

OPPENDAHL, Friedrich   W200742
Born in Nienburg. Sailed to America with the 1778 recruit shipment and was assigned as private in the 1st Company. Taken prisoner at Baton Rouge on 21 September 1779, he deserted from prisoner status at New Orleans on 15 July 1780.

OPPENHAEUSER, Peter   W200743
Born in Arzbach. Sailed to America with the 1777 recruit shipment and was assigned as private in the 1st Company. He deserted at Manchac on 9 July 1779.

OPPENHEIMER, Nikolaus   W201057
Sailed to America with the 1782 recruit shipment and was assigned as private in the 5th Company. He returned to Germany with his unit and was released at Korbach (W) on 22 October 1783.

OSCHMANN, Johann Konrad W200581
Born 1755/56 in Albertshausen (W). Evangelical. 5'4" tall. Sailed to America with the regiment in 1776 as private in the 5th Company. Taken prisoner at Baton Rouge on 21 September 1779, he died of illness at New Orleans on 28 November 1779.

OSTERHOLD, Konrad W200336
Born 1744 in Gellershausen (W). Evangelical. 5'5 1/4" tall. Sailed to America with the regiment in 1776 as private in the 3rd Company. He died of illness on 20 June 1777.

OSTMEYER, Henrich W201058
Sailed to America with the 1782 recruit shipment and was assigned as private in the 5th Company. He died of illness on 9 December 1782.

OTTO, Johann Friedrich W200337
Born 27 June 1744 in Oesdorf, Pyrmont. Baptized as Johann Friedrich Otten on 2 July, and confirmed in 1760 as Friedrich Otto. Evangelical. Father - Conrad Otten. Married. On 16 August 1777 Chaplain Waldeck (W40005) baptized twins born to Otto's wife. Sailed to America with the regiment in 1776 as private in the 3rd Company. He served in the 3rd Company throughout the war and apparently returned to Germany with the regiment in 1783. He had more than 11 years' previous military experience in the Waldeck 2nd Regiment.

PACKE, Wilhelm W200582
Born 1757/58 in Braunau (W). Evangelical. Shoemaker by trade. Sailed to America with the regiment in 1776 as private in the 5th Company. Taken prisoner at Baton Rouge on 21 September 1779, he died of illness at New Orleans on 25 November 1779. He had 7 months' previous military experience in the Waldeck 1st Regiment.

PAER, Emanuel W200446
Born 1752 in Mandern (W). Evangelical. Sailed to America with the regiment in 1776 as private in the 4th Company. He died of illness on 13 July 1777.

PAPE, Henrich Konrad W200828
Born in Oesdorf, Pyrmont (a twin); baptized Henrich Conrad Papen on 15 March 1754. Evangelical. Father - Johann Bernd Papen. Sailed to America with the 1779 recruit shipment and assigned as private in 4th Company. He boarded the *Santa Rosalia* on 29 May 1781 to return to New York after the capitulation of Pensacola. He returned to Germany with the regiment and was released at Korbach (W) on 20 Oct. 1783.

PAPE, Christofel Rudolf W200092
Born 15 January 1745 in Oesdorf, Pyrmont, and baptized on 18 January. Evangelical. Father - Johann Dietrich Papen. Sailed to America with the regiment as corporal in the 1st Company. He had originally been a private in the 4th Company, but was promoted and transferred on 21 May 1776. He deserted on 6 January 1777. He had 9 years' previous military experience in the Waldeck army.

PATERMANN, Friedrich   W200926
Sailed to America with the 1781 recruit shipment and was assigned as private in the 3rd Company. He was transferred to the 4th Company in July 1782, and apparently returned to Germany with the regiment in 1783.

PELZ, Lorenz   W201059
Sailed to America with the 1782 recruit shipment and was assigned as private in the 5th Company. He apparently returned to Germany with his unit in 1783.

PELZHAENGER, Johann Wilhelm   W201164
Date and manner of joining the regiment are uncertain, but by August 1780 he was a batman in the 4th Company. He died of illness on 27 August 1780.

PENTZEL, Christian Friedrich   W100005S
Born 21 March 1733 in Helsen (W), and on a 1 January 1773 roster he was listed as 39 years old. Lutheran. Father – Georg Samuel P., treasurer of the exchequer; Mother – Catherine Barbara, nee Wurffbain. Spoke German, Dutch, and French, and possibly English. According to his efficiency reports he was a talented artist and planner. Died on 23 September 1783 aboard ship on the Weser River south of Bremen from a self-inflicted gunshot wound, when returning home after the war. Sailed to America with the regiment in 1776 as captain commanding the 4th Company on the *Benjamin*. On 16 July 1778 he was living in the regimental baggage house in New York due to indisposition but on 27 July he and his company assumed duty at the Flagstaff on Staten Island. He was promoted to major with a date of rank of 14 April 1779. Between 3 February and 25 April 1780 he escorted Spanish officer prisoners from Pensacola to New Orleans aboard the sloop *Christiana* under a flag of truce. During the siege of Pensacola, he had command of an artillery position at the entrance to Pensacola Harbor. He boarded the *Santa Rosalia* with his batman on 29 May 1781 to return to New York after the capitulation of Pensacola. He returned to Germany aboard the transport *Ocean* with 170 Waldeck soldiers after the war, and was driven into Cuxhaven, Germany, about 9 September 1783 by a storm; he was then sent back to Bremerlehe to disembark. According to the 1773 roster he had been a cadet 10 months, a bombardier for 31 months with the 1st Battalion of the 1st Waldeck Regiment Artillery, 28 months as a 2nd lieutenant, and 130 months as a lieutenant, and at the time was stationed at Nijmegen, Holland. On a 1 January 1775 roster he was stationed at Brielle, Holland, and had been a captain for 21 months.

PERLE, Josef   W200744
Born in Hallstadt. Date and manner of joining the regiment are uncertain, but by April 1779 he was a private in the 2nd Company. Taken prisoner on the Amite River on 4 September 1779, he returned to duty in January 1782. He died of illness at Newtown on 12 July 1782.

PETER, Friedrich   W201144
Born 1769/70 in Crailsheim. Date and manner of joining the regiment
are uncertain, but by December 1779 he was a fifer in the 4th Company. He returned to Germany with the regiment and was released at
Korbach (W) on 16 October 1783.

PETER, Georg   W200745
Sailed to America with the 1778 recruit shipment and was assigned as
private in the 2nd Company. In December 1779 he was transferred to
the 4th Company, and in June 1782 he was transferred back to the 2nd
Company. He returned to Germany with the regiment and was released
at Korbach (W) on 16 October 1783.

PETER, Jakob   W200746
He received instructions in America from Chaplain Waldeck
(W400005) and was confirmed on 3 December 1780. Sailed to America
with the 1778 recruit shipment and was assigned as drummer in the
2nd Company. In December 1779 he was transferred to the 4th Company, and in June 1782 he was transferred back to the 2nd Company. He
returned to Germany with the regiment and was released at Korbach
(W) on 16 October 1783.

PETER, Samuel   W200448
Born 1752 in Magdeburg. Evangelical. 5'2 1/2" tall. Baker by trade.
Sailed to America with the regiment in 1776 as private in the 4th
Company. He deserted on 15 May 1781, after the fall of Pensacola,
and may have joined the Spanish army. A Samuel Peter is listed in
the 1790 census as living in Halfmoon, Albany County, New York, in
a household with one adult male and two females.

PETERS, Christian   W200927
Born in Linden. Sailed to America with the 1781 recruit shipment and
was assigned as private in the 3rd Company. He died of illness in the
hospital at Newtown on 20 September 1781.

PETERSON, Paul (Samuel)   W200928
Born in Nagelsberg. Sailed to America with the 1781 recruit shipment
and was assigned as private in the 3rd Company. He died of illness in
the hospital at New York on 9 September 1781.

PEUSTER, Johann Peter   W200447
Born 5 March 1756 in Nieder Werbe (W), and baptized Domini
Invocairt (1st Sunday of Lent?). Evangelical. 5'5" tall. Father –
Daniel P. Sailed to America with the regiment in 1776 as private in
the 4th Company. He boarded the *Santa Rosalia* on 29 May 1781 to
return to New York after the capitulation of Pensacola. Served
throughout the war in the 4th Company, and apparently returned to
Germany with the regiment in 1783.

PFEIFFER, Johannes   W200929
Born in Burgsolms. Sailed to America with the 1781 recruit shipment
and was assigned as private in the 3rd Company. He returned to
Germany with the regiment and was released at Bremen on 19 September 1783.

PFEIL, Henrich   W200209
Born 1759 in Hamburg. Evangelical. 5'3" tall. Shoemaker by trade. On
6-year enlistment. Sailed to America with the regiment in 1776 as
private in the 2nd Company. Taken prisoner on the Amite River on 4
September 1779, he deserted from prisoner status at New Orleans on
14 July 1780.

PFENNIG, Johann Jost   W201145
Born 25 May 1727 in Goddelsheim (W). Father - Johann Stephan P.;
Mother - Anna Catherina, nee Buntkirch. Third of 5 children. Married.
Father of 1 child, August Friedrich P., born 9 August 1773 in Wesel,
who died 9 July 1778, in Goddelsheim. Sailed to America with the
1777 recruit shipment and was assigned as private in the 1st Company. He died of illness in the hospital at Manchac on 27 August 1779.

PFENNIG, Karl   W201146
Born in Goddelsheim (W). Sailed to America with the 1777 recruit
shipment and was assigned as drummer in the 2nd Company. He died
of illness on 19 July 1777.

PFISTER, Karl (Friedrich)   W200134
Born 1747 in Schwerin, Meckelburg. Evangelical. Sailed to America
with the regiment on the *Adamant* in 1776 as medic in the 2nd Company. In December 1779 he was transferred to the 4th Company, and
transferred back to the 2nd Company in June 1782. He apparently
returned to Germany with the regiment in 1783.

PFITZER, Michael   W200747
Born in Goeppingen. Sailed to America with the 1778 recruit shipment
and was assigned as private in the 3rd Company. He was released at
Flatbush on 15 July 1783, and went to Nova Scotia where he received a
land grant for one man in June 1784.

PFLADO, Adam   W200930
Sailed to America with the 1781 recruit shipment and was assigned as
private in the 3rd Company. In July 1782 he was transferred to the 5th
Company. He returned to Germany with the regiment and was released
at Korbach (W) on 18 October 1783.

PFLANTZER, Johannes   W200748
Born in Linz. Date and manner of joining the regiment are uncertain,
but by April 1779 he was a private in the 5th Company. He did not
sail to West Florida with the regiment in 1778 but died of illness in
the hospital at New York on 6 May 1779.

PICKEL, Kaspar　　　　　　　　　　　　　　　　　W200583
Born 1760 in Weilar. Evangelical. Sailed to America with the regiment in 1776 as private in the 5th Company, having transferred from the 3rd Company on 30 May 1776. In December 1779 he was transferred to the 3rd Company, and in July 1782 he was transferred back to the 5th Company. He was released at Flatbush on 15 July 1783 and apparently went to Nova Scotia where he received a land grant for one man in June 1784.

PIEPER, Henrich　　　　　　　　　　　　　　　　　W200584
Born 22 September 1752 in Muehlhausen (W). Confirmed in 1765. Evangelical. Father - Johann Philipp P.; Mother - Marie Elisabeth, nee Schuettler. First of 9 children. Sailed to America with the regiment in 1776 as private in the 5th Company. He was wounded in the attack on Fort Washington on 16 November 1776. Taken prisoner at Baton Rouge on 21 September 1779, he returned to duty in January 1782, and apparently returned to Germany with the regiment in 1783.

PILGER, Konrad　　　　　　　　　　　　　　　　　W200449
Born 1753 in Bergfreiheit (W). Evangelical. Sailed to America with the regiment in 1776 as private in the 4th Company. By April 1779 he had been promoted to corporal. Wounded at the Advanced Redoubt at Pensacola on 4 May 1781, he was released in America and invalided back to Germany in December 1782. He had 5 years' previous military experience in the Waldeck army.

PINCK, Thomas　　　　　　　　　　　　　　　　　W201182
Date and manner of joining the regiment are uncertain, but by December 1781 he was a batman in the 3rd Company. By December 1782 he had been transferred to the 5th Company, and he apparently returned to Germany with the regiment in 1783.

PIPHARD, Johann Henrich　　　　　　　　　　　　　W200450
Born 1752 in Roerda bei Eschwege, Hesse. Shoemaker by trade. Sailed to America with the regiment in 1776 as private in the 4th Company. Wounded in January 1777, he died, apparently of his wounds, on 5 April 1777.

PIQUE, Friedrich Wilhelm　　　　　　　　　　　　　W200093
Born in Rhoden (W) and baptized 17 August 1751. He was confirmed in 1766. Evangelical. Father - Friedrich P. Sailed to America with the regiment in 1776 as private in the 1st Company. Taken prisoner at Baton Rouge on 21 September 1779, he deserted from prisoner status at New Orleans on 3 July 1780 and joined the Spanish army. He then deserted the Spanish army, went up the Mississippi River, and joined George Rogers Clark's forces in the Illinois Country. A William Pique is listed in Captain John Girault's company of the Illinois Regiment, having joined for the period of the war on 16 July 1780. He rose to the grade of sergeant but was then reduced for an unknown reason.

PITTIUS, Daniel   W201060
Sailed to America with the 1782 recruit shipment and was assigned as
free corporal in the 5th Company. He apparently returned to Germany
with his unit in 1783.

PITTIUS, Friedrich   W201061
Sailed to America with the 1782 recruit shipment and was assigned as
private in the 5th Company. He apparently returned to Germany with
his unit in 1783.

PLETZ, Reinhard   W200338
Born 1757 in Muenden (W). Evangelical. Married Catharine Louisa
Knipp on 14 October 1785. Sailed to America with the regiment in 1776
as private in the 3rd Company. He served in the 3rd Company throughout the war and apparently returned to Germany with the regiment in
1783.

PLEUGER, Johann Friedrich Philipp   W200095
Born 1741 in Luette, Lippe. Evangelical. Sailed to America with the
regiment in 1776 as private in the 1st Company. Taken prisoner in
New Jersey on 4 January 1777, he deserted from prisoner status at
Lancaster, Pennsylvania, on 4 June 1778.

POHLMANN, Anton   W200253
Born 1751 in Giebringhausen (W). Evangelical. Married with 1 child.
Sailed to America with the regiment in 1776 as captain at arms in the
3rd Company. Wounded in fighting on 27 October 1776 at Maroneck, he
died in the hospital of his wounds on 9 November 1776. He had 12
years and 6 months of previous military experience in the Waldeck
2nd Regiment.

PREISS, Henrich   W201062
Sailed to America with the 1782 recruit shipment and was assigned as
private in the 5th Company. He died of illness on 14 December 1782.

PREISS, Michael   W200931
Born in Vienna. Sailed to America with the 1781 recruit shipment and
was assigned as private in the 3rd Company. He was transferred to the
5th Company in July 1782. He returned to Germany with the regiment,
but deserted "on the Weser" on 23 September 1783.

PRIEUR, Claude   W200585
Born 1729 in Sugee, France. Catholic. Married. Sailed to America
with the regiment in 1776 as private in the 5th Company, but served as
servant for the Regimental Surgeon Mattern. In December 1779 he was
transferred to the 3rd Company, and on 25 April 1781 he was released
in America and invalided back to Germany. He had 8 years' previous
military experience in Holland, probably in a Waldeck unit.

PROBST, Georg   W200932
Sailed to America with the 1781 recruit shipment and was assigned as
private in the 3rd Company. In July 1782 he was transferred to the 5th
Company. He returned to Germany with the regiment and was released
at Korbach (W) on 16 October 1783..

PROBST, Johann Bernhard   W201175
Date and manner of joining the regiment are uncertain. He was released at Korbach (W) on 22 October 1783, together with other men
who had sailed to Halifax with the 1782 recruit shipment. Possibly he
had been inducted in Halifax as he had not been on the 1782 recruit
shipment.

PUETTMANN, Philipp   W200094
Born 1751 in Armsfeld (W). Evangelical. Sailed to America with the
regiment in 1776 as private in the 1st Company. He died of illness in
the hospital on 15 November 1776.

PUOLL, Anton (Andreas)   W200749
Born in Samariza, Italy. Sailed to America with the 1778 recruit
shipment and was assigned as private in the 3rd Company. He died of
illness at Pensacola on 18 July 1780.

QUANDS, Philipp   W200750
Born in Mainz. Sailed to America with the 1778 recruit shipment and
was assigned as private in the 4th Company. He boarded the *Santa
Rosalia* on 29 May 1781 to return to New York after the capitulation of
Pensacola. He returned to Germany with the regiment and was re-
leased at Bremen on 19 September 1783.

RAAB, Anton   W200623
Born 1751/52 in Nauroth (W). Evangelical. 5'6 3/4" tall. Tailor by
trade. Sailed to America with the regiment in 1776 as batman in the
5th Company, after having previously joined as a private. He became a
private in the 5th Company in August 1779, and died of illness on 28
September 1779. He had 5 years' previous military experience in
Holland, probably in a Waldeck unit.

RAABE, Christoph   W200339
Born 1758 in Sachsenberg (W). Evangelical. Sailed to America with
the regiment in 1776 as private in the 3rd Company. He died of illness
on 20 June 1777.

RAABE, Friedrich   W200340
Born 1757 in Bringhausen (W). Evangelical. 5'4" tall. Sailed to
America with the regiment in 1776 as private in the 3rd Company. He
served in the 3rd Company throughout the war and apparently returned
to Germany with the regiment in 1783.

RAABE, Henrich   W200341
Born 1759 in Bringhausen (W). Evangelical. 5'3" tall. Sailed to
America with the regiment in 1776 as private in the 3rd Company. He
served in the 3rd Company throughout the war and apparently returned
to Germany with the regiment in 1783.

RABANUS, Johannes   W200586
Born 26 May 1752 in Mehlen (W). Evangelical. Father - Elias R.;
Mother - Anna Elisabeth. Sixth of 6 children. Sailed to America with
the regiment in 1776 as private in the 5th Company. Taken prisoner at
Baton Rouge on 21 September 1779, he died of illness at New Or-
leans on 26 December 1779.

RABENSPROCK, Jost   W200933
Sailed to America with the 1781 recruit shipment and was assigned as
private in the 3rd Company. He was transferred to the 5th Company in
July 1782. He returned to Germany with the regiment and was released at Korbach (W) on 19 October 1783.

RABENSPROCK. Philipp   W200210
Born 1756 in Bergheim (W). Evangelical. 5' 3 1/2" tall. Sailed to
America with the regiment in 1776 as private in the 2nd Company.
Taken prisoner on the Amite River on 4 September 1779, he returned to
duty in January 1782. He apparently returned to Germany with the
regiment in 1783.

RANGE, Wilhelm   W200587
Born 1740/41 in Korbach (W). Evangelical. 5' 2" tall. Sailed to
America with the regiment in 1776 as private in the 5th Company. He
died of illness at Pensacola on 17 August 1779.

RAUCH, Johann Henrich   W200211
Born 1726 in Albertshausen (W). Evangelical. Married on 13 April
1764 to Anna Magdalena Otto, born 31 December 1730 and they had a
daughter Maria Catherina, born 24 February 1765, and at least one
other child. Sailed to America with the regiment in 1776 as private in
the 2nd Company. Died of illness in the hospital on 3 April 1778.

REESE, Georg   W200935
Born 27 August 1764 in Holzhausen, Pyrmont, and baptized 31 August. Lutheran. 5' 3" tall. Father - Christian R.; Mother - Anna
Margaretha, nee Schaper. Sailed to America with the 1781 recruit
shipment and was assigned as private in the 3rd Company. Died of
illness at Newtown on Long Island on 4 March 1782.

REHROHR, Johannes   W200936
Sailed to America with 1781 recruits as private in 3rd Company. He
was transferred to the 5th Company in June 1782. He returned to
Germany with the regiment and was released at Korbach (W) on 16
October 1783.

REICHHARD, Johannes   W200937
Born in Altenburg. Sailed to America with the 1781 recruit shipment
and was assigned as private in the 3rd Company. He was transferred to
the 5th Company in June 1782. He returned to Germany with the
regiment and was released at Bremen on 19 September 1783.

REINECK, Andreas   W200096 ′
Born 1737 in Tottleben, Saxony. Evangelical. Sailed to America with
the regiment in 1776 as private in the 1st Company. He deserted on 13
January 1777.

REINHARD, Georg   W201063
Sailed to America with the 1782 recruit shipment and was assigned as
private in the 5th Company. He returned to Germany with his unit, but
deserted at Bremen on 30 September 1783.

REINHARD, Henrich   W200212
Born 1758 in Braunsen (W). Evangelical. Sailed to America with
the regiment in 1776 as private in the 2nd Company. Taken prisoner on
the Amite River on 4 September 1779, he died of illness aboard ship
near Havana, while still in prisoner status, on 12 February 1781.

REINHARDT, Sebastian   W201165
Born 1760/61 in Sontheim. Sailed to America with the 1778 recruit
shipment and was sick upon arrival. He was assigned as private in
the 2nd Company. He died of illness in the hospital on 13 October
1778.

REISMANN, Philipp   W200503
Born 1746 in Kleinern (W). Evangelical. Sailed to America with the
regiment in 1776 as corporal in the 5th Company. Taken prisoner at
Springfield, New Jersey, on 5 January 1777, he was sent to Philadelphia to be exchanged on 18 June 1778. He died of illness in the hospital at Manchac on 24 August 1779. He had 3 years and 3 months of
previous military experience in the Waldeck army.

REISS, Michael   W200938
Born in Blaufelden. Sailed to America with the 1781 recruit shipment
and was assigned as private in the 3rd Company. He was transferred to
the 4th Company in July 1782, and died of illness on Long Island on
12 July 1782.

RENCKE, Johann Wilhelm   W200451
Born 1755/56 in Schwerin, Mecklenburg. Evangelical. 5'4" tall. Miller
by trade. Sailed to America with the regiment in 1776 as private in the
4th Company. Taken prisoner on 3 January 1777 in New Jersey, he
deserted from prisoner status at Lancaster, Pennsylvania, on 4 May
1778.

RENNE, Friedrich   W200939
Born in Hannover. Sailed to America with the 1781 recruit shipment
and was assigned as vice-corporal in the 3rd Company. In April 1781
he was promoted to corporal and in June 1782 he was transferred to the
5th Company. He returned to Germany with the regiment and was
released at Bremen on 19 October 1783.

RENNERT, Johann Jakob   W200452
Born 2 January 1757 in Buehle (W). Evangelical. Father - Johann
Daniel R.; Mother - Susanna Wilhelmina, nee Obenburg. Sixth of 9
children. Married Anna Elisabeth Butterweck on 24 November 1791.
Sailed to America with the regiment in 1776 as private in the 4th
Company. He boarded the *Santa Rosalia* on 29 May 1781 to return to
New York after the capitulation of Pensacola. He served in the 4th
Company throughout the war and returned to Germany with the regi-
ment in 1783.

RENNO, Gustav   W200495
Born 1749/50 in Schwartzenau, Witgenstein. Reformed. Sailed to
America with the regiment in 1776 as sergeant in the 5th Company.
Taken prisoner at Baton Rouge on 21 September 1779, he died of
illness on 24 December 1779. He had 2 years and 6 months of previous
military experience in Holland, probably in a Waldeck unit.

REPCKE, Friedrich   W201064
Sailed to America with the 1782 recruit shipment and was assigned as
private in the 5th Company. He returned to Germany with his unit and
was released in October 1783.

REPP, Theodor   W200015
Born 1755 in Mengeringhausen (W). Evangelical. Married. Sailed to
America with the regiment in 1776 as drummer in the 1st Company.
Taken prisoner at Baton Rouge on 21 September 1779, he returned to
duty in January 1782. He apparently returned to Germany with the
regiment in 1783. He had 9 years and 6 months of previous military
experience in the Waldeck army.

REUTER, Bernhard   W200940S
Born 1734/35 in Schmillinghausen (W). Evangelical (also listed as
Lutheran). 5'1/2" tall. Married with 2 children, one of whom was
possibly Bernhard Reuter (W201184). Sailed to America with the 1781
recruit shipment and was assigned as private in the 3rd Company. He
was transferred to the staff as a camp servant and assistant to the
provost on 24 February 1782, and died of illness in March 1782.

REUTER, Bernhard   W201184
Date and manner of joining the regiment are uncertain, but he was
enrolled as a batman in February 1782. Possibly the son of Bernhard
Reuter (W200940S). He apparently returned to Germany with the regiment in 1783.

REUTER, Johann Christian Philipp   W200262
Born 5 April 1731 in Rhena (W). Evangelical. Married with 5 children.
Father - Johann Christoph R. Sailed to America with the regiment in
1776 as fifer in the 3rd Company. He died of illness on 19 July 1777.
He had 30 years' previous military experience in the Waldeck army.

REUTER, Friedrich   W201065
(Possibly from Wirmighausen (W), as a Johann Georg R. was the son
of a Friedrich R. of Wirmighausen who had been in America and who
died on 7 July 1784.) Sailed to America with the 1782 recruit shipment
and was assigned as private in the 5th Company. He returned to
Germany with his unit and was released from the regiment at Korbach
(W) on 23 October 1783.

REUTER, Jakob   W200453
Born 1748 in Wirmighausen (W). Evangelical. 5'1" tall. Sailed to
America with the regiment in 1776 as private in the 4th Company. He
died of illness at Pensacola on 7 February 1780.

RHENA, Karl Adam Rudolf von   W200115
Born 16 January 1744 in Rhena (W). Evangelical. Father - Christian
Philipp v. R.; Mother - Katharine Wilhelmina, nee von Hatzfeld. Third
of 4 children. Sailed to America with the regiment in 1776 as cadet in
the 1st Company. He died of illness on 13 September 1777.

RIEMENSCHNEIDER, Franz Arnold   W200005
Born 3 March 1747 in Wildungen (W), and baptized on 6 March.
Evangelical. 5' 6 1/2" tall. Father - Jacob R.; Mother - Clara, nee
Mueller. Married with 3 children. Sailed to America with the regiment
in 1776 as quartermaster sergeant in the 1st Company. He was re-
leased in America on 16 July 1777 to return to Germany.

RIESE, Henrich   W200097
Born 1760/61 in Bringhausen, Koeln. Catholic. 5'5" tall. Sailed to
America with the regiment in 1776 as private in the 1st Company.
Taken prisoner at Baton Rouge on 21 September 1779, he deserted
from prisoner status at New Orleans on 4 January 1780.

RIPP, Adam   W201147
Sailed to America with the 1782 recruit shipment and was assigned as
drummer in the 5th Company. He returned to Germany with his unit
and was released from the regiment at Korbach (W) on 22 October
1783.

RISCH, Johannes   W200751
Born in Ulm. Sailed to America with the 1777 recruit shipment and
was assigned as private in the 5th Company. Taken prisoner at Baton
Rouge on 21 September 1779, he deserted from prisoner status at
Havana on 19 March 1782.

RISCHEBUSCH, Christian   W200942
Sailed to America with the 1781 recruit shipment and was assigned as
private in the 3rd Company. He was transferred to the 1st Company in
July 1782. He returned to Germany with the regiment and was released at Korbach (W) on 16 October 1783.

RISCHER, Josef   W200588
Born 1754 in Prauenitz. Silesia. Catholic. 5' 2 1/4" tall. Sailed to
America with the regiment in 1776 as private in the 5th Company.
Taken prisoner at Baton Rouge on 21 September 1779, he deserted
from prisoner status at New Orleans on 7 July 1780 and joined the
Spanish army.

RITTER, Friedrich   W200752
Born in Leipzig. Sailed to America with the 1778 recruit shipment and
was assigned as private in the 1st Company. He deserted at Manchac
on 13 August 1779.

RITTER, Johannes   W200454
Born 10 December 1760 in Goddelsheim (W). Evangelical. 5' tall.
Father - Johann Conrad R.; Mother - Engel Christina, nee Vach (or
Fach). Second of 8 children. Sailed to America with the regiment in
1776 as private in the 4th Company. He boarded the *Santa Rosalia* on
29 May 1781 to return to New York after the capitulation of Pensacola.
He served in the 4th Company throughout the war and apparently re-
turned to Germany with the regiment in 1783.

RITTMEYER, August   W200589
Born 1760 in Hildesheim. Evangelical. 5'3" tall. Sailed to America
with the regiment in 1776 as private in the 5th Company. He was
killed in fighting on 4 October 1777.

RODE, Johannes   W200342
Born 1727 in Strothe (W). Evangelical. Married. Sailed to America
with the regiment in 1776 as private in the 3rd Company. He died of
illness on 30 December 1777. He had more than 25 years' previous
military experience in the Waldeck 2nd Regiment.

RODEWALD, Johann Friedrich   W200590
Born in Oesdorf, Pyrmont, and baptized on 12 June 1757. Evangelical.
5' 6 1/4" tall. Father - Friedrich R. Sailed to America with the
regiment in 1776 as private in the 5th Company. Taken prisoner at
Elizabethtown, New Jersey, on 8 January 1777, he was sent to Philadelphia to be exchanged on 21 June 1778. Taken prisoner again at
Baton Rouge on 21 September 1779, he deserted from prisoner status
at Havana on 21 March 1782. He had 1 year of previous military experience in Holland in the Waldeck 2nd Regiment.

ROEGEL, Johannes   W200343
Born 1750 in Krimma, Saxony. Evangelical. Sailed to America with
the regiment in 1776 as private in the 3rd Company. He died of wounds
on 4 August 1777.

ROEHLING, Philipp   W200455
Born 1750 in Udorf, Koeln. Evangelical. Sailed to America with the
regiment in 1776 as private in the 4th Company. He boarded the *Santa
Rosalia* on 29 May 1781 to return to New York after the capitulation of
Pensacola. He served in the 4th Company throughout the war, and was
released at Flatbush on 15 July 1783.

ROEHRIG, Friedrich   W200753
Sailed to America with the 1777 recruit shipment and was assigned as
private in the 2nd Company. He was transferred to the 4th Company in
December 1779, and back to the 2nd Company in June 1782. He returned to Germany with the regiment and was released at Korbach (W)
on 21 October 1783.

ROELCKE, Friedrich   W200213
Born 1749 in Boehne (W). Evangelical. 5'4" tall. Teamster by trade.
Sailed to America with the regiment in 1776 as private in the 2nd
Company. Taken prisoner on the Amite River on 4 September 1779, he
died of illness at New Orleans on 20 October 1779.

ROEMER, Christoph   W200010
Born 1749 in Hesperinghausen (W). Evangelical. Sailed to America
with the regiment in 1776 as corporal in the 1st Company. Taken
prisoner at Baton Rouge on 21 September 1779, he deserted from
prisoner status at Havana on 31 March 1782. He rejoined his unit in
December of 1782, as a private, but deserted again at Flatbush on 2
July 1783. He had 10 years' previous military experience in the
Waldeck 1st Regiment.

ROEMER, Friedrich   W200344
Born 1757 in Hesperinghausen (W). Evangelical. 5'3" tall. Sailed to
America with the regiment in 1776 as private in the 3rd Company.
Taken prisoner at Springfield, New Jersey, on 5 January 1777, he was
sent to Philadelphia to be exchanged on 18 June 1778. He apparent-
ly returned to Germany with the regiment in 1783.

ROHDE, Johann Christian   W201066
Born in Ober Werbe (W); baptized 23 May 1751. Evangelical. Father -
supposedly a soldier not born in Waldeck; Mother - Anna Elisabeth
Rohde. Twin brother of Johann Christoph Rohde (W200263). Sailed to
America with the 1782 recruit shipment and assigned as private in the
5th Company. He apparently returned to Germany with his unit in 1783.

ROHDE, Johann Christoph   W200263
Born in Ober Werbe (W), and baptized on 23 May 1751. Evangelical.
Father - supposedly a soldier not born in Waldeck; Mother - Anna
Elisabeth Rohde. Twin brother of Johann Christian Rohde (W201066).
Sailed to America with the regiment in 1776 as drummer in the 3rd
Company. He served as drummer in the 3rd Company throughout the
war. He returned to Germany with the regiment and was released at
Korbach (W) on 20 October 1783. He had previous military experience
in Holland and Switzerland.

ROHDE, Johann Daniel   W200345A
Born 20 July 1757 in Meineringhausen (W). Evangelical. 5'4" tall.
Father - Johann Georg R. Ninth of 9 children. Sailed to America with
regiment in 1776 as private in the 3rd Company. In February 1779 he
was transferred to the artillery as a cannoneer. After the regiment lost
its guns at Pensacola, he was transferred back to the 3rd Company,
and apparently returned to Germany with the regiment in 1783.

ROLL, Johann Philipp   W200456
Born 1758 in Niederhill, Hohenloh. Evangelical. 5'5" tall. Tailor by
trade. Sailed to America with the regiment in 1776 as private in the
4th Company. He was wounded in fighting on 27 October 1776 at
Maroneck, near West Chester, New York, and then killed in the attack
on Fort Washington on 16 November 1776. He had 1 year of previous
military experience in Holland, probably in a Waldeck unit.

ROOSE, Konrad   W200943
Sailed to America with the 1781 recruit shipment and was assigned as
private in the 3rd Company. He was transferred to the 5th Company in
July 1782. He returned to Germany with the regiment and was released
at Korbach (W) on 19 October 1783.

ROQUETTE, Karl   W200934
Sailed to America with the 1781 recruit shipment and was assigned as
private in the 3rd Company. He was transferred to the 4th Company in
July 1782. He returned to Germany with the regiment and was released at Korbach (W) on 17 October 1783.

ROSE, Johannes   W200754
Born in Welda. Sailed to America with the 1778 recruit shipment and
was assigned as private in the 5th Company. Taken prisoner at Baton
Rouge on 21 September 1779, he deserted from prisoner status at New
Orleans on 1 July 1780 and joined the Spanish army.

ROSENBURG, Johann Peter   W200457
Born 1760 in Zierenberg, Hesse. Reformed. 5'5" tall. Sailed to
America with the regiment in 1776 as private in the 4th Company.
Taken prisoner on 5 January 1777 at Springfield, New Jersey, he
deserted from prisoner status at Lancaster, Pennsylvania, on 4 May
1778.

ROTHE, Georg   W201067
Sailed to America with the 1782 recruit shipment and was assigned as
private in th 5th Company. He apparently returned to Germany with his
unit in 1783.

RUDELBACH, Johannes   W200258
Born 12 January 1742 in Wildungen (W), and baptized on 14 January.
He was confirmed in 1755. (The confirmation book gives his date of
birth as 12 October 1742.) Evangelical. Father - Henrich R.; Mother -
Anna Elisabeth, nee Schallenberger. Married. Butcher by trade. Sailed
to America with the regiment in 1776 as corporal in the 3rd Company.

He served throughout the war in the 3rd Company, and apparently returned to Germany with the regiment in 1783. He had previous military experience in the Prussian army.

RUESEL, Johann Christian   W400007
Born in Mengeringhausen (W). Evangelical. Sailed to America with the regiment in 1776 as wagon servant on the staff. He died of illness on 8 December 1776.

RUMMEL, Georg   W200944
Sailed to America with the 1781 recruit shipment and was assigned as private in the 3rd Company. He was transferred to the 4th Company in July 1782, and apparently returned to Germany with the regiment in 1783.

RUMPELHARD, Michael   W201068
Sailed to America with the 1782 recruit shipment and was assigned as private in the 5th Company. He returned to Germany with his unit, but then deserted at Bremen on 30 September 1783.

RUNTE, Johannes   W200458
Born 2 April 1754 in Lelbach (W). Evangelical. 5'7" tall. Father – Johann Franz R.; Mother – Anna Gertrud, nee Grebe, of Adorf (W). Sixth of 7 children. Brother of Johann Justus Runte (W200214) below. First marriage in 1784. Second marriage on 21 December 1787 to Maria Elisabeth Wilke from Korbach (W). Daughter from first marriage, Marie Elisabeth, born 15 April 1784. Tailor by trade. Sailed to America with the regiment in 1776 as private in the 4th Company. By April 1779 he was a member of the 1st Company. Taken prisoner at Baton Rouge on 21 September 1779, he returned to duty in January 1782. He apparently returned to Germany with the regiment in 1783. He had 3 years' previous military experience in the Waldeck 2nd Regiment in Holland.

RUNTE, Johann Justus Friedrich   W200214
Born 26 November 1756 in Lelbach (W). Evangelical. 5'7 1/2" tall. Father – Johann Franz R.; Mother – Anna Gertrud, nee Grebe. Seventh of 7 children and brother of Johannes Runte (W200458) above. Sailed to America with the regiment in 1776 as private in the 2nd Company. In December 1779 he was transferred to the 4th Company. He deserted on 17 May 1781, after the fall of Pensacola, and may have joined the Spanish army. He had 2 years' previous military experience in the Waldeck 1st Regiment.

RUPP, Georg   W200755
Born in Grosssteinbach. Sailed to America with the 1778 recruit shipment and was assigned as corporal in the 3rd Company. Taken prisoner at Baton Rouge on 21 September 1779, he deserted from prisoner status at New Orleans on 12 July 1780 and joined the Spanish army.

RUPPERT, Ludwig   W200756
Born in Pyrmont. Sailed to America with the 1778 recruit shipment and
was assigned as private in the 5th Company. Taken prisoner at Baton
Rouge on 21 September 1779, he deserted from prisoner status at
New Orleans on 20 July 1780. It is possible that he then went up the
Mississippi River with Balthasar Kaltwasser (W200156) and, using the
name George Rupert, joined the American army under George Rogers
Clark in the Illinois Country on 14 August 1781 for the duration of the
war. He served initially in Captain John Girault's company of the
Illinois Regiment.

SACHS, Michael   W200757
Born in Weissenbach. Sailed to America with the 1778 recruit ship-
ment and was sick upon arrival. He was assigned as private in the 4th
Company. He died of illness at Pensacola on 14 August 1779.

SAENGER, Johann Henrich   W200625
Born 1758 in Boehne (W). Evangelical. Sailed to America with the
regiment in 1776 as batman in the 4th Company. He served as a
batman in the 4th Company throughout the war, and apparently returned to Germany with the regiment in 1783.

SAENGER, Ludwig   W201069
Sailed to America with the 1782 recruit shipment and was assigned as
private in the 5th Company. He apparently returned to Germany with
his unit in 1783.

SAHLMEYER, Andreas   W201166
Born 1750/51 in Gunzenhausen. Sailed to America with the 1777 recruit shipment and was assigned as private in the 3rd Company. He
deserted on 18 August 1778, but returned to duty on 25 October of the
same year. He then disappears from the record.

SALTZMANN, August   W200758
Born in Halberstadt. Sailed to America with the 1778 recruit shipment
and was assigned as private in the 1st Company. He died of illness in
the hospital at Manchac on 27 August 1779.

SALZMANN, Johannes   W200591
Born 1746 in Luetersheim (W). Sailed to America with the regiment
in 1776 as private in the 5th Company. Evangelical. Taken prisoner at
Elizabethtown, New Jersey, on 18 December 1776, he was sent to
Philadelphia to be exchanged on 21 June 1778. He was taken prisoner
again at Baton Rouge on 21 September 1779, and died of illness at
New Orleans on 15 November 1779.

SANDER, Karl   W200215
Born 1758 in Bevern, Braunschweig. Evangelical. 5'8 1/4" tall.
Sailed to America with the regiment in 1776 as private in the 2nd
Company. Taken prisoner at Springfield, New Jersey, on 5 January
1777, he was sent to Philadelphia to be exchanged on 13 July 1778. In

December 1779 he was transferred to the 4th Company. He was promoted to corporal in August 1780, and transferred back to the 2nd Company in June 1782. He apparently returned to Germany with the regiment in 1783. He had 2 years' previous military experience in the Waldeck 2nd Regiment.

SASSMANNSHAUSEN, Johannes   W200945
Born 1764 in Pente. Reformed. 5'1" tall. Sailed to America with the 1781 recruit shipment and was assigned as private in the 3rd Company. He died of illness at Newtown on 13 February 1782.

SAUER, Bernhard   W200383
Born 1751 in Radern (W). Evangelical. Sailed to America with the regiment in 1776 as corporal in the 4th Company. He deserted on 5 April 1777. He had 5 years' previous military experience in the Waldeck army.

SCHAAKE, Adolf   W200759
Born 1761 in Kohlgrund (W). Sailed to America with the 1778 recruit shipment and was assigned as private in the 2nd Company. Taken prisoner on the Amite River on 4 September 1779, he died of illness at New Orleans on 7 October 1779.

SCHAAKE, Johannes   W200760
Born in Kohlgrund (W). Sailed to America with the 1778 recruit shipment and was assigned as private in the 5th Company. Taken prisoner at Baton Rouge on 21 September 1779, he died there of illness on 23 September 1779.

SCHADE, Jakob   W201167
Born in Weinfeld, Switzerland. Sailed to America with the 1777 recruit shipment and was assigned as private in the 1st Company. He died of illness on 14 August 1777.

SCHADE, Peter   W200459
Born 1758 in Elberberg, Hesse. Evangelical. Sailed to America with the regiment in 1776 as private in the 4th Company. He boarded the *Santa Rosalia* on 29 May 1781 to return to New York after the capitulation of Pensacola. He served in the 4th Company throughout the war, and apparently returned to Germany with the regiment in 1783.

SCHADE, Willibald   W200761
Born in Herreden. Sailed to America with the 1778 recruit shipment and was sick upon arrival. He was assigned as private in the 3rd Company. He died of illness at Pensacola on 29 August 1779.

SCHAEFER, Andreas   W200461
Born 1750 in Braunsen (W). Evangelical. 5'3" tall. Married. Sailed to America with the regiment in 1776 as private in the 4th Company. He died of illness on 11 March 1777.

SCHAEFER, Christian   W200762

Sailed to America with the 1778 recruit shipment and was assigned as private in the 4th Company. He boarded the *Santa Rosalia* on 29 May 1781 to return to New York after the capitulation of Pensacola. He apparently returned to Germany with the regiment in 1783.

SCHAEFER, Henrich   W201070

Sailed to America with the 1782 recruit shipment and was assigned as private in the 5th Company. He apparently returned to Germany with his unit in 1783.

SCHAEFER, Johann Adam   W200460

Born 22 April 1759 in Mehlen (W). Evangelical. 5'6" tall. Linen weaver by trade. Father - Johannes S.; Mother - Anna Catharina, nee Hatzfeld. Ninth of 9 children. Sailed to America with the regiment in 1776 as private in the 4th Company. He boarded the *Santa Rosalia* on 29 May 1781 to return to New York after the capitulation of Pensacola. Served in the 4th Company throughout the war. and apparently returned to Germany with the regiment in 1783.

SCHAEFER, Johann Thomas   W200594

Born 1757 in Sachsenhausen (W). Evangelical. 5'5" tall. Sailed to America with the regiment in 1776 as private in the 5th Company. Taken prisoner in New Jersey on 19 January 1777, he is listed as a prisoner until 15 July 1783, and then as a deserter at Elizabethtown. He probably deserted much earlier, even as early as 1777.

SCHAEFER, Johannes   W200592

Born 1755 in Dehausen (W). Evangelical. Cartwright by trade. Sailed to America with the regiment in 1776 as private in the 5th Company. He was transferred to the 3rd Company in December 1779, and back to the 5th Company in July 1782. He apparently returned to Germany with the regiment in 1783.

SCHAEFER, Konrad   W201071

Sailed to America with the 1782 recruit shipment and was assigned as private in the 5th Company. He apparently returned to Germany with his unit in 1783.

SCHAEFER, Wilhelm   W200763

Born 1740 in Witzenhausen. Sailed to America with the 1778 recruit shipment and was assigned as private in the 1st Company. Taken prisoner at Baton Rouge on 21 September 1779, he died of illness on 17 October 1779.

SCHAEFFER, Johann Georg   W200593

Born 1752 in Petzigerode, Hesse. Reformed. 5'7" tall. Sailed to America with the regiment in 1776 as private in the 5th Company. He died of illness at Baton Rouge on 13 September 1779. He had 3 years' previous military experience in the Waldeck 1st Regiment.

SCHAEFFER, Johannes   W200098
Born 28 January 1755 in Meineringhausen (W). Evangelical. Father
- Johannes S.; Mother - Johanne Maria Gerdrut, nee Koehen. Fourth of
7 children. Sailed to America with the regiment in 1776 as private in
the 1st Company. He died of illness in the hospital at Manchac on 28
August 1779.

SCHAEFFER, Johannes   W200630
Born 1756 in Helsen (W). Evangelical. Sailed to America with the
regiment in 1776 as batman in the 1st Company. Taken prisoner at
Baton Rouge on 21 September 1779, his status was apparently changed
to private in November of that year. He returned to duty in January
1782. He deserted at Flatbush on 8 May 1783.

SCHAEFFER, Philipp   W200379
Born 1753 in Landau (W). Evangelical. Sailed to America with the
regiment in 1776 as corporal in the 4th Company. He was promoted to
captain at arms in April 1779, and died of illness at Pensacola on
17 October 1779. He had 4 years' previous military experience in the
Waldeck army.

SCHAEFFER, Wilhelm   W200595
Born 1757 in Kloster Merxhausen, Hesse. Reformed. Sailed to America with the regiment in 1776 as corporal in the 5th Company. Taken
prisoner at Baton Rouge on 21 September 1779, he deserted from
prisoner status at New Orleans on 9 July 1780 and joined the
Spanish army. He had 2 years' previous military experience in Holland, probably in a Waldeck unit.

SCHAPER, Bernhard   W200216
Born in Holzhausen, Pyrmont. Hans Bernhard Schaper was confirmed
at age 14 in 1766. Johann Bernhard Schaper married Anna Maria Christina Grothen, 2nd daughter of Weiland Friedrich Grothen, on 28
September 1772. Sailed to America with the regiment in 1776 as private in the 2nd Company. Taken prisoner on the Amite River on 4
September 1779, he returned to duty in January 1782. He apparently
returned to Germany with the regiment in 1783.

SCHAPER, Georg   W200946
Sailed to America with the 1781 recruit shipment and was assigned as
vice corporal in the 3rd Company. Promoted to corporal in April 1781,
he was transferred to the 2nd Company in July 1782. He returned to
Germany with the regiment and was released at Korbach (W) on 24
October 1783.

SCHAPPE, Lorenz   W200947
Born in Nass, Saarbruecken. Date and manner of joining the regiment
are uncertain, but in April 1781 he was a private in the 3rd Company.
He deserted at Pensacola on 9 May 1781, the day of the surrender of
the Pensacola garrison, and may have joined the Spanish army.

SCHARSCHMID, Johann Jakob   W200596
Born 15 June 1758 in Nieder Werbe (W). Evangelical. 5' 2 1/2" tall.
Father - Daniel Wilhelm S., a Dutch soldier whose wife was a resi-
dent of Nieder Werbe (W). Sailed to America with the regiment in
1776 as private in the 5th Company. Taken prisoner at Baton Rouge on
21 September 1779, he returned to duty in January 1782. He apparently
returned to Germany with the regiment in 1783.

SCHART, Michael   W200764
Born 1750/51 in Kaltenthal. Sailed to America with the 1778 recruit
shipment and was assigned as private in the 4th Company. He died of
illness at Pensacola on 11 May 1779.

SCHEER, Lorenz   W201186
Born in Reinhardshausen (W). Date and manner of joining the regiment
are uncertain, but he was a batman by November 1781. He died of
illness at New York on 29 November 1781.

SCHEIDELER, Daniel   W200100
Born 1754 in Adorf (W). Evangelical. Shoemaker by trade. Sailed to
America with the regiment in 1776 as private in the 1st Company.
Wounded on 16 November 1776 during the attack on Fort Washington,
he died of his wounds on 23 November 1776, probably in the
hospital at Harlem. He had 5 years' previous military experience in
the Waldeck 1st Regiment.

SCHELE, Friedrich   W200597
Born 1760 in Hannover. Evangelical. 5'2" tall. Wig maker by trade. On
6-year enlistment. Sailed to America with the regiment in 1776 as
private in the 5th Company. He was transferred to the 3rd Company in
December 1779, and back to the 5th Company in July 1782. He was
released from the regiment at Flatbush on 15 July 1783.

SCHENCKEL, Konrad   W200948
Born in Wiesenbach. Sailed to America with the 1781 recruit shipment
and was assigned as private in the 3rd Company. He died of illness in
the hospital at New York on 30 August 1781.

SCHEPP, Jakob (Josef)   W200217
Born 1754 in Hamburg, Darmstadt. Evangelical. 5'5 1/4" tall. Sailed
to America with the regiment in 1776 as private in the 2nd Company.
He was transferred to the 4th Company in December 1779, and back to
the 2nd Company in June 1782. He returned to Germany with the
regiment, but deserted at Korbach (W) on 18 October 1783. He had 4
years' previous military experience in the Waldeck 1st Regiment.

SCHEUERMANN, Christoph (Konrad)   W200101
Born 1752 in Wrexen (W). Evangelical. Sailed to America with the
regiment in 1776 as private in the 1st Company. He died of illness in
the hospital at Manchac on 4 August 1779.

SCHILLING, Johannes   W201072
Sailed to America with the 1782 recruit shipment and was assigned as
private in the 5th Company. He died of illness on 10 January 1783.

SCHIMANECK, Gottfried   W201073
Sailed to America with the 1782 recruit shipment and was assigned as
private in the 5th Company. He died of illness at Halifax On 7 May
1783.

SCHIMMEL, Anton (Jost)   W200765
Sailed to America with the 1778 recruit shipment and was assigned as
private in the 4th Company. He boarded the *Santa Rosalia* on 29 May
1781 to return to New York after the capitulation of Pensacola. He
returned to Germany with the regiment and was released at Korbach
(W) on 16 October 1783.

SCHIMMEL, Johann Georg   W200598
Born 1757 in Heuchelheim, Darmstadt. Evangelical. Sailed to America with the regiment in 1776 as private in the 5th Company. Taken
prisoner at Baton Rouge on 21 September 1779, he deserted from
prisoner status at Havana on 25 March 1782. A John Scimmel is listed
in the 1790 census as living in Watervliet, Albany County, New York,
in a household with one adult male, one male under sixteen years of
age, and two females.

SCHIMMEL, Johann Jost   W200218
Born 15 April 1747 in Meineringhausen (W). Evangelical. Father
Johann Henrich S. Third of 3 children. Sailed to America with the
regiment in 1776 as private in the 2nd Company. He died of illness on
17 March 1777.

SCHIRR, Franz Philipp   W200346
Born 16 September 1751 in Wildungen (W). Baptized 19 September,
and confirmed in 1765. Evangelical. 5'4" tall. Father – Franz S.;
Mother – Anna Sybilla Magda. Hat maker by trade. Sailed to America
with the regiment in 1776 as private in the 3rd Company. Taken prisoner at Baton Rouge on 21 September 1779, he was transferred to the
5th Company in December 1779. He returned to duty in January 1782,
and was transferred back to the 3rd Company in July 1782. He apparently returned to Germany with the regiment in 1783.

SCHLAUDERBECK, Michael   W200766
Born in Nuernberg. Sailed to America with the 1777 recruit shipment
and was assigned as private in the 3rd Company. He served in the 3rd
Company throughout the war, and was released from the regiment at
Flatbush on 15 July 1783. In 1784 he received a land grant in Nova
Scotia for one man and one woman.

SCHLEIERMACHER, Henrich   W200347
Born 19 March 1739 in Wildungen (W), baptized on 22 March, and confirmed in 1752. Evangelical. 5'4" tall. Father - Henrich S.; Mother - Anna Margaretha, nee Hubert. Married with 3 children. Hat maker by trade. Sailed to America with the regiment in 1776 as private in the 3rd Company. He served throughout the war in the 3rd Company, being promoted to corporal in August 1780. He apparently returned to Germany with the regiment in 1783. He had 16 years' previous military experience in the Waldeck 2nd Regiment.

SCHLEIERMACHER, Johannes   W200102
Born in 1733 in Wildungen (W). Evangelical. Married with 1 child. Sailed to America with the regiment in 1776 as private in the 1st Company. He died in the hospital at Manchac on 15 August 1779. He had 7 years and 3 months of previous military experience in the Waldeck 1st Regiment.

SCHLOSSMUELLER, Johann Henrich   W200462
Born 4 May 1727 in Holzhausen, Pyrmont, and baptized on 9 May. Evangelical. 5'3" tall. Father - Henrich S. Married with 6 children, including: Georg Friedrich, born 15 July 1753; Johann Friedrich, born 5 October 1755; and Johann Ludwig, born 24 January 1762. Sailed to America with the regiment in 1776 as private in the 4th Company. He died of illness on 4 April 1777.

SCHLUCKEBIER, Johann Henrich   W200002
Born in Sachsenhausen (W), and baptized on 17 October 1735. Evangelical (also noted as Lutheran). 5'8" tall. Father - Johann Ernst S. Sailed to America with the regiment in 1776 as sergeant in the 1st Company. Taken prisoner at Baton Rouge on 21 September 1779, he was apparently released by the Spaniards sometime after 23 May 1781 and died at Kingston, Jamaica, on 24 September 1781. He had more than 21 years of previous military experience in the Waldeck army.

SCHMECK, Jakob   W200220
Born 1750 in Mandern (W). Evangelical. 5'5" tall. Sailed to America with the regiment in 1776 as private in the 2nd Company. He was transferred to the 4th Company in December 1779, and back to the 2nd Company in June 1782. He apparently returned to Germany with the regiment in 1783.

SCHMECK, Johann Georg   W200219
Born 14 January 1757 in Helsen (W). Evangelical. Father - Johann Conrad S., grenadier. Mother - Marie Catharina, nee Vormittag. Second of 7 children. Sailed to America with the regiment in 1776 as private in the 2nd Company. Taken prisoner at Springfield, New Jersey, on 5 January 1777, he enlisted in the American army on 21 March 1777. He apparently deserted back to his own regiment as he was transferred to the 4th Company in December 1779. He boarded the *Santa Rosalia* on 29 May 1781 to return to New York after the capitulation of Pensacola. He was transferred to the 2nd Company in June 1782, and apparently returned to Germany with the regiment in 1783.

SCHMECK, Johannes   W200221
Born 1759 in Mandern (W). Evangelical. 5'3" tall. Sailed to America
with the regiment in 1776 as private in the 2nd Company. He died of
illness on 21 October 1777.

SCHMID, Henrich   W200949
Sailed to America with the 1781 recruit shipment and was assigned as
private in the 3rd Company. He was transferred to the 5th Company in
July 1782. He returned to Germany with the regiment and was released at Korbach (W) on 19 October 1783.

SCHMID(T), Johann Adam   W200348
Born 30 December 1750 in Bringhausen (W), and baptized on 6 Janu-
ary 1751. Evangelical. 5'4" tall. Father - Johann Adam S., school-
master. Mother - Marie Elisabeth, nee Kohlhoeber. Fifth of 8 children.
Tailor by trade. Sailed to America with the regiment in 1776 as private
in the 3rd Company, and was the school master for the regiment when
it returned from America. He served throughout the war in the 3rd
Company, being wounded in the attack on Fort Washington on 16
November 1776. He served as the song leader for Chaplain Waldeck
(W400005) at religious services. He apparently returned to Germany
with the regiment in 1783. He had 8 years' previous military experience in the Waldeck 2nd Regiment.

SCHMID, Johannes   W201187
Date and manner of joining the regiment are uncertain, but by
December 1781 he was batman for Captain August Alberti
(W100008) in the 5th Company. He was transferred to the 2nd
Company in August 1782, and apparently returned to Germany with
the regiment in 1783.

SCHMID, Konrad   W200599
Born 1756 in Frankenau, Hesse. Evangelical. 5'6 1/4" tall. Sailed to
America with the regiment in 1776 as private in the 5th Company.
Taken prisoner at Baton Rouge on 21 September 1779, he returned to
duty in January 1782. He apparently returned to Germany with the
regiment in 1783. He had 2 years' previous military experience in the
Waldeck 2nd Regiment.

SCHMID, Peter   W200767
Born 1751/52 in Hohenfeld, Fulda. Sailed to America with the 1778
recruit shipment and was assigned as private in the 3rd Company. He
deserted at Pensacola on 21 March 1780.

SCHMIDMANN, Wilhelm   W201074
Sailed to America with the 1782 recruit shipment and was assigned as
private in the 5th Company. He returned to Germany with his unit and
was released from the regiment at Korbach (W) on 23 October 1783.

SCHMIDT, Christian (Ludwig)   W200626C
Born 1759/60 in Arolsen (W). Evangelical. Sailed to America with the
regiment in 1776 as free corporal in the 3rd Company. He was commissioned an ensign with date of rank of 14 April 1779 . Records indicate that he was then assigned to the 2nd, 3rd, and 4th Companies,
all at about the same time, but that he was finally a member of the
4th Company by April 1780. On 5 December 1780 he rode to The
Cliffs with Chaplain Waldeck (W400005) to visit Captain Pentzel
(W100005S). He was transferred to the 2nd Company in June 1782 and
apparently returned to Germany with the regiment in 1783. He had 1
year of previous military experience as a cadet in the Waldeck 2nd
Regiment.

SCHMIDT, Felix   W200768
Sailed to America with the 1777 recruit shipment and was assigned as
private in the 4th Company. He apparently returned to Germany with
the regiment in 1783.

SCHMIDT, Franz   W200463
Born 1737 in Oberdufenbach, Runckel. Catholic. 5'9" tall. Sailed to
America with the regiment in 1776 as private in the 4th Company. He
died of illness on 18 March 1777. He had previous military experience
in the Prussian army.

SCMHIDT, Friedrich, Sr.   W200600
Born 1751 in Holzhausen, Pyrmont. Evangelical. 5'3" tall. Sailed to
America with the regiment in 1776 as private in the 5th Company.
Taken prisoner at Springfield, New Jersey, on 5 January 1777, he was
sent to Philadelphia to be exchanged on 21 June 1778. He was taken
prisoner again at Baton Rouge on 21 September 1779, and died of
illness at New Orleans on 21 October 1779.

SCHMIDT, Friedrich   W201194
Born in Leipzig. Date and manner of joining the regiment are uncer-
tain, but by September 1779 he was a private in the 5th Company.
Taken prisoner at Baton Rouge on 21 September 1779, he deserted
from prisoner status at New Orleans on 11 July 1780 and joined the
Spanish army.

SCHMIDT, Friedrich, Jr.   W200769
Born in Holzhausen, Pyrmont. Sailed to America with the 1777 recruit
shipment and was assigned as private in the 5th Company. He was
apparently taken prisoner at Baton Rouge on 21 September 1779, returned to duty in January 1782, then returned to Germany with the
regiment in 1783.

SCHMIDT, Friedrich   W201183
He is on the 1782 recruit list, but does not appear in the HETRINA or
on any other documents found to date.

SCHMIDT, Georg   W200349
Born 1758 in Kaltholzhausen, Nassau. Reformed. Sailed to America
with the regiment in 1776 as private in the 3rd Company. He was
killed in fighting at Elizabethtown, New Jersey, on 27 December 1776.

SCHMIDT, Henrich   W200103
Born 1750 in Romersberg, Hesse. Reformed. Married. Sailed to America with the regiment in 1776 as private in the 1st Company. He died of
illness on 30 April 1777.

SCHMIDT, Henrich   W200633
Born in Berndorf (W). Sailed to America with the 1778 recruit ship-
ment and was assigned as private in the 1st Company. He deserted at
Manchac on 9 July 1779.

SCHMIDT, Henrich   W200770
Sailed to America with the 1778 recruit shipment and was assigned as
private in the 2nd Company. He was transferred to the 4th Company in
December 1779, and back to the 2nd Company in August 1782. He
then disappears from the record.

SCHMIDT, Jakob Philipp   W200464
Born 1749 in Ristein, Witgenstein. Evangelical (also listed as Lutheran). 5'5 1/2" tall. On 4-year enlistment. Sailed to America with the
regiment in 1776 as private in the 4th Company. He died of illness on
25 July 1777.

SCHMIDT, Johannes   W200350
Born 1746 in Kaltholzhausen, Nassau. Reformed. Tailor by trade.
Sailed to America with the regiment in 1776 as private in the 3rd
Company. He was wounded in fighting in December 1776, and died of
illness at Pensacola on 11 August 1779. He had 5 years' previous
military experience in the Prussian army from which he had deserted.

SCHMIDT, Johannes   W200104
Born 1754/55 in Wellen (W). Evangelical. Tailor by trade. Sailed to
America with the regiment in 1776 as private in the 1st Company. He
was apparently taken prisoner at Baton Rouge on 21 September 1779 as
he died of illness at New Orleans on 8 November 1779. He had 5 years
and 3 months of previous military experience in the Waldeck army.

SCHMIDT, Konrad   W200603
Born 1736 in Affoldern (W). Evangelical. 5'4" tall. Miller by trade.
Sailed to America with the regiment in 1776 as private in the 5th
Company. He originally was assigned to the 3rd Company, which
listed his age as 26, but transferred on 30 May 1776. He died of ill-
ness on 30 June 1777.

SCHMIDT, Konrad   W200771
Born in Stadtbergen. Sailed to America with the 1778 recruit shipment
and was assigned as private in the 2nd Company. He was transferred
to the 4th Company in December 1779, and deserted at Pensacola on
17 May 1781. He must have returned to duty as he was transferred to
the 2nd Company in June 1782 and apparently returned to Germany
with the regiment in 1783.

SCHMIDT, Ludwig   W200772
Born in Erfurt. Sailed to America with the 1778 recruit shipment and
was assigned as private in the 4th Company. He and his wife boarded
the *Santa Rosalia* on 29 May 1781 to return to New York after the
capitulation of Pensacola. He returned to Germany with the regiment
and was released at Bremen on 19 September 1783.

SCHMIDT, Philipp   W200602
Born 1752 in Muehlhausen (W). Evangelical. 5'5" tall. Sailed to
America with the regiment in 1776 as private in the 5th Company. He
died of illness in the hospital at New York on 24 December 1778.

SCHMIDTMANN, Christian   W200950
Born in Heselbrik, Schwarzb. Sailed to America with the 1781 recruit
shipment and was assigned as private in the 3rd Company. In July
1782 he was transferred to the 5th Company, and he died of illness at
New York on 5 November 1782.

SCHNABEL, Karl   W200222
Born 1758 in Zweibruecken. Evangelical. 5'2 1/2" tall. Sailed to
America with the regiment in 1776 as private in the 2nd Company. In
December 1779 he was transferred to the 4th Company, and was
promoted to corporal in April 1780. Demoted to private in June 1781,
he was promoted back to corporal in October of the same year. In
June 1782 he was transferred to the 2nd Company. He deserted in
August 1782, but returned to duty in December 1782 as a private in the
2nd Company. He was released from the regiment in January 1783,
apparently in New York.

SCHNEIDER, David, Sr.   W200774
Born in Wetzlar. Sailed to America with the 1778 recruit shipment and
was assigned as private in the 3rd Company. He was released from the
regiment at Flatbush on 15 July 1783.

SCHNEIDER, David   W201200
Born in Lauterbach. Date and manner of joining the regiment are
uncertain, but he was a private in the 3rd Company in April 1779. He
was released from the regiment at Pensacola on 12 April 1779, for
theft.

SCHNEIDER, Franz   W200775
Born in Billigheim. Sailed to America with the 1778 recruit shipment
and was sick upon arrival. He was assigned as private in the 5th
Company. He died of illness at Pensacola on 14 July 1779.

SCHNEIDER, Henrich W200223
Born 1758 in Ober Waroldern (W). Evangelical. Sailed to America with the regiment in 1776 as private in the 2nd Company. He deserted on 19 April 1777.

SCHNEIDER, Philipp W201075
Sailed to America with the 1782 recruit shipment and was assigned as private in the 5th Company. He returned to Germany with his unit and was released from the regiment at Korbach (W) on 23 October 1783.

SCHNEIDER, Philipp (Georg) W200106
Born 1739/40 in Muehlhausen (W). Evangelical. 5' 8 1/2" tall. Married with 2 children. Sailed to America with the regiment in 1776 as private in the 1st Company. He was killed in fighting at Springfield, New Jersey, on 5 January 1777. He had 18 years' previous military experience in the Waldeck 1st regiment.

SCHNEIDER, Thomas W200951
Born in Endebrueck, Witgenstein. Sailed to America with the 1781 recruit shipment and was assigned as private in the 3rd Company. He was transferred to the 5th Company in July 1782, and was released from the regiment at Flatbush on 15 July 1783.

SCHNEPPER, Friedrich W201076
Sailed to America with the 1782 recruit shipment and was assigned as private in the 5th Company. He apparently returned to Germany with his unit in 1783.

SCHNEPPER, Henrich W200830
Born 1762/63 in Landau (W). Sailed to America with the 1779 recruit shipment and was assigned as private in the 3rd Company. He apparently returned to Germany with the regiment in 1783.

SCHNITZIUS, Ludwig W200224
Born 1756 in Hogheim, Leiningen. Evangelical. Sailed to America with the regiment in 1776 as private in the 2nd Company. Taken prisoner on the Amite River on 4 September 1779, he deserted from prisoner status at New Orleans on 12 July 1780 and joined the Spanish army. He had 3 years and 6 months of previous military experience in the Waldeck 2nd Regiment.

SCHOENBERGER, Johannes W200776
Born in Salzburg. Date and manner of joining the regiment are uncertain, but he was a private in the 4th Company by April 1779. He deserted on 12 May 1781, after the fall of Pensacola, and may have joined the Spanish army.

SCHOENEFELD, Christian W200777
Born in Crimitzchen/Heit. Sailed to America with the 1778 recruit shipment and was assigned as private in the 3rd Company. He deserted at Baton Rouge on 12 September 1779.

SCHOTTE, Dietrich (Friedrich)   W200131
Born 1751 in Carlshaven, Hesse. Reformed. Sailed to America with
the regiment in 1776 as sergeant in the 2nd Company. Taken prisoner
at Baton Rouge on 21 September 1779, he returned to duty in January
1782. He returned to Germany with the regiment and was released at
Korbach (W) on 17 October 1783.

SCHRAGE, Friedrich   W200778
Born 1745/46 in Oerzen. Sailed to America with the 1778 recruit
shipment and was assigned as medic in the 3rd Company. He was
transferred to the 5th Company in April 1779. Taken prisoner at Baton
Rouge on 21 September 1779, he died of illness on 3 November 1779.

SCHRAMM, Johannes (Zacharias)   W200952
Sailed to America with the 1781 recruit shipment and was assigned as
private in the 3rd Company. He died of illness at Newtown on 1
November 1781.

SCHRANTZ, Josef   W200225
Born 1759 in Canstein, Koeln. Catholic. Sailed to America with the
regiment in 1776 as private in the 2nd Company. Taken prisoner on
5 January 1777, at Springfield, New Jersey, he was sent to Philadelphia to be exchanged on 18 June 1778. Taken prisoner again on the
Amite River on 4 September 1779, he deserted from prisoner status at
Havana on 5 October 1780.

SCHRAUFF, Georg   W200107
Born 1751 in Mandern (W). Evangelical. 5' 5" tall. Sailed to America
with the regiment in 1776 as private in the 1st Company. Taken prisoner at Baton Rouge on 21 September 1779, he died of illness aboard
ship on 22 September 1780, while still in prisoner status and being
moved from New Orleans to Havana.

SCHRAUFF, Konrad   W200627
Born 1752/53 in Zueschen (W). Reformed. Shoemaker by trade.
Married with 1 child. Sailed to America with the regiment in 1776 as
private in the 1st Company. Taken prisoner at Baton Rouge on 21
September 1779, he died of illness on 8 December 1779. He had
more than 5 years' previous military experience in the Waldeck army.

SCHREIBER, Bernhard   W200779C
Born 1762 in Helsen (W), and was 41 years old in 1802. Sailed to
America with the 1778 recruit shipment and was assigned as free
corporal in the 2nd Company. Taken prisoner on the Amite River on 4
September 1779, he returned to duty in January 1781. He was transferred to the 5th Company as an ensign in June 1782, and returned to
Germany with the regiment in 1783. He sailed to the Cape of Good
Hope in Dutch service in 1802 as captain commanding the 3rd Company of the 5th Waldeck Battalion. During his career in the Waldeck
army he spent 4 years as free corporal, 2 years and 8 months as an
ensign, 2 months as a 2nd lieutenant, and 17 years and 5 months as a

1st lieutenant, having a date of rank of 15 November 1784. His date of rank as captain was 18 May 1802. He was a prisoner of war of the English in June 1806.

SCHREIBER, Ulrich W200108
Born 1748 in Hundsdorf (W). Evangelical. 5'5 1/2" tall. Sailed to America with the regiment in 1776 as private in the 1st Company. Taken prisoner in New Jersey in early January 1777, his exchange or escape date is unknown. He was taken prisoner again on 21 September 1779 at Baton Rouge, and he returned to duty in January 1782. He returned to Germany with the regiment and was released at Korbach (W) on 21 October 1783. He had 9 years' previous military experience in the Waldeck 1st Regiment.

SCHREIER, Johannes W200921
Born in Berlin. Sailed to America with the 1781 recruit shipment and was assigned as corporal in the 3rd Company. He was demoted to private in September 1781. He returned to Germany with the regiment and was released at Bremen on 19 September 1783.

SCHREYER, Franz Friedrich Josef W200465
Born 1757 in Stirtzenhart, Mainz. Catholic. Linen weaver by trade. Married Maria Dorothea Friederike Boetz of Korbach (W) at Massenhausen (W) on 10 February 1787. Sailed to America with the regiment in 1776 as private in the 4th Company. He boarded the *Santa Rosalia* on 29 May 1781 to return to New York after the capitulation of Pensacola. He served in the 4th Company throughout the war and returned to Germany with the regiment. He was released at Korbach (W) on 16 Ootober 1783.

SCHREYER, Leonhard W200780
Born 1760/61 in Hagen. Sailed to America with the 1778 recruit shipment and was assigned as private in the 4th Company. He died of illness on 29 February 1780.

SCHROEDER, Johann Friedrich W200351
Born in Bergheim (W), and baptized on 19 January 1746. Evangelical. 5'5 1/2" tall. Married with 4 children. Linen weaver by trade. Sailed to America with the regiment in 1776 as private in the 3rd Company. He died of illness at Baton Rouge on 6 September 1779.

SCHUESSLER, Christoph W200781
Sailed to America with the 1778 recruit shipment and was sick upon arrival. He was assigned as private in the 2nd Company. He was transferred to the 4th Company in December 1779, and back to the 2nd Company in June 1782. He returned to Germany with the regiment and was released at Korbach (W) on 16 October 1783.

SCHUETTE, Henrich W201077
Sailed to America with the 1782 recruit shipment and was assigned as private in the 5th Company. He apparently returned to Germany with his unit in 1783.

SCHUETTLER, Adam (Adolph) W200109
Born 1750 in Neudorf (W). Evangelical. 5'5" tall. Married with 1 child. Sailed to America with the regiment in 1776 as private in the 1st Company. He died of illness in the hospital at Manchac on 7 August 1779.

SCHUETTLER, Georg David W200604
Born 1746/47 in Helmighausen (W). Evangelical. 5'2" tall. Married with 1 child. Sailed to America with the regiment in 1776 as private in the 5th Company. He was wounded in the attack on Fort Washington on 16 November 1776. Taken prisoner at Baton Rouge on 21 September 1779. He died of illness on 27 November 1779.

SCHUETZ, Anton W200831
Born 1760/61 in Dehringhausen (W). Sailed to America with the 1779 recruit shipment and was assigned private in the 3rd Company. He was transferred to the 5th Company in July 1782. He returned to Germany with the regiment and was released at Korbach (W) on 19 Oct. 1783.

SCHUETZ, Johann Henrich W200832
Born 23 March 1759 in Volkhardinghausen (W). Father - Johann Adam S., herdsman; Mother - Johanna Katharina, nee Heise. Brother of Johann Wilhelm Schuetz (W200605). Married Anna Katharina Elisabeth Rossener, from France, on 22 March 1784. They had 4 children of whom the first was born in Coeverden, Holland. Sailed to America with the 1779 recruit shipment and was assigned as private in the 4th Company. He boarded the *Santa Rosalia* on 29 May 1781 to return to New York after the capitulation of Pensacola. He returned to Germany with the regiment and was released at Korbach (W) on 20 Oct. 1783.

SCHUETZ, Johann Wilhelm W200605
Born 20 November 1754 in Volkhardinghausen (W). Evangelical. 5'3" tall. Father - Johann Adam S., herdsman; Mother - Johanna Katharina, nee Heise. First of 4 children. Brother of Johann Henrich Schuetz (W200832). Sailed to America with the regiment in 1776 as private in the 5th Company. Taken prisoner at Baton Rouge on 21 September 1779, he died there of illness the next day.

SCHULTZE, Andreas W200628
Born 1751 in Bornighausen, Koeln. Catholic. Tinsmith by trade. Sailed to America with the regiment in 1776 as private in the 4th company. He boarded the *Santa Rosalia* on 29 May 1781 to return to New York after the capitulation of Pensacola. He died of illness in Newtown on 22 April 1782.

SCHULTZE, Johann Christoph W200226
Born in Holzhausen, Pyrmont, and baptized on 13 April 1753. Evangelical. 5'5" tall. Father - Hermann S. Linen weaver by trade. Sailed to America with the regiment in 1776 as private in the 2nd Company. He was transferred to the 4th Company in December 1779, and back to the 2nd Company in June 1782. He apparently returned to Germany with the regiment in 1783.

SCHULTZE, Karl   W201079
Sailed to America with the 1782 recruit shipment and was assigned as
medic in the 5th Company. He returned to Germany with his unit, but
deserted at Bremen on 30 September 1783.

SCHULTZE, Michael   W200953
Born 1759 in Weissenbach. Lutheran. 5'3 1/2" tall. Sailed to
America with the 1781 recruit shipment and was assigned as private in
the 3rd Company. He died of illness at Newtown on 3 March 1782.

SCHULTZE, Johann Stefan   W200466
Born 1758 in Netze (W). Evangelical. 5'4" tall. Sailed to America
with the regiment in 1776 as private in the 4th Company. He boarded
the *Santa Rosalia* on 29 May 1781 to return to New York after the
capitulation of Pensacola. He served in the 4th Company throughout
the war and returned to Germany with the regiment. He was released at
Korbach (W) on 20 October 1783.

SCHULTZE, Martin   W200601
Bcrn in Hassenberg. Date and manner of joining the regiment are
uncertain, but by September 1777 he was a private in the 4th Company. He died of illness on 14 September 1777.

SCHULTZE, Wilhelm   W300014
Born in Pyrmont. Evangelical. 5'8" tall. Father of 1 child. Sailed to
America with the regiment in 1776 as bombardier in the artillery
section. He was transferred to the 3rd Company in June 1781 after the
regiment lost its guns at Pensacola. He was transferred to the 5th
Company in the summer of 1782 and returned to Germany with the
regiment. He was released at Korbach (W) on 16 October 1783.

SCHUM, Friedrich   W200782
Born 1746/47 in Schmalfelden (or Schmalkalden). Sailed to America
with the 1778 recruit shipment and was assigned as sergeant in the
2nd Company. Taken prisoner on the Amite River on 4 September
1779, he died of illness at New Orleans on 9 September 1779.

SCHUMACHER, Andreas   W201078
Sailed to America with the 1782 recruit shipment and was assigned as
private in the 5th Company. He returned to Germany with his unit and
was released from the regiment at Korbach (W) on 22 October 1783.

SCHUMACHER, Arnold   W200833
Born in Korbach (W), and baptized on 27 March 1743. Evangelical.
Father - Tilemann Arnold Henrich S., lawyer. Mother - Gertrud, nee
Schultheiss. Married Justine Christine Elisabeth Wildstach, born 4
October 1748 in Korbach Neustadt (W) at Sachsenhausen on 17 October
1770. She died at Korbach (W) in late October or early November
1779. They had 4 children, all born in Sachsenhausen (W): Justine
Christine, born prematurely on 30 June 1771 and died a few days later;
Wilhelmine Catharine Philippine Fredricke, born 10 November

1772; Johann Christoph Wilhelm, born 27 February 1775 who died 2 October 1781; and Maria Christine, born 4 February 1777. After he failed his examination to become the preacher at Freienhagen (W), he became a drunkard and joined the 3rd Regiment, leaving his wife and children in Germany. Sailed to America with the 1779 recruit shipment and was assigned as cadet in the 4th Company. He died of illness in camp at Pensacola on 29 July 1780.

SCHUMACHER, Johann Henrich Christian   W200252
Born in Mengeringhausen (W), and baptized on 20 May 1748. Evangelical. Father – Henrich Andreas, medic with the grenadiers; Mother – Sophia Margaretha, nee Hagemann. Surgeon by trade. Sailed to America with the regiment in 1776 as sergeant in the 3rd Company. He was released from the regiment on 15 July 1777 and returned to Germany. He had 6 months' previous military experience in the Hessian army from which he had deserted, 9 years in the Prussian army, and 1 year in the Waldeck 2nd Regiment.

SCHUMACHER, Philipp   W200954
Born in Lauterbach. Sailed to America with the 1781 recruit shipment and was assigned as private in the 3rd Company. He died of illness in the hospital at New York on 13 August 1781.

SCHUMANN, Peter   W200783
Born in Frankfurt. Sailed to America with the 1777 recruit shipment and was assigned as private in the 4th Company. He deserted at Havana on 1 October 1781 while being transported to New York after the fall of Pensacola.

SCHURCK, Ludwig   W200917
Sailed to America with the 1782 recruit shipment and was assigned as private in the 5th Company. He died of illness at Halifax on 7 March 1783.

SCHWALBACH, Wilhelm   W200504
Born 1757 in Elmershausen, Hesse. Evangelical. Goldsmith by trade. Sailed to America with the regiment in 1776 as corporal in the 5th Company. He did not sail to West Florida with the regiment in 1778 but died of illness in the hospital at New York on 3 February 1779.

SCHWARTZ, Jakob   W201080
Sailed to America with the 1782 recruit shipment and was assigned as private in the 5th Company. He returned to Germany with his unit and was released at Korbach (W) on 23 October 1783.

SCHWENCKE, Johann Georg Friedrich   W200227
Born 19 June 1757 in Helsen (W). Evangelical. Father – Johann Jakob S., grenadier; Mother – Elisabeth, nee Ebersbach. First of 8 children. Sailed to America with the regiment in 1776 as private in the 2nd Company. Taken prisoner at Springfield, New Jersey, on 5 January 1777, he enlisted in the American army on 2 February 1777. He

apparently deserted back to his own regiment and was assigned to the 1st Company. He was taken prisoner again at Baton Rouge on 21 September 1779, and deserted from prisoner status at Havana on 4 October 1780.

SCHWENDER, Wilhelm   W201081
Sailed to America with the 1782 recruit shipment and was assigned as private in the 5th Company. He apparently returned to Germany with his unit in 1783.

SCHWERD(T), Johann Henrich   W200467
Born 14 June 1750 in Neersen, Pyrmont. Evangelical. 5'7 1/4" tall. Father - Johann Henrich S.; Mother - Maria Elisabeth, nee Pfennigs. Sailed to America with the regiment in 1776 as private in the 4th Company. He boarded the *Santa Rosalia* on 29 May 1781 to return to New York after the capitulation of Pensacola. He died of illness at Newtown on 7 September 1781.

SCRIBA, Wilhelm   W200785
Date and manner of joining the regiment are uncertain, but he was a corporal in the 5th Company by April 1779. Taken prisoner at Baton Rouge on 21 September 1779, he returned to duty in January 1782. He was promoted to captain at arms in June of 1782, and apparently returned to Germany with the regiment in 1783.

SECK, Friedrich (Joseph)   W200786
Born in Hildburghausen. Sailed to America with the 1778 recruit shipment and was assigned as private in the 2nd Company. He was transferred to the 4th Company in December 1779, and back to the 2nd Company in June 1782. He was released from the regiment at New York on 18 July 1783.

SEIL, Hermann   W200352
Born 1758 in Schweinsburg, Ober Hesse. Evangelical. Sailed to America with the regiment in 1776 as private in the 3rd Company. Taken prisoner at Baton Rouge on 21 September 1779, he died of illness at New Orleans on 17 October 1779.

SELTSAM, Johannes (Georg Wilhelm)   W200468
Born 5 July 1747 in Wildungen and confirmed in 1761. Evangelical. Cloth maker by trade. Sailed to America with the regiment in 1776 as private in the 4th Company. He was released in America as an invalid on 19 December 1782, and may have returned to Germany.

SEMPER, Adam   W200787
Born in Reichenbach. Sailed to America with the 1778 recruit shipment and was assigned as private in the 4th Company. He boarded the *Santa Rosalia* on 29 May 1781 to return to New York after the capitulation of Pensacola. He returned to Germany with the regiment and was released at Bremen on 19 September 1783.

SENFT, Georg   W201082
On 3 December 1788 a Johann Georg Senft, master tailor from Asel
and son of Johann Henrich S., married Anna Elisabeth Knust of Meineringhausen. They had 7 children. Johann Georg S. died 8 February
1826. Sailed to America with the 1782 recruit shipment and was assigned as private in the 5th Company. He returned to Germany with his
unit and was released at Korbach (W) on 23 October 1783.

SIEBEL, Franz Adolf   W200469
Born in Korbach (W), and baptized on 31 March 1756. Evangelical.
5'1" tall. Hatmaker by trade. Father - Johannes; Mother - Susanna
Louisa. Sailed to America with the regiment in 1776 as private in the
4th Company. He served in the 4th Company throughout the war, being
wounded in the attack on Fort Washington on 16 November 1776. He
boarded the *Santa Rosalia* on 29 May 1781 to return to New York after
the capitulation of Pensacola. He apparently returned to Germany with
the regiment in 1783.

SIEBEL, Johann Dietrich   W200353
Born 18 November 1756 in Buehle (W). Evangelical. Father - Johann
Franz S., herdsman; Mother - Maria Catharina Margaretha, nee Kann.
Second of 3 children. Sailed to America with the regiment in 1776 as
private in the 3rd Company. He served throughout the war in the 3rd
Company, but then deserted at New York on 16 July 1783.

SIEBERT, Friedrich   W200788
Born 1763/64 in Gronau. Sailed to America with the 1778 recruit
shipment and was sick upon arrival. He was assigned as private in
the 4th Company. He died of illness on 6 April 1780.

SIEBERT, Johann Jakob   W200470
Born 1762/63 in Elberberg, Hesse. Evangelical. 5' tall. Sailed to
America with the regiment in 1776 as private in the 4th Company.
Apparently captured in New Jersey in early 1777, he deserted from
prisoner of war status at Lancaster, Pennsylvania, on 4 May 1778.

SIEGLER, Alexander   W200110
Born 1737 in Falckenbourg, Koeln. Catholic. 5'6" tall. Sailed to
America with the regiment in 1776 as private in the 1st Company. He
was apparently promoted to corporal and to quartermaster sergeant
prior to April 1779. Taken prisoner at Baton Rouge on 21 September
1779, he died of illness at New Orleans on 29 April 1780. He had 12
years' previous military experience in the Danish army.

SIEMON, Christian   W200829
Born in Weissenfels. Sailed to America with the 1781 recruit shipment
and was assigned as private in the 3rd Company. He was transferred to
the 5th Company in July 1782, and died of illness at New York on 2
October 1782.

SIEMON, Christian (Johannes)   W201163
Born in Augsburg. Sailed to America with the 1781 recruit shipment
and was assigned as private in the 3rd Company. He was transferred to
the 5th Company in July 1782. He returned to Germany with the regiment and was released "on the Weser" on 20 September 1783.

SIEMON, Friedrich   W201148
Sailed to America with 1782 recruit shipment and was assigned as
drummer in the 5th Company. He apparently returned to Germany with
his unit in 1783.

SIEMON, Friedrich   W201083
Sailed to America with the 1782 recruit shipment and was assigned
private in the 5th Company. He apparently returned to Germany with
his unit in 1783.

SIEVER, Johann Hermann (Henrich)   W200354
Born in Holzhausen, Pyrmont, and baptized on 5 June 1757. Evangelical. 5'4 1/2" tall. Father – Johann S. Sailed to America with the
regiment in 1776 as private in the 3rd Company. He was killed in the
attack on The Village on 7 January 1781.

SIMSHAEUSER, Justus (August)   W200502
Born 1751 in Sachsenhausen (W). Evangelical. Sailed to America
with the regiment in 1776 as corporal in the 5th Company. Taken
prisoner at Baton Rouge on 21 September 1779. He returned to duty in
January 1781. He was promoted to quartermaster sergeant in June
1782, and apparently returned to Germany with the regiment in 1783.

SINEMUS, Christian   W200955
Born in Rhoden (W). Sailed to America with the 1781 recruit shipment
and was assigned as private in the 3rd Company. He was transferred to
the 5th Company in July 1782, and apparently returned to Germany
with the regiment in 1783.

SINEMUS, Johannes   W200956
Born in Rhoden (W). Sailed to America with the 1781 recruit shipment
and was assigned as private in the 3rd Company. He was transferred
to the 5th Company in July 1782, and apparently returned to Germany
with the regiment in 1783.

SINN, Konrad   W200957
Born in Wegenfeld, Swabia. Sailed to America with the 1781 recruit
shipment and was assigned as private in the 3rd Company. He was
transferred to the 4th Company in July 1782, and died of illness at
Flatbush on 8 June 1783.

SIX, Georg   W200228
Born 1757 in Erdenbrick, Witgenstein. Reformed. 5'6" tall. Sailed to
America with the regiment in 1776 as private in the 2nd Company. He
was transferred to the 4th Company in December 1779, and back to the

2nd Company in June 1782. He returned to Germany with the regiment and was released at Korbach (W) on 19 October 1783. He had 3 years' previous military experience in the Waldeck 2nd Regiment.

SOMMER, Josef   W201117
Sailed to America with the 1782 recruit shipment and was assigned as private in the 5th Company. He apparently returned to Germany with his unit in 1783.

SOMMER, Thomas   W201085
Sailed to America with the 1782 recruit shipment and was assigned as private in the 5th Company. He died of illness at Halifax on 29 March 1783.

SONDERMANN, Daniel   W200789
Born in Oberense. Married. His wife accompanied him to America and died there in July 1779. Sailed to America with the 1777 recruit shipment and was assigned as private in the 1st Company. He died of illness in the hospital at Manchac on 19 August 1779.

SONNENSCHEIN, Johann Friedrich   W200229
Born 10 December 1757 in Sachsenhausen (W), and baptized on 14 December. Evangelical. Father - Johann Ernst S. Sailed to America with the regiment in 1776 as private in the 2nd Company. Taken prisoner on the Amite River on 4 September 1779, he died of illness at New Orleans on 11 October 1779.

SORG, Andreas   W200790
Born in Unterreichenbach. Sailed to America with the 1778 recruit shipment and was assigned as private in the 3rd Company. He died of illness at Pensacola on 28 June 1780.

SPERLING, Georg Wilhelm   W200230
Born 1755 in Ellingerode, Hesse. Reformed. 5'3" tall. Sailed to America with the regiment in 1776 as private in the 2nd Company. He was transferred to the 4th Company in December 1779, and back to the 2nd Company in June 1782. He apparently returned to Germany with the regiment in 1783. He had 2 years' previous military experience in the Waldeck 2nd Regiment.

SPIEGEL, Schoenberg von   W200629
Born 1759 in Pickeleheim, Paderborn. Evangelical. Sailed to America with the regiment in 1776 as a free corporal in the 2nd Company. He died of a burning fever in the hospital on 12 August 1777.

STABROTH, Gottfried   W300013
Born 1753 in Berlin. Evangelical. 5'6" tall. Sailed to America with the regiment in 1776 as cannoneer in the artillery section. He was transferred to the 3rd Company after the regiment lost its guns at Pensacola. He returned to Germany with the regiment and was released at Korbach (W) on 16 October 1783.

141

STALLMANN, Henrich　　　　　　　　　　　W200356
Born 1758 in Elleringhausen (W). Evangelical. Sailed to America with the regiment in 1776 as private in the 3rd Company. He died of illness on 27 August 1777, at which time he was listed as a drummer.

STARCKE, Konrad　　　　　　　　　　　　W200958
Sailed to America with the 1781 recruit shipment and was assigned as corporal in the 3rd Company. He was promoted to sergeant in April 1781, and transferred to the 1st Company in July 1782. He apparently returned to Germany with the regiment in 1783.

STAUDINGER, Karl　　　　　　　　　　　　W201086
Sailed to America with the 1782 recruit shipment and was assigned as private in the 5th Company. He returned to Germany with his unit, but deserted at Bremen on 30 September 1783.

STEIGER, Emanuel　　　　　　　　　　　　W201087
Sailed to America with the 1782 recruit shipment and was assigned as private in the 5th Company. He returned to Germany with his unit, but deserted at Bremen on 30 September 1783.

STEIN, Valentin　　　　　　　　　　　　　W201149
Born 1750/51 in Kassel. Sailed to America with the 1777 recruit shipment and was assigned as private in the 3rd Company. He died of fatigue on the march on 25 August 1778.

STEINBACH, Friedrich　　　　　　　　　　W201088
Sailed to America with the 1782 recruit shipment and was assigned as private in the 5th Company. He died of illness at Halifax on 4 March 1783.

STEINBACH, Henrich　　　　　　　　　　　W200111
Born 1746 in Hanebach, Spangenb. Reformed. Sailed to America with the regiment in 1776 as private in the 1st Company. He died of illness in the hospital on 7 December 1776.

STEINECK, Konrad　　　　　　　　　　　　W200357
Born 1751 in Heimershausen, Hesse. Reformed. Sailed to America with the regiment in 1776 as private in the 3rd Company. He served in the 3rd Company throughout the war, and was released from the regiment at Flatbush on 15 July 1783. He had 4 years' previous military experience in the Waldeck 1st Regiment.

STEINMETZ, Albrecht　　　　　　　　　　W200959
Born in Nuernberg. Sailed to America with the 1781 recruit shipment and was assigned as private in the 3rd Company. He died of illness at Newtown on 24 November 1781.

142

STEINMEYER, Johann Henrich Christoph   W200013
Born in Oesdorf, Pyrmont, and baptized on 27 May 1759. Evangelical. Father - Henrich Georg S. Brother of Johann Friedrich Philipp Steinmeyer (W200231). Sailed to America with the regiment in 1776 as fifer in the 1st Company. Taken prisoner at Baton Rouge on 21 September 1779, he returned to duty in January 1782. He apparently returned to Germany with the regiment in 1783. He had 1 year and 9 months of previous military experience in the Waldeck army.

STEINMEYER, Johann Friedrich Philipp   W200231
Born in Oesdorf, Pyrmont, and baptized on 5 August 1753. Evangelical. Father - Henrich Georg S. Brother of Johann Henrich Christoph Steinmeyer (W200013). Sailed to America with the regiment in 1776 as private in the 2nd Company. Wounded in fighting on 27 October 1776 at Maroneck, near West Chester, New York, he died of his wounds in the hospital on 7 November 1776. He had 6 years and 3 months of previous military experience in the Waldeck army.

STEMPEL, Johann Stephan   W200471
Born 18 September 1757 in Goddelsheim (W). Evangelical. 5'4" tall. Father - Johannes; Mother - Catharina Margaretha Anna, nee Schroeder. Second of 3 children. Sailed to America with the regiment in 1776 as private in the 4th Company. He boarded the *Santa Rosalia* on 29 May 1781 to return to New York after the capitulation of Pensacola. He served in the 4th Company throughout the war, and apparently returned to Germany with the regiment in 1783.

STEMPFLER, Kaspar   W200792
Sailed to America with the 1777 recruit shipment and was assigned as private in the 3rd Company. Taken prisoner at Baton Rouge on 21 September 1779, he deserted from prisoner status at New Orleans on 3 July 1780 and joined the Spanish army.

STERNER, Henrich   W201089
Sailed to America with the 1782 recruit shipment and was assigned as private in the 5th Company. He deserted at Halifax on 6 August 1783.

STEUERNAGEL, Carl Philipp   W200380
Born 15 November 1754 in Helsen (W). Evangelical. Father - Johannes S., cantor; Mother - Dorothea Sophia, nee Esau. Possibly an only child. Sailed to America with the regiment in 1776 aboard the transport *Benjamin* as corporal in the 4th Company. After the battle at Fort Washington on 16 November 1776, which he graphically described in his diary, he and medic Beck (W200255) escorted the Waldeck casualties to the hospital at Harlem. About 1 December 1776 he came down sick with fever and spent 14 weeks in the hospital and 14 weeks recovering. Originally the hospital was at Harlem but then moved closer to New York. He thought his illness might have been a contagious scurvy caught from new arrivals. He served throughout the war in the 4th Company, being promoted to quartermaster sergeant in April 1780. He boarded the *Santa Rosalia* on 29 May 1781 to return to New York after the capitulation of Pensacola. He returned to Germany

with the regiment in 1783. He had 1 year and 9 months of previous military experience in the Waldeck army. He marched to Holland in the Waldeck 5th Battalion in 1785, and back to Waldeck the following year. (A copy of his memoirs, translated by this writer, is in the New York Public Library in both German and English, and is the source of considerable information on the Waldeck Regiment and life in America during the late 18th century.)

STIEGLER, Michael   W200112
Born 1738 in Waltenbourg, Saxony. Evangelical. 5'6 1/4" tall. Married. Carpenter by trade. Sailed to America with the regiment in 1776 as private in the 1st Company. Prior to 1779 he was transferred to the 5th Company. Taken prisoner at Baton Rouge on 21 September 1779, he deserted from prisoner status at New Orleans on 11 July 1780 and joined the Spanish army. He had 8 years' previous military experience in the Hannoverian army.

STIEHL, Johannes (Henrich)   W200472
Born 8 June 1756 in Wildungen (W), baptized on 10 June, and confirmed in 1770. Evangelical. 5'2 1/2" tall. Father - Johann Christoph S.; Mother - Anna. Died 9 December 1801. Sailed to America with the regiment in 1776 as private in the 4th Company. He boarded the *Santa Rosalia* on 29 May 1781 to return to New York after the capitulation of Pensacola. He served in the 4th Company throughout the war. He returned to Germany with the regiment and was released at Korbach (W) on 20 October 1783.

STIERLEIN, Johann Henrich   W100018S
Born in Stuttgart. Sailed to America with the regiment in 1776 as ensign and adjutant on the staff. He was promoted to 2nd lieutenant in October 1780, and on 5 December made a two-hour ride to The Cliffs with Chaplain Waldeck (W400005) to visit Captain Pentzel (W100005S). He was killed in the attack on The Village on 7 January 1781.

STIESING, Henrich   W200232
Born 1758 in Dehausen (W). Evangelical. Sailed to America with the regiment in 1776 as private in the 2nd Company. Taken prisoner on the Amite River on 4 September 1779, he deserted from prisoner status at Havana on 28 March 1782.

STOECKER, Johannes   W200233
Born 1758 in Wrexen (W). Evangelical. Sailed to America with the regiment in 1776 as private in the 2nd Company. Taken prisoner on the Amite River on 4 September 1779, he deserted from prisoner status at Havana on 14 April 1782.

STOESSEL, Eberhard   W200793
Born in Altenkirchen. Sailed to America with the 1777 recruit shipment and was assigned as private in the 2nd Company. Taken prisoner on the Amite River on 4 September 1779, he deserted from prisoner status at New Orleans on 19 July 1780.

STOLTZ, Jakob W201090
Sailed to America with the 1782 recruit shipment and was assigned as private in the 5th Company. He returned to Germany with his unit, but deserted at Bremen on 30 September 1783.

STOLTZ, Wilhelm W200358
Born 1744/45 in Elsoff, Witgenstein. Reformed. 5'9" tall. Sailed to America with the regiment in 1776 as private in the 3rd Company. Taken prisoner at Springfield, New Jersey, on 5 January 1777, he was sent to Philadelphia to be exchanged on 18 June 1778. He was killed in the attack on The Village on 7 January 1781.

STRACKE, Johannes W200113
Born 21 December 1752 in Wildungen (W). Baptized on 24 December, and confirmed in 1765. Evangelical. Father – Sergeant Stracke; Mother – Elisabeth. Sailed to America with the regiment in 1776 as private in the 1st Company. He had been a corporal, but he deserted on 16 May 1776 and returned to duty on 31 May as a private. He died of illness in the hospital at Manchac on 4 September 1779. He had 6 years and 6 months of previous military experience in the Waldeck army.

STREHLE, Johannes W201150
Born in Hohenhard. Date and manner of joining the regiment are uncertain, but he was a private in the 3rd Company by September 1778. He returned to Germany with the regiment and was released at Korbach (W) on 16 October 1783.

STREMME, Johannes W200473
Born 1758 in Usseln (W). Evangelical. 5'5" tall. Smith by trade. Sailed to America with the regiment in 1776 as private in the 4th Company. He died of illness on 6 January 1777.

STREMME, Jost W200359
Born 1759 in Usseln (W). Evangelical. 5'3" tall. Sailed to America with the regiment in 1776 as private in the 3rd Company. Taken prisoner at Baton Rouge on 21 September 1779, he died of illness at New Orleans on 7 December 1779.

STREMMEL, Ludwig W200960
Sailed to America with the 1781 recruit shipment and was assigned as private in the 3rd Company. He was transferred to the 5th Company in July 1782. He returned to Germany with the regiment and was released at Korbach (W) on 16 October 1783.

STRIEPECKE, Henrich W200114
Born 1750 in Wrexen (W). Evangelical. 5'5" tall. Married with 2 children. Sailed to America with the regiment in 1776 as private in the 1st Company. Taken prisoner at Baton Rouge on 21 September 1779, he returned to duty in January 1782. He apparently returned to Germany with the regiment in 1783.

STRUBBERG, Friedrich Carl Henrich   W100009
Born 9 March 1740 in Korbach (W). Father - Johann Wilhelm S.,
treasurer in the exchequer; Mother - Anna Dorothea, nee Lueders. A
lieutenant in the service of Solms-Laubach in 1775, Friedrich Carl
was found innocent of a paternity suit on 21 March 1776. Sailed to
America with the regiment in 1776 as 2nd lieutenant in the 1st
Company. He sailed up the Hudson River on 14 Oct. 1777 as part of a
relief force for General Burgoyne, but then returned down river on 16
Oct. and to Staten Island on the 21st. He was promoted to 1st lieutenant with a date of rank of 5 March 1777. Taken prisoner at Baton
Rouge on 21 Sept. 1779, he returned to duty in May 1781. He boarded
the *San Pedro and San Pablo* on 29 May 1781 to return to New York
after the capitulation of Pensacola. He apparently returned to Germany with the regiment in 1783. He died on 18 July 1808 at the castle in
Waldeck (W), a colonel and castle commandant, still unmarried.

STRUCK, Karl   W200962
Sailed to America with the 1781 recruit shipment and was assigned as
private in the 3rd Company. He was transferred to the 1st Company in
July 1782. He returned to Germany with the regiment, and was released at Korbach (W) on 16 October 1783.

STRUEBE, Johann Stefan   W200234
Born 1756 in Benkhausen (W). Evangelical. 5'4" tall. Sailed to
America with regiment in 1776 as private in the 2nd Company. Taken
prisoner on the Amite River on 4 Sept. 1779, he returned to duty in
Jan. 1782. He apparently returned to Germany with regiment in 1783.
He had 3 years' prior military experience in Waldeck 2nd Regiment.

STUCKENBROCK, Johann Henrich Bernhard (Ludwig)   W200235
Born in Holzhausen, Pyrmont, and baptized on 14 May 1760. Evangelical. Father - Johann Georg S. One of the godparents was a Ludwig
Grote. Sailed to America with the regiment in 1776 as private in the
2nd Company. Taken prisoner on the Amite River on 4 September
1779, he died of illness aboard ship near Havana, while still in prisoner status, on 4 September 1780.

STUHLDREHER, Georg Friedrich   W200236
Born 23 June 1755 in Muehlhausen (W), and confirmed in 1769.
Evangelical. Father - Johann Georg S.; Mother - Katharine Elisabeth,
nee Fisseler. Second of 4 children. Sailed to America with regiment in
1776, private in the 2nd Company. He died of illness on 3 Sept. 1777.

SUDE, Friedrich Christoph Julius (Philipp)   W200834
Born 3 September 1756 in Waldeck (W), and baptized on 12 September. Evangelical. Father - Otto Friedrich S., lawyer; Mother - Elisabeth Abertina, nee Lapin. Sailed to America with the 1779 recruit
shipment and was assigned as cadet in the 4th Company. In August
1780 he was promoted to free corporal. He boarded the *Santa Rosalia*
on 29 May 1781 to return to New York after the capitulation of Pensacola. He returned to Germany with the regiment and was released at
Korbach (W) on 16 October 1783.

SUDE, Wilhelm Philipp   W200237
Born 10 March 1754 in Muehlhausen (W). Evangelical. 5'7" tall.
Father – Johann Henrich S.; Mother – Marie Christine, nee Schreiber. Fifth of 5 children. Sailed to America with the regiment in 1776 as
private in the 2nd Company. He died of illness on 9 August 1777. He
had 1 year of previous military experience in Holland, from which he
had deserted, and 6 months in the Prussian army, from which he had
also deserted.

SUISS, Johannes   W200360
Born 1746 in Nieder Buehl, Braunfels. Reformed. 5'4" tall. Sailed to
America with the regiment in 1776 as private in the 3rd Company. He
died of illness on 7 July 1777. He had 15 years' previous military
experience in the Prussian army, from which he had deserted.

TABROTH, Wilhelm   W200873
Born in Neimen. Sailed to America with the 1781 recruit shipment and
was assigned as private in the 3rd Company. He was transferred to the
2nd Company in June 1782. He returned to Germany with the regiment
and was released at Bremen on 19 September 1783.

TANNER, Martin   W200014
Born 1762 in Strasbourg. Evangelical. Sailed to America with the
regiment in 1776 as fifer in the 1st Company. He had originally been
assigned to the 2nd Company, but was transferred to the 1st Company
on 29 May 1776. He died of illness on 21 February 1777.

TAUBERT, Wilhelm   W200116
Born 1754 in Korbach (W). Evangelical. 5'4 1/2" tall. Sailed to
America with the regiment in 1776 as private in the 1st Company.
Taken prisoner on 5 January 1777 in New Jersey, he was sent to
Philadelphia to be exchanged on 18 June 1778. He boarded the *Santa
Rosalia* on 29 May 1781 to return to New York after the capitulation of
Pensacola. He returned to Germany with the regiment and was re-
leased at Korbach (W) on 20 October 1783.

TEICHLER, Johannes   W200963
Born in Stuhlweissenburg. Sailed to America with the 1781 recruit
shipment and was assigned as private in the 3rd Company. He was
transferred to the 4th Company in July 1782. He returned to Germany
with the regiment and was released at Bremen on 19 September 1783.

TENT, Georg Wilhelm   W200606
Born 1758 in Mengeringhausen (W). Evangelical. 5'4" tall. Baker by
trade. A sergeant at the time of his marriage to Wilhelmine Luise,
widowed Emde, on 18 April 1789, Johann Georg Tent was the host of
an inn near the local forge. He married a second time on 29 May 1795
to Johannette Elisabeth Nelle, of Meineringhausen (W) and had one
child by her, a son, Georg Karl Wilhelm, born 7 March 1796. Sailed to
America with the regiment in 1776 as private in the 5th Company.
Taken prisoner at Baton Rouge on 21 September 1779, he returned to

duty in January 1782. He was promoted to corporal in June 1782, and apparently returned to Germany with the regiment in 1783. He had 7 months' previous military experience in the Waldeck 1st Regiment.

TENTE, Christian W200239
Born 1759 in Sachsenhausen (W). Evangelical. 5'3 1/2" tall. Sailed to America with the regiment in 1776 as private in the 2nd Company. Taken prisoner on the Amite River on 4 September 1779, he died of illness at New Orleans on 13 January 1780.

TESCHEL, Georg W200964
Born in Bavaria. Sailed to America with the 1781 recruit shipment and was assigned as private in the 3rd Company. He died of illness on 19 October 1781.

TEWES, Johannes W200361
Born 1758 in Sachsenberg (W). Evangelical. Sailed to America with the regiment in 1776 as private in the 3rd Company. He served in the 3rd Company throughout the war, and apparently returned to Germany with the regiment in 1783.

TEWES, Philipp W200794
Sailed to America with the 1777 recruit shipment and was assigned as private in the 2nd Company. He was transferred to the 4th Company in December 1779, and back to the 2nd Company in June 1782. He apparently returned to Germany with the regiment in 1783.

THALER, Lorenz W200795
Born in Ammendorf. Sailed to America with the 1777 recruit shipment and was assigned as private in the 3rd Company. He deserted at Pensasola on 1 April 1781.

THEILE, Johannes W201091
Sailed to America with the 1782 recruit shipment and was assigned as private in the 5th Company. He returned to Germany with his unit and was released at Korbach (W) on 22 October 1783.

THIELE, Friedrich W200965
Born in Hamburg. Date and manner of joining the regiment are uncertain, but by April 1781 he was a private in the 3rd Company. He deserted at Pensacola on 9 May 1781, the day the surrender of Pensacola was signed, and may have joined the Spanish army.

THIELE, Konrad W200003
Born 1743 in Neerdar (W). Evangelical. Sailed to America with the regiment in 1776 as sergeant in the 1st Company. He died of illness in the hospital at Manchac on 12 August 1779. He had 12 years' previous military experience in the Waldeck army.

THIELEMANN, Georg   W200117

Born 1750 in Mandern (W). Evangelical. Sailed to America with the regiment in 1776 as private in the 1st Company. Taken prisoner in New Jersey in early January 1777, he was carried on the rolls as a prisoner throughout the war, and then listed as a deserter at Elizabethtown, New Jersey, on 15 July 1783. He probably deserted much earlier, even as early as 1777.

THIEMANN, Henrich (Friedrich)   W200796

Born in Minden. Date and manner of joining the regiment are uncertain, but by April 1779 he was a private in the 4th Company. He boarded the *Santa Rosalia* on 29 May 1781 to return to New York after the capitulation of Pensacola. He died of illness at Newtown, on Long Island, on 18 September 1781.

THIETKE, Christian   W300015

Born 1737 in Lueder. Evangelical. 5'6" tall. Sailed to America with the 1778 recruit shipment and was assigned as cannoneer in the artillery section. He was wounded in the Advanced Redoubt at Pensacola on 7 May 1781. After the regiment lost its guns at Pensacola, he was transferred to the 3rd Company. He returned to Germany with the regiment and was released at Korbach (W) on 16 October 1783. He had 16 years' previous military experience in the Hessian and Hannoverian armies.

THOMAS, Christoph   W201151

Born in Boxberg. Sailed to America with the 1778 recruit shipment and was sick upon arrival. He was assigned as private in the 2nd Company. He died of illness in the hospital at New York on 7 January 1779.

THOR, Johannes   W200607

Born 28 January 1749 in Bringhausen (W). Evangelical. 5'4 1/2" tall. Father - Adam T.; Mother - Marie Katharine, nee Zuerges. Fourth of 4 children. Sailed to America with the regiment in 1776 as private in the 5th Company. Taken prisoner at Baton Rouge on 21 September 1779, he deserted from prisoner status at New Orleans on 1 July 1780 and joined the Spanish army. He had 2 years' previous military experience in Holland, probably in a Waldeck unit.

THUMERNICH(T), Johann Peter   W200362

Born in Bergheim (W), and baptized on 26 December 1735. Evangelical. Married with 4 children. Sailed to America with the regiment in 1776 as private in the 3rd Company. He died of illness on 8 March 1777.

TODT, Christian   W200835

Born 1762/63 in Dehringhausen (W). Sailed to America with the 1779 recruit shipment and was assigned as private in the 4th Company. He boarded the *Santa Rosalia* on 29 May 1781 to return to New York after the capitulation of Pensacola. He apparently returned to Germany with the regiment in 1783.

TODT, Johann Henrich   W200372
Born 18 May 1721 in Gembeck (W). Lutheran. Father - Johann Jost T., Mother - Anna Maria, nee Fingerhut. Sailed to America with the regiment in 1776 as sergeant in the 4th Company. He died of illness at Pensacola on 22 October 1779. He had 26 years' previous military experience in the Waldeck army.

TODT, Johann Jakob   W200129
Born 14 February 1728 in Helsen (W). Evangelical. 5'9 1/2" tall. Father - Henrich Johann Ludwig T., shoemaker; Mother - Maria Elisabeth, nee Spiess. Married an Anna Catherina Hennefreund, with whom he had 2 children. Died on 14 December 1804. Sailed to America with the regiment in 1776 as sergeant in the 2nd Company. He was transferred to the 4th Company in December 1779, and back to the 2nd Company in June 1782. In September 1782 he was released from the regiment, as an invalid, in America, but was transferred back to Germany in December 1782. He had 30 years' previous military experience in the Waldeck 2nd Regiment, and at a later date became an ensign in the Waldeck army.

TOENGES, Henrich   W200797
Sailed to America with the 1778 recruit shipment and was assigned as private in the 4th Company. He boarded the *Santa Rosalia* on 29 May 1781 to return to New York after the capitulation of Pensacola. He apparently returned to Germany with the regiment in 1783.

TRAINER, Marcus   W200474
Born 1740 in Somenhart, Wuertemberg. Evangelical. 5'1 1/2" tall. Baker by trade. Sailed to America with the regiment in 1776 as private in the 4th Company. He boarded the *Santa Rosalia* on 29 May 1781 to return to New York after the capitulation of Pensacola. He served in the 4th Company throughout the war. He returned to Germany with the regiment and was released at Korbach (W) on 18 October 1783.

TRAND, Johann Conrad   W200264
Born 18 November 1757 in Wildungen (W), baptized 24 November, and confirmed in 1771. Evangelical. Father - Johannes T.; Mother - Maria Elisabeth, nee Andraein. Chimney sweep by trade. Sailed to America with the regiment in 1776 as drummer in the 3rd Company. He served in the 3rd Company throughout the war, and apparently returned to Germany with the regiment in 1783.

TREITLING, Christian   W200475
Born 1759 in Memmingen. Shoemaker by trade. Sailed to America with the regiment in 1776 as private in the 4th Company. Taken prisoner in New Jersey on 5 January 1777, he died of illness while still a prisoner on 24 May 1778.

TROLL, Friedrich   W201092
Sailed to America with the 1782 recruit shipment and was assigned as private in the 5th Company. He returned to Germany with his unit, but deserted at Bremen on 30 September 1783.

TROLL, Johann Philipp W200476
Born in Mengeringhausen (W), and baptized on 15 November 1750.
Evangelical. 5'5 1/2" tall. Father - Stephan Friedrich T.; Mother -
Eva Catharina, nee Marioth. Tailor by trade. Sailed to America with
the regiment in 1776 as private in the 4th Company. He died of illness
in the hospital at New York on 19 December 1778.

TROST, Friedrich W201093
Sailed to America with the 1782 recruit shipment and was assigned as
private in the 5th Company. He apparently returned to Germany with
his unit in 1783.

TROST, Johann Conrad W200132
Born 21 September 1743 in Landau (W). Evangelical. Father - Johann
Christian T., master carpenter; Mother - Susanna Catharina, nee Hil-
debrand. Fifth of 9 children. Married. His sister married Conrad
Theodor Zimmermann (W200493). Sailed to America with the regiment
in 1776 as captain at arms in the 2nd Company. In August 1779 he was
demoted to private. Taken prisoner on the Amite River on 4 September 1779, he died of illness at New Orleans on 5 September 1779. He
had 3 years' previous military experience in the Waldeck 2nd Regiment.

TRUEBENDOERFER, Leonhard W200798
Born 1760/61 in Marsbach. Sailed to America with the 1778 recruit
shipment and was sick upon arrival. He was assigned as private in
the 5th Company. He died of illness at Pensacola on 3 June 1779.

TUCHSCHEER, Georg W200966
Born in Westernau, Nassau. Sailed to America with the 1781 recruit
shipment and was assigned as private in the 3rd Company. He was
transferred to the 2nd Company in June 1782, and was released from
the regiment at Flatbush on 15 July 1783.

TUITEL, Jean W201152
Born in Laasphe. Sailed to America with the 1778 recruit shipment and
was assigned as corporal in the 5th Company. Taken prisoner at Baton
Rouge on 21 September 1779, he deserted at Havana on 31 March 1782,
while still in prisoner status.

UHLE, Philipp W200608
Born 1751 in Stadtberg, Koeln. Catholic. Smith by trade. Sailed to
America with the regiment in 1776 as private in the 5th Company.
Taken prisoner at Baton Rouge on 21 September 1779, he deserted
from prisoner status at New Orleans on 8 July 1780 and joined the
Spanish army.

UHLMANN, Friedrich W200799
Sailed to America with the 1778 recruit shipment and was sick upon
arrival. He was assigned as private in the 3rd Company. He returned
to Germany with the regiment and was released at Korbach (W) on 19
October 1783.

ULENBRUCH, Henrich   W200099
Born 1757 in Schmillinghausen (W). Evangelical. Sailed to America
with the regiment in 1776 as batman, possibly for Lieutenant Johann
Wilhelm Leonhardi (W100016), in the 1st Company. Taken prisoner
at Baton Rouge on 21 September 1779, he deserted from prisoner
status at Havana on 13 August 1780.

ULM, Jakob   W201094
Sailed to America with the 1782 recruit shipment and was assigned as
private in the 5th Company. He returned to Germany with his unit and
was released at Korbach (W) on 22 October 1783.

ULMER, Kaspar (Adam)   W201095
Sailed to America with the 1782 recruit shipment and was assigned as
private in the 5th Company. He returned to Germany with his unit, but
deserted at Bremen on 30 September 1783.

ULNER, Georg   W200254
Born 1757 in Marburg, Hesse. Reformed (also listed as Evangelical). 5'3 1/2" tall. Sailed to America with the regiment in 1776 as
quartermaster sergeant in the 3rd Company. He served throughout the
war in the 3rd Company, being promoted to sergeant in April 1780,
and apparently returned to Germany with the regiment in 1783.

ULRICH, Christian   W200800
Born 1759/60 in Gemmingen, Swabia. Sailed to America with the 1778
recruit shipment and was sick upon arrival. He was assigned as private in the 5th Company. Taken prisoner at Baton Rouge on 21 September 1779, he died of illness on 8 November 1779.

ULRICH, Johannes   W200363
Born 1759 in Gellershausen (W). Evangelical. 5'4" tall. Sailed to
America with the regiment in 1776 as private in the 3rd Company. He
served in the 3rd Company throughout the war, and apparently returned
to Germany with the regiment in 1783.

ULRICH, Johann Peter   W200477
Born 13 February 1752 in Frebershausen (W). Evangelical. Father -
Johannes U.; Mother - Magdalina, nee Caspar. Sailed to America with
the regiment in 1776 as private in the 4th Company. Taken prisoner at
Maroneck, near West Chester, New York, on 27 October 1776, he was
listed throughout the war as a prisoner, and as a deserter at West
Chester, New York, on 15 July 1783. He probably deserted much
earlier, even as early as 1777.

ULRICH, Lorenz   W200364A
Born 1755 in Gellershausen (W). Evangelical. 5'5" tall. Sailed to
America with the regiment in 1776 as private in the 3rd Company. He
was transferred to the artillery section in February 1776, and after the
regiment lost its guns at Pensacola, he was transferred back to the 3rd
Company in June 1781. He apparently returned to Germany with the
regiment in 1783.

UNGER, Johann Bernhard   W200143
Born 24 August 1760 in Strothe. Evangelical. 4'8" tall. Father -
Anthon U.; Mother - Margarette Elisabeth, nee Berthold. Sailed to
America with the regiment in 1776 as drummer in the 2nd Company.
Taken prisoner on the Amite River on 4 September 1779, he deserted
from prisoner status at Havana on 2 April 1782.

URBACH, Andreas   W200968
Sailed to America with the 1781 recruit shipment and was assigned as
drummer in the 3rd Company. He was transferred to the 1st Company
in July 1782. He returned to Germany with the regiment and was
released at Korbach (W) on 26 October 1783.

URBACH, Joseph   W200969
Sailed to America with 1781 recruit shipment and assigned as private
in the 3rd Company. Transferred to the 1st Company in July 1782. He
returned to Germany with the regiment and was released in Oct. 1783.

URSALL, Wilhelm Theodor   W200250C
Born 1753 in Holzmuenden, Braunschweig. Evangelical. Sailed to
America with the regiment in 1776 as sergeant in the 3rd Company. He
was commissioned an ensign in April 1780 and killed by a cannonball
on 4 May 1781 in the advanced redoubt at Pensacola. He had 4 years'
previous military experience in the Braunschweig army and 1 year in
the English army.

URSPRUNG, Georg Henrich   W200240
Born 1754 in Reinhardshausen (W). Evangelical. Linen weaver by
trade. Sailed to America with the regiment in 1776 as private in the
2nd Company. He was transferred to the 4th Company in December
1779, and back to the 2nd Company in June 1782. He apparently returned to Germany with the regiment in 1783.

VAHLF, Johannes   W200509
Born 1760 in Welda, Paderborn. Catholic. Sailed to America with the
regiment in 1776 as drummer in the 5th Company. Taken prisoner at
Baton Rouge on 21 September 1779, he deserted from prisoner status
at New Orleans on 2 July 1780 and joined the Spanish army.

VALAND, Johannes   W200478
Born 1760 in Berndorf (W). Evangelical. 5'4" tall. Sailed to America
with the regiment in 1776 as private in the 4th Company. He boarded
the *Santa Rosalia* on 29 May 1781 to return to New York after the
capitulation of Pensacola. He served in the 4th Company throughout
the war, and apparently returned to Germany with the regiment in 1783.

VALENTIN, Johann Jost   W200479
Born 1754 in Sintz, Graubuenderland. Reformed. Married with 2 children. Mason by trade. Sailed to America with the regiment in 1776 as
private in 4th Company. Taken prisoner at Springfield, N.J., on 5
January 1777, he was sent to Philadelphia to be exchanged on 21 June
1778. He was released from the regiment at Flatbush on 15 July 1783.

VERCKEN, Konrad   W201153
Born in Hameln. Evangelical. Married Katherina Rebekka Schneider
and they had a daughter, Anna Justine Elisabeth. Date and manner of
joining the regiment are uncertain, but by September 1777 he was a
private in the 1st Company. He died of illness on 5 September 1777.

VERGLASS, Johann Konrad   W200480
Born 1755 in Hannover. Evangelical. 5'3" tall. Tailor by trade. On 6-
year enlistment. Sailed to America with the regiment in 1776 as private in the 4th Company. He deserted on 7 April 1777.

VESPER, Johannes   W201154
Sailed to America with the 1782 recruit shipment and was assigned as
drummer in the 5th Company. He apparently returned to Germany with
his unit in 1783.

VOEPEL, Christoph   W200241
Born 1759 in Neudorf (W). Evangelical. 5'2" tall. Sailed to America
with the regiment in 1776 as private in the 2nd Company. Taken prisoner on the Amite River on 4 September 1779, he died of illness at
New Orleans on 22 October 1779.

VOEPEL, Henrich   W200609
Born 1758 in Dehausen (W). Evangelical. Sailed to America with the
regiment in 1776 as private in the 5th Company. Taken prisoner at
Springfield, New Jersey, on 5 January 1777, he was sent to Philadel-
phia to be exchanged on 18 June 1778. He died of illness at Baton
Rouge on 13 September 1779.

VOEPEL, Johann Wilhelm   W200242
Born 24 August 1756 in Sachsenhausen (W). Evangelical. Father –
Johannes V. Sailed to America with the regiment in 1776 as private in
the 2nd Company. He was transferred to the 4th Company in December
1779, and back to the 2nd Company in June 1782. He apparently returned to Germany with the regiment in 1783.

VOGEL, Kaspar Anton   W201155
Born 1756/57 in Meerhof. Sailed to America with the 1778 recruit
shipment and was sick upon arrival. He was assigned as private on
the 5th Company. He died of illness in the hospital on 19 September
1778.

VOLAND, Friedrich   W201096
Sailed to America with the 1782 recruit shipment and was assigned as
private in the 5th Company. He apparently returned to Germany with
his unit in 1783.

VOLCKE, Philipp Henrich   W200481
Born 1751 in Kohlgrund (W). Evangelical. Sailed to America with the
regiment in 1776 as private in the 4th Company, having transferred to
the transport *Adamant* at Spithead on 24 June 1776. Although carried on
the rolls as a private, he served as Chaplain Philipp Waldeck's

batman until he was invalided back to Germany on 25 April 1781. While making the rounds of the transports at Plymouth, England, on 7 July 1776, with Chaplain Waldeck (W400005), he fell out of the boat but was pulled out of the water by the English sailors.

VOLLMAR, Johannes   W200610
Born 1737 in Wehr, Hesse. Evangelical. Sailed to America with the regiment in 1776 as private in the 5th Company. Taken prisoner at Baton Rouge on 21 September 1779, he returned to duty in January 1782. He was invalided back to Germany in December 1782. He had 15 years' previous military experience in Sardinia.

VOLLMUELLER, Georg   W201156
Born in Lauterbach. Date and manner of joining the regiment are uncertain, but by September 1777 he was a private in the 3rd Company. He died of illness on 23 September 1777.

VOLMAR, Friedrich   W200801
Sailed to America with the 1778 recruit shipment and was assigned as private in the 5th Company. Taken prisoner at Baton Rouge on 21 September 1779, he died of illness in October 1779.

WAGENER, Caspar   W200483
Born 14 February 1748 in Mehlen (W). Evangelical. Linen weaver by trade. Father - Nicolaus W., granary supervisor; Mother - Anna Martha, nee Dalwig, Nicolaus's first wife. Half-brother of Johannes Wagener (W200482). First of 3 children. Sailed to America with the regiment in 1776 as private in the 4th Company. Taken prisoner on 27 October 1776 at Maroneck, near West Chester, New York, he was carried on the rolls as a prisoner throughout the war, and then listed as a deserter at West Chester on 15 July 1783. He probably deserted much earlier in the war, even as early as 1776.

WAGENER, Daniel   W400006
Born 1753 in Anraff (W). Evangelical. Married. Sailed to America with the regiment in 1776 as wagon servant on the staff. There is no further information available.

WAGENER, Georg   W201097
Sailed to America with the 1782 recruit shipment and was assigned as private in the 5th Company. He returned to Germany with his unit, but then deserted at Bremen on 30 September 1783.

WAGENER, Johannes   W200243
Born 1752 in Inzig. Evangelical. Sailed to America with the regiment in 1776 as private in the 2nd Company. Taken prisoner at Springfield, New Jersey, on 5 January 1777, he was sent to Philadelphia to be exchanged on 21 June 1778. Taken prisoner again on the Amite River on 4 September 1779, he deserted from prisoner status at New Orleans on 18 July 1780. He had 4 months of previous military experience in the Waldeck 1st Regiment.

WAGENER, Johannes   W200482
Born 21 June 1758 in Mehlen (W). Evangelical. 5'7" tall. Father -
Nicolaus W., granary supervisor; Mother - Maria Fatherina, nee
Hoehne, Nicolaus's second wife. Third of 9 children. Half-brother of
Caspar Wagener (W200483). Sailed to America with the regiment in
1776 as private in the 4th Company. He boarded the *Santa Rosalia* on
29 May 1781 to return to New York after the capitulation of Pensacola.
He served in the 4th Company throughout the war. Returned to Germa-
ny with the regiment and was released at Korbach (W) 20 Oct. 1783.

WAGENER, Nikolaus   W200970
Born in Zell. Sailed to America with the 1781 recruit shipment and
was assigned as private in the 3rd Company. He was transferred to the
5th Company in June 1782, and released at New York on 18 July 1783.
He received a land grant in Nova Scotia for one man in June 1784.

WAGENER, Werner   W200484
Born 1756 in Luetersheim (W). Evangelical. Sailed to America with
the regiment in 1776 as private in the 4th Company. He and his wife
boarded the *Santa Rosalia* on 20 May 1781 to return to New York after
the capitulation of Pensacola. He served in the 4th Company throughout the war, and apparently returned to Germany with the regiment in
1783. He had 3 years' previous military experience in the Waldeck
army.

WAGENSTAHL, Johannes   W200971
Sailed to America with the 1781 recruit shipment and was assigned as
private in the 3rd Company. He was transferred to the 5th Company in
July 1782. He returned to Germany with the regiment and was released at Korbach (W) on 18 October 1783.

WAGES, Andreas   W201104
Sailed to America with the 1782 recruit shipment and was assigned as
private in the 5th Company. He returned to Germany with his unit and
was released from the regiment at Korbach (W) on 23 October 1783.

WAHL, Henrich Carl   W200485
Born 30 July 1753 in Wildungen (W), baptized on 1 August, and con-
firmed in 1767. Evangelical. 5'4 1/2" tall. Father - Henrich Carl W.;
Mother - Anna Catharina, nee Schleiermacher. Died in 1832. Sailed to
America with the regiment in 1776 as private in the 4th Company.
Taken prisoner at Elizabethtown, New Jersey, on 8 January 1777, he
was sent to Philadelphia to be exchanged on 13 July 1778. He appar-
ently returned to Germany with the regiment in 1783.

WALDECK, Philipp Franz   W400005
Born 9 March 1750 in Hemfurth (W), and confirmed in 1764. Evangelical. Preacher and tutor by profession. Son of a clergyman, he studied
theology at University of Jena. Died of a fever on 20 March 1784 at
Mengeringhausen (W), and was buried there. Sailed to America with
the regiment in 1776 as chaplain on the staff, having transferred to the
transport *Adamant* at Spithead, England, on 24 June 1776. On 14

October 1777 he sailed up the Hudson River on the *Klenehorn* as part of a relief force for General Burgoyne, but returned down river on the 16th and to Staten Island on the 21st. On 5 December 1780 he made a two-hour ride from Pensacola to The Cliffs to visit Captain Pentzel (W100005S). He served in America with the regiment throughout the war, recording in his diary (which I believe is the most interesting diary written by any of the so-called Hessians during the Revolutionary War) his duties and observations on all aspects of life where the regiment saw duty. He returned to Germany with the regiment in 1783.

WALTER, Anton   W201098
Sailed to America with the 1782 recruit shipment and was assigned as private in the 5th Company. He died of illness on 9 December 1782.

WALTER, Jakob   W200118
Born 1746 in Basdorf, Darmstadt. Evangelical. Sailed to America with the regiment in 1776 as private in the 1st Company. Taken prisoner at Baton Rouge on 21 September 1779, he deserted from prisoner status at Havana on 31 March 1782. He had 13 years and 3 months of previous military experience in the Waldeck 1st Regiment.

WALTER, Leonhard   W200119
Born 1735 in Kirch Bergfort, Erberg. Evangelical. Sailed to America with the regiment in 1776 as private in the 1st Company, having joined on the march to Bremerlehe. He deserted on 6 January 1777. He had 9 years and 3 months of previous military experience in the Prussian army, from which he had deserted.

WALTER, Wilhelm   W201099
Sailed to America with the 1782 recruit shipment and was assigned as private in the 5th Company. He returned to Germany with his unit, but then deserted at Bremen on 30 September 1783.

WARLICH, Jeremias   W200142
Born 24 Nov. 1751 in Wildungen (W); baptized 26 Nov. Evangelical. Father - Paulus W.; Mother - Dorothea. Sailed to America with regiment in 1776 as drummer in 2nd Company. By April 1779 he had been promoted to corporal. Taken prisoner on the Amite River 4 Sept. 1779, he deserted from prisoner status at Havana on 21 March 1782. He had 8 years' previous military experience in the Waldeck army.

WASSERFELD, Henrich   W200486
Born 1756 in Helsen (W). Evangelical. Locksmith by trade. Sailed to America with the regiment in 1776 as private in the 4th Company. He died of illness on 8 April 1777.

WAY, Johannes (John)(Tom)   W201188
Date and manner of joining the regiment are uncertain, but by December 1781 he was a batman, probably for Lieutenant Wilhelm Keppel (W100010), then with the 4th Company. It is possible that he was a former Negro slave. He was transferred to the 5th Company in August 1782, and may have returned to Germany with the regiment.

WEBER, Andreas   W201100
Sailed to America with the 1782 recruit shipment and was assigned as
private in the 5th Company. He returned to Germany with his unit, but
then deserted at Bremen on 30 September 1783.

WEBER, Franz Henrich   W200365
Born in Loewensen, Pyrmont, and baptized on 28 February 1755.
Evangelical. Father - Franz W.; Mother - Anna Catharina, nee
Frohmann. Sailed to America with the regiment in 1776 as private in
the 3rd Company. He served in the 3rd Company throughout the war,
and apparently returned to Germany with the regiment in 1783. He had
2 years and 9 months of previous military experience in the Waldeck
army.

WEBER, Johann Henrich   W200802
Born in Wahlen. Sailed to America with the 1778 recruit shipment and
was assigned as private in the 1st Company. Taken prisoner at Baton
Rouge on 21 September 1779, he deserted from prisoner status at
Havana on 31 March 1782.

WEBER, Johann Jost   W200120
Born 1751 in Anraff (W), and confirmed in 1765. Evangelical. Father
- Henrich W.; Mother - Anna Elisabeth, nee Welker. Sailed to
America with the regiment in 1776 as private in the 1st Company. He
died of illness in the hospital at Manchac on 23 August 1779.

WEICHSEL, Matthias   W201157
Born 1744/45 in Mainz. Date and manner of joining the regiment are
uncertain, but by March 1780 he was a private in the 3rd Company. He
was released from the regiment in August 1780, and taken back as a
batman the same month. He deserted at Pensacola on 26 April 1781.

WEIDENHAGEN, Johannes   W200611
Born 1754 in Mandern (W). Evangelical. 5'4 1/2" tall. Sailed to
America with the regiment in 1776 as private in the 5th Company. He
was wounded in the attack on Fort Washington on 16 November 1776.
Taken prisoner at Baton Rouge on 21 September 1779, he returned to
duty in January 1782. He apparently returned to Germany with the
regiment in 1783. He had 4 years' previous military experience in
Holland, probably in a Waldeck unit.

WEIL, Jost   W201101
Sailed to America with the 1782 recruit shipment and was assigned as
private in the 5th Company. He returned to Germany with his unit and
was released from the regiment at Korbach (W) on 22 October 1783.

WEIL, Wilhelm   W201102
Sailed to America with the 1782 recruit shipment and was assigned as
private in the 5th Company. He died of illness at Halifax on 23 March
1783.

WEINECK, Hermann   W200487
Born 1758 in Falckenburg, Hesse. Reformed. 5'5" tall. Hunter by trade. Sailed to America with the regiment in 1776 as private in the 4th Company. Possibly taken prisoner in late 1776 or early 1777, he died of illness in prisoner status on 8 July 1778. He had 1 year of previous military experience in the Holland regiment Oranien, from which he had deserted.

WEINHOLD, Anton   W200366
Born 1757 in Troppau, Silesia. Catholic. 5'5" tall. Cloth maker by trade. Sailed to America with the regiment in 1776 as private in the 3rd Company. Taken prisoner at Springfield, New Jersey, on 5 January 1777, he enlisted in the American army on 19 March 1777. He apparently deserted back to his regiment and served the remaining years of the war in the 3rd Company. He returned to Germany with the regiment and was released at Korbach (W) on 17 October 1783.

WEINKAUFF, Adam   W200803
Sailed to America with the 1778 recruit shipment and was assigned as private in the 2nd Company. He was transferred to the 4th Company in December 1779, and back to the 2nd Company in June 1782. He apparently returned to Germany with the regiment in 1783.

WEIRAUCH, Adam   W200367
Born 1757 in Waldbolau, Erbach. Evangelical. Sailed to America with the regiment in 1776 as private in the 3rd Company. He was wounded in the attack on Fort Washington on 16 November 1776. He deserted on 17 May 1781, after the fall of Pensacola, and may have joined the Spanish army. He had 2 years' previous military experience in the Kurpfalz army.

WEISHAUPT, Christoph   W200012
Born 1732 in Wrexen (W). Evangelical. 5'9" tall. Sailed to America with the regiment in 1779 as corporal in the 1st Company. Taken prisoner at Baton Rouge on 21 September 1779, he returned to duty in January 1782. He was promoted to sergeant in June 1782, and apparently returned to Germany with the regiment in 1783. He had 15 years' previous military experience in the Waldeck 1st Regiment.

WEISS, Adam   W200973
Born in Vienna. Sailed to America with the 1781 recruit shipment and was assigned as private in the 3rd Company. He was transferred to the 2nd Company in June 1782. He returned to Germany with the regiment and was released at Bremen on 19 September 1783.

WEISS, Gottlieb   W200804
Born in Waldenburg. Sailed to America with the 1777 recruit shipment and was assigned as private in the 1st Company. Taken prisoner at Baton Rouge on 21 September 1779, he deserted from prisoner status at New Orleans on 15 July 1780.

WEISS, Johannes   W200974
Born in Kupferzell. Sailed to America with the 1781 recruit shipment
and was assigned as private in the 3rd Company. He was transferred to
the 4th Company in July 1782, and died of illness at Flatbush on 16
February 1783.

WEISSE, Christian   W201103
Sailed to America with the 1782 recruit shipment and was assigned as
private in the 5th Company. He apparently returned to Germany with
his unit in 1783.

WEISSENBORN, Johannes   W200805
Born in Muehlhausen (W). Sailed to America with the 1778 recruit
shipment and was assigned as private in the 3rd Company. He was
released from the regiment on 15 July 1783 at Flatbush, and received
a land grant in Nova Scotia for one man in June 1784.

WEITENKAMP, Christoph   W200244
Born 1758 in Goettingen. Evangelical. 5'2 1/2" tall. Bookbinder by
trade. Sailed to America with the regiment in 1776 as private in the
2nd Company. He died of illness on 12 August 1777.

WEITNER, Johannes   W200806
Born 1761/62 in Hamburg. Sailed to America with the 1778 recruit
shipment and was sick upon arrival. He was assigned as private in
the 1st Company. Taken prisoner at Baton Rouge on 21 September
1779, he died of illness on 26 October 1779.

WEITNER, Leonhard   W200807
Born in Unterscheffach, Swabia. Sailed to America with the 1778 recruit shipment and was assigned as private in the 2nd Company. He
deserted in June 1779, and returned to duty the same month. He died
of illness at Pensacola on 4 December 1779.

WEITZEL, Nikolaus   W200975
Born in Echzell. Sailed to America with the 1781 recruit shipment and
was assigned as private in the 3rd Company. He died of illness in the
hospital at Newtown on 17 September 1781.

WELCKER, Ludwig   W200612
Born in 1759 in Eichelsachsen, Darmstadt. Evangelical. 5'5" tall.
Shoemaker by trade. Sailed to America with the regiment in 1776 as
private in 5th Company. Taken prisoner at Baton Rouge 21 September
1779, he deserted from prisoner status at New Orleans 14 July 1780.

WELNER, Johannes   W200488S
Born 1754 in Braunau (W). Evangelical. Blacksmith by trade. Sailed
to America with the regiment in 1776 as private in the 4th Company.
By April 1779 he was carried on the regimental rolls as a batman, and
by June 1780 as a wagon servant. He deserted at Pensacola on 8 May
1781.

WENDOLPH, Jakob   W200808
Born in Giebelhausen, Mainz. Sailed to America with the 1778 recruit
shipment and was assigned as private in the 4th Company. He deserted on 11 May 1781, after the fall of Pensacola, and may have joined
the Spanish army.

WENTHE, Johann Christian   W300016
Born 26 October 1739 in Hameln. Father - Jobst W.; Mother - Anna
Magdalena, nee Freymann. Married Anna Katharina Fricke in 1769, to
whom was born a daughter, Marie Elizabeth in 1772, and a son, Karl
Philipp, in 1775. Sailed to America with the regiment in 1776 as
cannoneer in the artillery section. He was wounded on 7 May 1781 at
the advanced redoubt at Pensacola, and died of his wounds on 16 May
1781.

WERBEIN, Carl Ludwig (Georg)   W200121
Born in Holzhausen, Pyrmont, and baptized on 26 May 1755. Evangelical. Father - Johann Friedrich W. Sailed to America with the
regiment in 1776 as private in the 1st Company. He died of illness in
the hospital at Manchac on 26 July 1779.

WERLE, Johannes   W200245
Born 1752 in Bendorf, Ansbach. Evangelical. 5'6 1/2" tall. Sailed to
America with the regiment in 1776 as private in the 2nd Company.
Wounded in the attack on Fort Washington on 16 November 1776, he
died of his wounds the next day. He had 6 years' previous military
experience in the Waldeck 2nd Regiment.

WERNER, Henrich   W200489
Born 1755 in Odershausen (W). Evangelical. Sailed to America with
the regiment in 1776 as private in the 4th Company. He died in the
hospital at Manchac on 30 August 1779. He had 2 years' previous
military experience in the Waldeck army.

WERNER, Jakob   W200122
Born 1755 in Wildungen (W). Evangelical. Sailed to America with the
regiment in 1776 as private in the 1st Company. By April 1779, he was
a private in the 2nd Company, and in December 1779, he was transferred to the 4th Company. He deserted on 17 May 1781, after the fall
of Pensacola, and may have joined the Spanish army.

WERSINGER, Wilhelm   W200809
Sailed to America with the 1777 recruit shipment and was assigned as
private in the 4th Company. He boarded the *Santa Rosalia* on 29 May
1781 to return to New York after the capitulation of Pensacola. He
returned to Germany with the regiment and was released at Korbach
(W) on 16 October 1783.

WESSERLEIN, August   W201190
Born 1759 in Zittau. Lutheran. 5'3" tall. Sailed to America with the
1781 recruit shipment and was assigned as private in the 3rd Company. He died of illness at Newtown on 28 January 1782.

WESTE, Henrich   W200976
Born in Reine. Sailed to America with the 1781 recruit shipment and was assigned as private in the 3rd Company. He was transferred to the 1st Company in July 1782. He returned to Germany with the regiment and was released at Bremen on 19 September 1783.

WESTMEYER, August (Justus)   W200836
Born in 1762/63 in Immighausen (W). Sailed to America with the 1779 recruit shipment and was assigned as private in the 3rd Company. He deserted at Flatbush on 2 July 1783.

WETTERHACKE, Johannes   W200246
Born 1750 in Goddelheim, Corvey. Catholic. 5'3" tall. Married with 2 children. Sailed to America with the regiment in 1776 as private in the 2nd Company. He deserted on 2 April 1777.

WETTERWALD, Martin   W200810
Born in Vilisan, Switzerland. Sailed to America with the 1777 recruit shipment and was assigned as private in the 5th Company. Taken prisoner at Baton Rouge on 21 September 1779, he deserted from prisoner status at New Orleans on 7 July 1779 and joined the Spanish army.

WEYBRENNER, Georg   W200811
Born in Loehnberg. Sailed to America with the 1777 recruit shipment and was assigned as private in the 1st Company. Taken prisoner at Baton Rouge on 21 September 1779, he died of illness at New Orleans on 19 July 1780.

WIBBECKE, Henrich   W200490
Born 1746 in Netze (W). Evangelical. Sailed to America with the regiment in 1776 as private in the 4th Company. He served in the 4th Company throughout the war, and apparently returned to Germany with the regiment in 1783. He had 6 years' previous military experience in Holland, probably in a Waldeck unit.

WICHARD, Stefan   W200123
Born 1754 in Netze (W). Evangelical. 5'5 3/4" tall. Sailed to America with the regiment in 1776 as private in the 1st Company. Wounded and taken prisoner at Baton Rouge on 21 September 1779, he returned to duty in January 1782. He apparently returned to Germany with the regiment in 1783.

WIEDLAAKE, Otto   W200138
Born 1753 in Polle, Hannover. Evangelical. 5'5" tall. Sailed to America with the regiment in 1776 as corporal in the 2nd Company. He was wounded in the attack on Fort Washington on 16 November 1776, and transferred to the English army on 8 September 1778. He had 1 year and 6 months of previous military experience in the Hannoverian army.

WIEGAND, Gottfried   W200613
Born 1757 in Mengeringhausen (W). Evangelical. Sailed to America
with the regiment in 1776 as private in the 5th Company. By April
1779 he had been promoted to corporal and been transferred to the 1st
Company. Taken prisoner at Baton Rouge on 21 September 1779, he
deserted from prisoner status at New Orleans on 20 July 1780. He had
4 years and 6 months of previous military experience in Holland,
probably in a Waldeck unit.

WIEGAND, Karl Theodor   W100022S
Born 1747 in Korbach (W). Evangelical. Sailed to America with the
regiment in 1776 as regimental quartermaster and 2nd lieutenant on
the staff, with a date of rank of 2 March 1776. He sailed up the Hudson
River on the Klenehorn as part of a relief force for General Burgoyne
on 14 October 1776 but returned down river on the 16th and went to
Staten Island on the 21st. He boarded the *San Pedro and San Pablo* on
29 May 1781 to return to New York after the capitulation of Pensacola.
He served on the staff as regimental quartermaster throughout the war
and apparently returned to Germany with the regiment in 1783.

WIEGMANN, Christoph   W200812
Born in Koenigsberg. Sailed to America with the 1777 recruit shipment
and was assigned as private in the 3rd Company. He was released
from the regiment at Flatbush on 15 July 1783, and received a land
grant for one man in Nova Scotia in June 1784.

WIEGOLD, Daniel   W200837
Born 1762/63 in Herzhausen (W). Sailed to America with the 1779
recruit shipment and was assigned as private in the 2nd Company.
Transferred to the 4th Company sometime in late 1779 or early 1780,
and back to the 2nd Company in June 1782. Returned to Germany with
the regiment and was released at Korbach (W) on 16 October 1783.

WIENAND, Christian   W200257
Born 1749 in Rhenegge (W). Evangelical. Sailed to America with
regiment in 1776 as corporal in 3rd Company. Died of illness on 27
July 1777. Eight years' previous military experience in Waldeck army.

WIES(S)ER, Josef Thomas   W200614
Born 1727 in Weissenheim, Pfalz. Catholic. 5'5 1/2" tall. Hunter by
trade. Sailed to America with the regiment in 1776 as private in the
5th Company. Taken prisoner at Springfield, N.J., on 5 January 1777,
he was sent from Lancaster, Pa., to Philadelphia to be exchanged on
29 July 1778. Transferred to the 3rd Company in Dec. 1779, and died
of illness in the hospital at Pensacola on 15 April 1781. He had 6
years' previous military experience in the French army.

WIETH, Samuel   W200977
Born in Wittgenstein. Sailed to America with the 1781 recruit shipment and was assigned as private in the 3rd Company. He was transferred to the 5th Company in July 1782. He returned to Germany with
the regiment and was released at Korbach (W) on 23 October 1783.

WIGAND, Philipp   W200508
Born 1759 in Helmighausen (W). Evangelical. Sailed to America with
the regiment in 1776 as drummer in the 5th Company. Taken prisoner
at Baton Rouge on 21 September 1779, he deserted from prisoner
status at New Orleans on 12 July 1780 and joined the Spanish army.

WILDSTACH, Theodor Franz   W200496
Born 1753 in Korbach (W). Evangelical. 5'8 1/2" tall. Sailed to
America with the regiment in 1776 as sergeant in the 5th Company.
Taken prisoner at Baton Rouge on 21 September 1779, he returned to
duty in January 1782. He died of illness at Flatbush on 10 November
1782. He had 5 years' previous military experience in Holland, probably in a Waldeck unit.

WILHELM, Christian (Johannes)   W200124
Born 1728 in Berlin. Evangelical. Married. Sailed to America with the
regiment in 1776 as private in the 1st Company. He was released in
America on 24 October 1778 as an invalid. He returned to Europe on
the *Echo* on 8 October 1778, arriving at Portsmouth, England, on 1
January 1779.

WILHELM, Georg Jakob   W200368
Born 1754 in Ober Werbe (W). Evangelical. 5'5 3/4" tall. Sailed to
America with the regiment in 1776 as private in the 3rd Company. He
served in the 3rd Company throughout the war, and apparently returned
to Germany with the regiment in 1783. He had 3 years' previous military experience in the Waldeck 2nd Regiment.

WILKE, Johann Henrich   W200491
Born in Anraff (W), and baptized on 4 August 1757. Evangelical. 5'5"
tall. Father - Johannes W.; Mother - Marie Elisabeth, nee Melwig.
Tailor by trade. Died in an accident on 5 January 1807. Sailed to
America with the regiment in 1776 as private in the 4th Company.
Taken prisoner at Elizabethtown, New Jersey, on 8 January 1777, he
was sent to Philadelphia to be exchanged on 21 June 1778. He boarded the *Santa Rosalia* on 29 May 1781 to return to New York after the
capitulation of Pensacola. He served in the 4th Company throughout
the remainder of the war, and apparently returned to Germany with the
regiment in 1783.

WILMOWSKY, Josias Theodor Friedrich Ludwig von   W100012
Born in Korbach (W), and baptized on 31 March 1758. Evangelical.
Father - Philibert Zachaeus Noee W., who died 8 January 1766;
Mother - Christiane Elisabeth Philippine, nee von Noelting. Seventh of
9 children and oldest of 2 sons. His godparents were Count Hermann
Josias von Waldeck, hunt master Friedrich von Leliva, Lieutenant
Colonel von Noelting, the widow Eleonore Dorothea von Huyssen, and
Miss Louise von Spiegel zu Kohlgrund. He married Henriette Frieder-
ike Charlotte von Noelting, daughter of Johann Friedrich Wilhelm von
Noelting and his wife, Caroline, nee Ziegenberg, at Adorf (W) on 16
May 1780. They had 2 sons: Ludwig Friedrich Karl August, born 27
February 1801 in Korbach, and Wilhelm Karl Ludwig, born 6 June

1802 in Korbach, one of whose godparents was the then Major Karl Mueller (W200378C). Von Wilmowsky and his family drowned when the transport *De Vreede* sank near Dover, England, during the night of 21/22 November 1802, as he was en route to the Cape of Good Hope to assume duty as the commander of the 5th Waldeck Battalion in Dutch service. Sailed to America with the regiment in 1776 as 1st lieutenant, date of rank of 8 March 1776, in the 3rd Company. He served in the 3rd Company throughout the war, and returned to Germany with the regiment in 1783. He was promoted to captain in the 5th Battalion on 5 November 1784, and marched into Holland with the battalion in 1785 and back to Waldeck in 1786. On 1 April 1794, when the then Lieutenant Colonel Gerhard Henrich Heldring (W100014) was promoted to colonel, von Wilmowsky became a lieutenant colonel. He assumed command of the 5th Battalion on 25 April 1802 when Heldring transferred to the 1st Battalion, prior to the 5th Battalion's departure for the Cape of Good Hope. The birth of his second son delayed von Wilmowsky's departure until November.

WINCKELMANN, Johann Karl   W200369
Born 1761 in Hamburg. Evangelical. 5'2" tall. Sailed to America with the regiment in 1776 as private in the 3rd Company. He deserted on 15 May 1781, after the fall of Pensacola, and may have joined the Spanish army.

WINTERBERG, Johannes   W200247
Possibly born 19 May 1755 in Gembeck (W), the illegitimate son of Luise Henrette Scheele. Evangelical. Sailed to America with the regiment in 1776 as private in the 2nd Company. He died of illness on 16 June 1777.

WIRTH, Christian   W200978
Born in Geschwind, Limburg. Sailed to America with the 1781 recruit shipment and was assigned as private in the 3rd Company. He died of illness at Newtown on 11 April 1782.

WIRTHS, Franz Philipp   W200376C
Born 1757 in Thalitter, Darmstadt. Evangelical. Sailed to America with the regiment in 1776 as quartermaster sergeant in the 4th Company. He was promoted to sergeant in April 1779. He boarded the *Santa Rosalia* on 29 May 1781 to return to New York after the capitulation of Pensacola. He was commissioned an ensign in March 1782. He was transferred to the 3rd Company in August 1782, and returned to Germany with the regiment in 1783. He had 2 years' previous military experience in Holland, probably in a Waldeck unit. In 1802 he was a captain commanding the 1st Company of the 5th Battalion, and sailed to the Cape of Good Hope with the battalion. He retired in mid-August 1804 and apparently returned to Germany.

WISSELER, Johannes   W201159
Sailed to America with the 1782 recruit shipment and was assigned as drummer in the 5th Company. Returned to Germany with his unit and was released from the regiment at Korbach (W) on 22 October 1783.

WISSEMANN, Georg   W200125
Born 1751 in Hoeringhausen, Darmstadt. Evangelical. 5'8 1/4" tall.
Married with 1 child. Sailed to America with the regiment in 1776 as
private in the 1st Company. Taken prisoner in New Jersey on 4 January 1777, he was exchanged, probably in July 1778. He deserted from
Manchac on 17 July 1779. He had 1 year of previous military experience in the Waldeck 1st Regiment.

WOLFF, Anton   W200248
Born 1740 in Brincksen, Paderborn. Catholic. 5'2" tall. Smith by
trade. Sailed to America with the regiment in 1776 as private in the
2nd Company. He died of illness on 21 January 1778. He had 7 years
and 6 months of previous military experience in the Paderborn army,
from which he had deserted.

WOLFF, Anton   W200624
Born in Neuburg. Sailed to America with the 1778 recruit shipment and
was assigned as private in the 4th Company. He deserted at Pensacola
on 8 April 1781.

WOLFF, Veit   W200979
Born in Swabia. Sailed to America with the 1781 recruit shipment and
was assigned as private in the 3rd Company. He died of illness on 21
October 1781.

WOLLENHAUPT, Johannes   W200492
Born 1752 in Zueschen (W). Evangelical. 5'2 1/4" tall. Sailed to
America with the regiment in 1776 as private in the 4th Company. He
boarded the *Santa Rosalia* on 29 May 1781 to return to New York after
the capitulation of Pensacola. He served in the 4th Company throughout the war, but died of illness aboard ship on the North Sea on 6
September 1783, on the return to Germany.

WUERTZ, Johannes   W200813
Born in Gruenewik, Berg. Sailed to America with the 1777 recruit
shipment and was assigned as private in the 1st Company. Taken
prisoner at Baton Rouge on 21 September 1779, he died of illness at
Havana on 26 May 1781, while still in prisoner status.

ZAHNER, Johannes   W200814
Sailed to America with the 1778 recruit shipment and was assigned as
private in the 4th Company. He boarded the *Santa Rosalia* on 29 May
1781 to return to New York after the capitulation of Pensacola. He
returned to Germany with the regiment and was released at Korbach
(W) on 16 October 1783.

ZANGE, Johann Gottfried   W200615
Born 1760 in Bautzen, Lausiez. Evangelical. 5' 2" tall. Cloth maker
by trade. Sailed to America with the regiment in 1776 as private in the
5th Company. He was killed in the fighting near Springfield, New
Jersey, on 5 January 1777.

ZEIGER, Kaspar W200616
Born 1752 in Altenlotheim, Darmstadt. Evangelical. 5'4 3/4" tall. Sailed to America with the regiment in 1776 as private in the 5th Company. Taken prisoner at Baton Rouge on 21 September 1779, he returned to duty in January 1782. He was promoted to corporal in June 1782, and apparently returned to Germany with the regiment in 1783. He had 4 years' previous military experience in the Waldeck 2nd Regiment.

ZENECKE, Erdmann W300017
Born in Goeritz. Sailed to America with the 1777 recruit shipment and was assigned as cannoneer in the artillery section. He was transferred to the 3rd Company in June 1781 after the regiment lost its guns at Pensacola. He was released from the regiment at Flatbush on 15 July 1783, and received a land grant in Nova Scotia for one man, one woman, and one child under ten years, in June 1784.

ZENTLER, Michael W200370
Born 1754 in Tiefensaal, Hohenloh. Evangelical. Sailed to America with the regiment in 1776 as private in the 3rd Company. He died of illness in the hospital on 2 November 1776. He had 6 months of previous military experience in the Waldeck 1st Regiment.

ZICK, Ludwig W200006
Born 1754 in Arolsen (W). Evangelical. Sailed to America with the regiment in 1776 as medic in the 1st Company. Taken prisoner at Baton Rouge on 21 September 1779, he died of illness there on 4 October 1779. He had 1 year and 6 months of previous military experience in the Waldeck army.

ZIEGENHAINER, Peter W200815
Born in Altenkirchen. Sailed to America with the 1777 recruit shipment and was assigned as private in the 3rd Company. He deserted at Pensacola on 2 April 1783.

ZIEGLER, Franz W200617
Born 1734 in Untersterode, Hesse. Reformed. 5'5 3/4" tall. Sailed to America with the regiment in 1776 as private in the 5th Company. He was transferred to the 3rd Company in December 1779, and back to the 5th Company in July 1782. He was released at Flatbush on 15 July 1783, and received a land grant in Nova Scotia for one man in June 1784.

ZIMMERMANN, Henrich Hermann (Christoph) W200618
Born in Oesdorf, Pyrmont, and confirmed in 1772 at the age of 15. Evangelical. 5'3 1/4" tall. Tobacco worker by trade. On 6-year enlistment. Sailed to America with the regiment in 1776 as private in the 5th Company. Taken prisoner at Springfield, New Jersey, on 5 January 1777, he was sent to Philadelphia to be exchanged on 18 June 1778. Taken prisoner again at Baton Rouge on 21 September 1779, he deserted at Havana on 19 March 1782 while still in prisoner status.

ZIMMERMANN, Johann Friedrich   W200126
Born 20 February 1749 in Dringenau, Pyrmont, baptized 23 February,
and confirmed in 1766 at the age of 17. Evangelical. 5'4 1/4" tall.
Father - Christian Z. Sailed to America with the regiment in 1776 as
private in the 1st Company. Taken prisoner at Baton Rouge on 21
September 1779, he probably returned to duty in January 1782. He
apparently returned to Germany with the regiment in 1783.

ZIMMERMANN, Konrad Theodor   W200493
Born 12 July 1749 in Landau (W). Evangelical. Father - Carl Ludwig
Z.; Mother - Anna Margaretha, nee Butterweck. Second of 3 children.
Married Maria Elisabeth Trost, sister of Johann Conrad Trost
(W200132) on 10 February 1774. They had 1 child before he went to
America and 2 children after his return. Tailor by trade. Sailed to
America with the regiment in 1776 as a private in the 4th Company,
although he had deserted on the march to the port, on 22 May at
Borgentreich, and returned the same day. He boarded the *Santa Rosalia*
on 29 May 1781 to return to New York after the capitulation of Pensa-
cola. He served in the 4th Company until December 1782 when he was
invalided back to Germany.

ZIPP, Peter   W200816
Born in Dillhausen. Sailed to America with the 1777 recruit shipment
and was assigned as private in the 1st Company. He deserted at
Manchac on 7 August 1779.

ZOELLNER, Johann Friedrich   W200249
Born in Hagen, Pyrmont, and confirmed in 1766 at age 15. Evangelical. Sailed to America with the regiment in 1776 as private in the 2nd
Company. Wounded in the fighting near West Chester, New York, on
27 October 1776, he was invalided back to Germany on 21 February
1777. He may have sailed on the transport *Ann*, Master James Rudd,
going on board at New York on 17 February 1777, and arriving at Dept-
ford, England, on 23 March 1777.

ZOELTNER, (Henrich) Friedrich   W200355
Born 9 March 1756 in Goddelsheim (W). Evangelical. 5'6" tall. Father
- Johann Bernhard Franz Z.; Mother - Anna Maria. Fourth of 4 chil-
dren. Sailed to America with the regiment in 1776 as private in the 3rd
Company. He served in the 3rd Company throughout the war and appar-
ently returned to Germany with the regiment in 1783.

ZURMUEHLEN, Johann Henrich   W200631
Born 16 October 1744 in Baarsen, Pyrmont, and baptized on 21 October. Evangelical. Father - Caspar Z.; Mother - Anna Elisabeth, nee
Meyer of Neersen. Sailed to America with the regiment in 1776 as
batman in the 2nd Company. As he then disappears from the record, he
may have been batman for Lieutenant Colonel von Dalwigk
(W100002S) and returned to Germany with him in 1777. He had 7
years' previous military experience in the Waldeck army.

ZWICK, Karl Ludwig   W200127
Born 1740 in Rosswick, Anhalt Zerbst. Evangelical. 5'6 1/2" tall.
Sailed to America with the regiment in 1776 as private in the 1st
Company. Promoted to corporal in late 1776 or early 1777, he died
of illness on 20 May 1777. He had previous military experience in the
Prussian and Danish armies.

SPELLING ALTERNATES

The following is a list of alternate spellings of names used in preparing the Mini-Bios. The first name on the line is the alternate spelling and the second name is the name as listed in the preceding pages. All possible alternate spellings are not listed but only those which have been encountered. When only a single letter in the name has varied, and the alphabetical sequence is not affected, the single-letter variation has been shown in parentheses. The reader should remember that some names were anglicized in America, often as translations of the German name, e.g., 'Coldwater' for 'Kaltwasser', and first names were often changed in America. Names such as Meyer or Schaefer should be checked under all possible variations. Also, many times the letters are or have been changed or mistakenly read by persons copying from the old documents. Finally, the combinations ae, oe, and ue are used to denote the umlauted vowels a, o, and u.

Albracht = Albrecht
Albrecht = Albracht
Antrae = Andre
Arens = Arend
Arnd = Arend
Arnt = Arend
Aschenhauer = Aschenhausen
Bab = Bob
Bachstaeter = Bachstaedter
Bachus = Backes
Bap = Bob
Barghenn = Burghenn
Baumler = Baumueller
Baur = Bauer
Baurschmid(t) = Bauerschmidt
Beckenhauer = Birckenhauer
Berckenhauer = Birckenhauer
Berger = Berges
Berges = Berger
Bestelmeier = Besselmeier
Bickell = Pickel
Bikmann = Bickmann
Bohne = Boehne
Bothe = Bethe
Brandenstein = Brandstein
Breininger = Breuninger

Bruckhauser = Bruckhaeuser
Bruene = Bruehne
Buddeker = Buddecker
Buettmann = Puettmann
Clemens = Clementz
Clumann = Kleemann
Cramer = Kraemer
Cruelpath = Crollpath
D'Amour = Diamor
Daemmer = Demmer
Dammer = Demmer
Daubert = Taubert
Dehmuth = Demuth
Delader = de la Dior
Deuerlein = Deierlein
Deylinger = Deilinger
Diedrich = Dietrich
Dingel = Dengel
Doetike = Doedecke
Dommer = Demmer
Drebes = Drewes
Drillmann = Dullmann
Duelmann = Dullmann
Dumerich = Thumernich(t)
Duttmann = Dullmann
Ehrhardt = Erhard

171

Emde = Embde
Ewe = Ebe
Fabroth = Tabroth
Faschauer = Fasshauer
Feiger = Jaeger
Fersch = Ferst
Flammo = Flamme
Fleishut = Fleischhut
Frade = Frede
Francer = Frantzer
Freese = Frese
Frentz = Frantz
Gabel = Kabel
Gebhard = Gerhard
Gercke = Goercke
Gilde = Giede
Goedeke = Goedecke
Grebing = Graebing
Guerger = Gerger
Guillaume = Wilhelm
Gunkel = Kunckel
Haan = Hahn(e)
Hagen, van = Hugen
Haimemann = Heinemann
Hase = Haase
Hausschildt = Hauschild
Heineke = Heinecke
Hense = Hentze
Hertes = Herdes
Hoele = Hoehle
Homann = Hohmann
Humberger = Homberger
Huneke = Hunecke
Irdenkauff = Indenkauff
Jerger = Gerger
Jungermann = Junckermann
Kels = Kelfs
Keesemeyer = Kaesemeyer
Kestering = Kesting
Kienold = Kinold
Klahotz = Klahold
Klappenmoefer = Koppenhoeffer
Klass = Kluss
Kneiet = Kneile
Knocke = Kocke
Koester = Kuester
Koesting = Kesting
Koocke = Kocke
Kramer = Kremer
Kreye = Kreyer
Kuehn = Kuhn
Kuehnhold = Kinold

Kumpel = Kuempel
Kuschenbauer = Kussenbauer
Kuster = Kuester
Laake = Packe
Laar = Lahr
Lamering = Lemmering
Lawe = Laue
Lecher = Lercher
Leinbach = Leimbach
Leitenberg = Leydenberg
Leitmann = Leutmann
Lenger = Saenger
Leser = Leeser
Linte(n) = Linde(n)
Littled = Littlet
Loebelein = Loeblein
Loormann = Lohrmann
Luckel = Lueckel
Lunert = Luenert
Malcus = Malches
Marterns = Materns
Mattheus = Matthias
Maurer = Mauer
Mauske = Meuske
Meckel = Mechel
Meier = Meyer
Meiser = Meuser
Mengerhausen = Mengeringhausen
Merckert = Marckert
Merz = Mertz
Meusch = Meuske
Mey = May
Meyer = Meier
Michael = Michel
Mieting = Mieding
Minke = Mincke
Mock = Moock
Moehr = Moer
Moeller = Mueller
Muehlich = Mielig
Muelich = Mielig
Munch = Muench
Muncke = Mincke
Munder = Muender
Mundhenke = Mundhenck(e)
Mundhenken = Mundhenck(e)
Muss = Muus
Muus = Muss
Nastler = Nassler
Neuhoefer = Neuschaeffer
Neumeier = Neumeyer
Neuscheffer = Neuschaeffer

172

Niemann = Neumann
Nolte = Nolle
Obkirchen = Obkircher
Otten = Otto
Paake = Packe
Paar = Paer
Peister = Peuster
Petzhaenger = Pelzhaenger
Pfitzer = Pfister
Piper = Pieper
Pipphardt = Piphard
Piquae = Pique
Preuss = Preiss
Proll = Puoll
Purr = Burr
Rabanaus = Rabanus
Rabensburg = Rabeneprock
Rapensprock = Rabensprock
Raquette = Roquette
Reinshartd = Reinhard
Relcke = Roelcke
Reuther = Reuter
Risse = Riese
Roehmer = Roemer
Roeling = Roehling
Romer = Roemer
Rosenberg = Rosenburg
Rothe = Rohde
Rothewald = Rodewald
Rysel = Ruesel
Saltzmann = Salzmann
Saure = Sauer
Schaacke = Schaake
Schaber = Schaper
Schanz = Schrantz
Scheffer = Schaeffer
Scheidler = Scheideler
Scheurmann = Scheuermann
Schitz = Schuetz
Schleuderbeck = Schlauderbeck
Schmit = Schmid(t)
Schneideler = Schneider
Schneppel = Schnepper
Schreier = Schreyer
Schueller = Schuetler
Schuhmacher = Schumacher
Schulz(e) = Schultz(e)
Schurch = Schurck
Schurg = Schurck
Scimmel = Schimmel
Seigling = Leugling
Seltzam = Seltsam

Siebers = Siebert
Siegeler = Siegler
Simshauser = Simshaeuser
Steinchel = Heinschel
Stiegeler = Stiegler
Stiel = Stiehl
Stieling = Stiesing
Stripecke = Striepecke
Stuerner = Sterner
Stuldreher = Stuhldreher
Stumpler = Stempler
Suese = Suiss
Teigmeyer = Teigtmeyer
Tentin = Tente
Teuchler = Teichler
Tewes = Drewes
Thillemann = Thielemann
Tibes = Tewes
Toeld = Todt
Toett = Todt
Totelmann = Thielemann
Trant = Trand
Trebes = Drewes
Triebendoerfer = Truebendoefer
Trube = Drube
Urspruch = Ursprung
Ursprug = Ursprung
Verst = Ferst
Vleischhut = Fleischhut
Voland = Valand
von Rhene = von Rhena
Wagner = Wagener
Walentin = Valentin
Webe = Weber
Wehrbein = Werbein
Weit = Weil
Werlich = Warlich
Wesserfeld = Wasserfeld
Weyrauch = Weirauch
Wiebeke = Wibbecke
Wiedlacke = Wiedlaake
Wiegand = Wigand
Wieghard = Wichard
Wiehl = Wieth
Wiesemann = Wissemann
Wilcke = Wilke
Wilker = Welcker
Wilstach = Wildstach
Wuertz = Wirths
Zeyger = Zeiger
Zuck = Zick

BIBLIOGRAPHY

ALGEMEEN, Rijksarchief. Raad von State, nr. 1969, "1744-1793." The Haag, Netherlands.

ANONYMOUS. "Stammtafel der Familie Marc aus Arolsen." A typescript in the archives of the Waldeck Historical Society, Arolsen, Germany.

AUERBACH, Inge and FROEHLICH, Otto (eds.). *Hessische Truppen im amerikanischen Unabhaengigkeitskrieg (HETRINA)*. 5 vols. Marburg, Germany, 1972-76.

BAURMEISTER, Carl L. *Revolution in America: Confidential Letters and Journals, 1776-1784*. Bernard A. Uhlendorf, ed. and trans. Second ed. Westport, Conn., 1973.

BRACHT, Karl and Hilda. Correspondence with compiler regarding church records in Rhoden, Germany, 1985.

CLINTON, George. *Public Papers of George Clinton, First Governor of New York, 1777-1795, 1801-1804*. 10 vols. New York, 1973.

DALWIGK, Linde Freifrau von. Conversations with compiler at Dalwigsthal, Germany, 1985.

DEMANDT, Karl E. *Geschichte des Landes Hessen*. Cassel, Germany, 1972.

DeMARCE, Virginia. *The Settlement of Former German Auxiliary Troops in Canada after the War of Independence, 1776-1783*. Sparta, Wis., 1984.

EELKING, Max von. *The German Allied Troops in the North American War of Independence, 1776-1783*. Joseph G. Rosengarten, trans. and abr. Baltimore, Md., 1969.

FARMAR, Robert. "Robert Farmar's Journal of the Siege of Pensacola." *The Historical Magazine*, vol. IV. New York, 1860.

FAYE, Stanley. *The Spanish and British Fortifications of Pensacola, 1698-1821*. Pensacola, Fla., 1977.

FORCE, Peter (ed.). *American Archives: Fifth Series. Containing a Documentary History of the United States of America from the Declaration of Independence (July 4, 1776 - September 8, 1788)*. 3 vols. Washington, D.C., 1848-53.

GALVEZ, Bernardo de. "Bernardo de Galvez's Combat Diary for the Battle of Pensacola, 1781." Maury Baker and Margaret Bissler Haas, eds. *The Florida Historical Quarterly.* Vol. LXI, nr. 1. Gainesville, Fla., July 1977.

HAARMANN, Albert W. "The Spanish Conquest of British West Florida, 1779-1781." *The Florida Historical Quarterly,* vol. XXXIX, nr. 1. Gainesville, Fla., 1960.

_____. "The 3rd Waldeck Regiment in British Service, 1776-1783." *Army Historical Research,* vol. 48, nr. 95. Manhattan, Kans., Autumn 1970.

HAZARD, Samuel. "Colonial Records." *Pennsylvania Collected Records.* Vol. II. Harrisburg, Pa., 1952.

_____. "Papers Relating to the British Prisoners." *Pennsylvania Archives.* 2nd Series. Vol. 1. Philadelphia, 1880.

_____. *Pennsylvania Archives.* 1st Series, vol. 5, 1776-1777. Philadelphia, 1853.

HEISEY, John W. (trans. and ed.). "Extracts from the Diaries of the Moravian Pastors of the Hebron Church, Lebanon, 1755-1814." *Pennsylvania Historical Association Quarterly Journal,* vol. XXXIV. Philadelphia, January 1967.

HELLWIG, Wilhelm. Correspondence with compiler regarding church records in Korbach, Germany, 1988.

HORN, D.B. (ed.). *British Diplomatic Representatives, 1689-1789.* London, 1932.

JONES, Thomas. *History of New York During the Revolutionary War.* Edward Floyd DeLancey, (ed.). 2 vols. New York, 1968.

KIRCHENBUECHER (Church Records) of various localities in Waldeck, Germany, 1984-88.

LANGER, Aloys. Correspondence with compiler regarding church records in Bad Pyrmont, Germany, 1985.

LUNDIN, Leonard. *Cockpit of the Revolution: The War for Independence in New Jersey.* New York, 1972.

MARSHALL, Douglas and PECKHAM, Howard H. *Campaigns of the American Revolution: An Atlas of Manuscript Maps.* Ann Arbor, Mich., 1976.

MEDDING, Wolfgang. "Waldecker Soldaten kaempften in amerikanischen Unabhaengigkeitskrieg." *Mein Waldeck,* nr. 5, *Waldeckische Landeszeitung.* Arolsen, Germany, March 1964.

MIRANDA, Francisco de. "Miranda's Diary of the Siege of Pensacola, 1781," Donald E. Worcester, trans. *The Florida Historical Quarterly*, vol. XXIX, nr. 3. Gainesville, Fla., January 1951.

NEUSS, Erich. *Geschichte des Geschlectes von Wilmowsky*. Halle, Germany, 1938.

RUDOLPH, Martin (comp.). "Die Nachkommen des Curt Sohumacher aus Eversberg und seiner beiden Frauen Magd. Schreiber u. Magd. Benn--Versuch einer Nachfahrentafel, zusammengestellt von Dr. Martin Rudolph." *Korbacher Burgerfamilien*. Goettingen, Germany, 1976.

RUPERT, J. Daniel. Correspondence with compiler regarding George Rupert mentioned by the Virginia Commission on Revolutionary Claims. Kalamazoo, Mich., 1988.

SMITH, William. *Historical Memoirs from 26 August 1778 to 12 November 1783 of William Smith*. William H. W. Sabine, (ed.). New York, 1971.

STAATSARCHIV, Hamburg. "Manuscript 10,897, Ritzebuttel. Abt VII, Fach. 7, vols. B and C and Amtsarch. Ritzebuttel, Abt VII, Fach. 6, vol. G."

STAATSARCHIV Marburg. "Fuerstlich Waldeckisches Kabinett," nrs. 978, 1002, 1003, 1004, and 1008.

STEINMETZ, Hermann. *Die Waldeckischen Beamten von Mittelalter bis zur Zeit der Befreiungskrieg*. 2 vols. n.p. (Korbach ?), 1983.

STEUERNAGEL, Carl Philipp. "Eine kurze Beschreibung ..." A manuscript in the New York Public Library Bancroft Collection.

STRYKER, William S. (ed.). *Documents Pertaining to the Revolutionary War of the State of New Jersey*. Vol. 1. Trenton, N.J., 1901.

SUTHERLAND, Maxwell. "Case History of a Settlement." *The Dalhousie Review*, vol. XLI. Halifax, Nova Scotia, Spring 1961.

WALDECK, Philipp. "Tagebuch." A manuscript in the New York Public Library Bancroft Collection.

WALDECKISCHE Ortssippenbuecher (Genealogical Books) for various localities in Waldeck, Germany, 1984-88.

WALDECKISCHES Intelligenz-Blatt (Newspaper). Korbach, Germany, 19 August 1777, 18 April 1780, and 4 February 1783.

WARNECKE, Wolfgang. Correspondence with compiler regarding church records in Pyrmont, Germany, 1985.

INDEX

All names on pages xi-xxix are indexed. For pages 1-169, the only names indexed are those of individuals whose surnames differ from that of the soldier under discussion.

Other books by the author:

Eighteenth Century America (A Hessian Report On the People, the Land, the War) As Noted in the Diary of Chaplain Philipp Waldeck (1776-1780)
Enemy Views: The American Revolutionary War as Recorded by the Hessian Participants
Hessian Chaplains: Their Diaries and Duties
Hesse-Hanau Order Books, A Diary and Roster: A Collection of Items Concerning the Hesse-Hanau Contingent of "Hessians" Fighting Against the American Colonists in the Revolutionary War
Most Illustrious Hereditary Prince: Letters to Their Prince from Members of Hesse-Hanau Military Contingent in the Service of England During the American Revolution
Order Book of the Hesse-Cassel von Mirbach Regiment
A Hessian Officer's Diary of the American Revolution Translated From An Anonymous Ansbach-Bayreuth Diary and The Prechtel Diary
Journal of the Hesse-Cassel Jaeger Corps
Journal of a Hessian Grenadier Battalion
Hessian Letters and Journals and A Memoir
The Trenton Commanders: Johann Gottlieb Rall and George Washington, as noted in Hessian Diaries
Defeat, Disaster, and Dedication
Revolutionary War Letters Written by Hessian Officers: Generals Wilhelm von Knyphausen, Carl Wilhelm Von Hachenberg, Friedrich Wilhelm von Lossberg, Johann Friedrich Cochenhausen, Friedrich Von Riedesel and Major Carl Leopold von Baurmeister
English Army and Navy Lists, Compiled During the American Revolutionary War by Ansbach-Bayreuth Lieutenant Johann Ernst Prechtel
Journal of the Prince Charles Regiment
The Diary of Lieutenant von Bardeleben and Other von Donop Regiment
Georg Pausch's Journal and Reports of the Campaign in America, as Translated from the German Manuscript in the Lidgerwood Collection in the Morristown Historical Park Archives, Morristown, N.J.

CD: The Hessian Collection, Volume 1: Revolutionary War Era
CD: Diaries of Two Ansbach Jaegers
CD: Waldeck Soldiers of The American Revolutionary War
CD: Canada During the America Revolutionary War
CD: A Hessian Report on the People, the Land, the War of Eighteenth Century America, As Noted in the Diary of Chaplain Philipp Waldeck 1776-1780
CD: They Also Served. Women with the Hessian Auxiliaries
CD: A Hessian Diary of the American Revolution
CD: A Hessian Officer's Diary of The American Revolution
CD: Ansbach-Bayreuth Diaries from the Revolutionary War

www.ingramcontent.com/pod-product-compliance
Lightning Source LLC
Chambersburg PA
CBHW070910270326
41927CB00011B/2513